First World War
and Army of Occupation
War Diary
France, Belgium and Germany

1 DIVISION
2 Infantry Brigade
Northamptonshire Regiment
1st Battalion
12 August 1914 - 20 May 1919

WO95/1271

The Naval & Military Press Ltd
www.nmarchive.com
Published in association with The National Archives

Published by

The Naval & Military Press Ltd

Unit 10 Ridgewood Industrial Park,

Uckfield, East Sussex,

TN22 5QE England

Tel: +44 (0) 1825 749494

www.naval-military-press.com

www.nmarchive.com

This diary has been reprinted in facsimile from the original. Any imperfections are inevitably reproduced and the quality may fall short of modern type and cartographic standards.

© **Crown Copyright**
Images reproduced by permission of The National Archives, London, England, 2015.

Contents

Document type	Place/Title	Date From	Date To
Heading	1st Division 2nd Brigade 1st Battalion Northamptonshire Regt. Aug-Dec 1914		
Heading	2nd Brigade 1st Division. 1st Battalion Northamptonshire Regiment August 1914.		
Miscellaneous	The Qtrs. 1st Division		
War Diary		12/08/1914	16/08/1914
War Diary	Esqueheries	17/08/1914	20/08/1914
Miscellaneous	I have the honour to be Sir Your obedient Servant		
Miscellaneous	Etreux		
War Diary		12/08/1914	16/08/1914
War Diary	Esqueheries	17/08/1914	20/08/1914
War Diary	Etrosungt	21/08/1914	22/08/1914
War Diary	Givret	23/08/1914	24/08/1914
War Diary	Marbaix	25/08/1914	31/08/1914
Heading	2nd Brigade. 1st Division. 1st Battalion Northamptonshire Regiment September 1914		
War Diary		01/09/1914	05/10/1914
Diagram etc	1st Nov to Aug ln Shire Rgt.		
Miscellaneous	Head Quarters 2nd Infantry Brigade		
Heading	2nd Brigade. 1st Division.1st Battalion Northamptonshire Regiment October 1914		
War Diary		01/10/1914	17/11/1914
Heading	2nd Brigade. 1st Division.1st Battalion Northamptonshire Regiment November 1914		
War Diary		26/10/1914	20/12/1914
Heading	2nd Brigade. 1st Division. 1st Battalion Northamptonshire Regiment December 1914		
Heading	1st Division 2nd Inf. Bde. War Diary 1st Battalion Northampton Regiment December 1914 (26.11.14-31.12.14)		
War Diary		26/11/1914	31/12/1914
Heading	1st Division 2nd Brigade 1st Battalion Northamptonshire Regt. Jan-Dec 19155		
Heading	2nd Infantry Brigade. 1st Division. War Diary 1st Northamptonshire Regiment. January 1915		
War Diary		01/01/1915	30/01/1915
War Diary		31/01/1915	04/02/1915
Heading	2nd Infantry Brigade. 1st Division. War Diary 1st Northamptonshire Regiment. February 1915		
War Diary		31/01/1915	28/02/1915
Heading	2nd Infantry Brigade. 1st Division. War Diary 1st Northamptonshire Regiment March 1915		
War Diary		01/03/1915	08/03/1915
War Diary	Oblinghem	09/03/1915	31/03/1915
Heading	2nd Infantry Brigade. 1st Division. War Diary 1st Northamptonshire Regiment. April 1915		
War Diary	Billets (Cornet-Le-Malo)	01/04/1915	06/04/1915
War Diary	(Trenches)	07/04/1915	12/04/1915
War Diary	Billets (Les Facous)	13/04/1915	14/04/1915
War Diary	Billets (Les Harisoires)	15/04/1915	23/04/1915

War Diary	Billets (Riche Bourg)	24/04/1915	26/04/1915
War Diary	Support Trenches	27/04/1915	30/04/1915
Heading	2nd Infantry Brigade. 1st Division. 1st Northamptonshire Regiment. May 1915		
War Diary	In Support Trenches in front of Riche Bourg St Vaast	01/05/1915	02/05/1915
War Diary	Oblingham Billets	03/05/1915	05/05/1915
War Diary	(Le Touret) Billets	06/05/1915	10/05/1915
War Diary	Oblingham (Billets)	11/05/1915	11/05/1915
War Diary	Bethune (Billets)	12/05/1915	14/05/1915
War Diary	Gorre Bridge (Billets)	15/05/1915	18/05/1915
War Diary	Bethune (Billets)	19/05/1915	20/05/1915
War Diary	Annequin (Billets)	21/05/1915	23/05/1915
War Diary	Trenches	24/05/1915	27/05/1915
War Diary	Annequin Billets	28/05/1915	28/05/1915
War Diary	Trenches	29/05/1915	31/05/1915
Heading	2nd Infantry Brigade. 1st Division. War Diary 1st Northamptonshire Regiment. June 1915		
War Diary	In Trenches (Cuinchy Section)	01/06/1915	01/06/1915
War Diary	Billets In Cambrin	02/06/1915	04/06/1915
War Diary	Billets at Labeuvriere	05/06/1915	10/06/1915
War Diary	Billets at Allouagne	11/06/1915	16/06/1915
War Diary	Trenches in Cuinchy Area	17/06/1915	19/06/1915
War Diary	Billets at Bethune	20/06/1915	23/06/1915
War Diary	Bethune	24/06/1915	24/06/1915
War Diary	Allouagne	25/06/1915	27/06/1915
War Diary	Cambrin & Annequin	28/06/1915	30/06/1915
Heading	2nd Infantry Brigade. 1st Division. War Diary 1st Northamptonshire Regiment. July 1915		
War Diary	(Billets at Cambrin & Annequin)	01/07/1915	02/07/1915
War Diary	(Trenches)	03/07/1915	07/07/1915
War Diary	Billets (Sailly-La-Bourse)	08/07/1915	12/07/1915
War Diary	(Billets Laboures)	13/07/1915	18/07/1915
War Diary	(Trenches)	19/07/1915	25/07/1915
War Diary	(Billets Noyelles)	26/07/1915	31/07/1915
Heading	2nd Infantry Brigade. 1st Division. War Diary 1st Northamptonshire Regiment. August 1915		
War Diary	Billets Annezin	01/08/1915	06/08/1915
War Diary	Cambrin (Billets & dugouts)	07/08/1915	08/08/1915
War Diary	Billets Cambrin	09/08/1915	12/08/1915
War Diary	Trenches Z	12/08/1915	17/08/1915
War Diary	Billets Annezin	18/08/1915	22/08/1915
War Diary	Billets Vermelles	23/08/1915	23/08/1915
War Diary	Trenches Y	24/08/1915	27/08/1915
War Diary	Vermelles	28/08/1915	28/08/1915
War Diary	Trenches	29/08/1915	31/08/1915
Heading	1st Division. 2nd Brigade. War Diary of 1st Northamptons September 1915		
War Diary	Trenches in front of Vermelles	01/09/1915	02/09/1915
War Diary	Vermelles Burbure	03/09/1915	07/09/1915
War Diary	Burbure	08/09/1915	20/09/1915
War Diary	Lapugnoy	21/09/1915	23/09/1915
War Diary	Bivouac	24/09/1915	24/09/1915
War Diary	Trenches	25/09/1915	27/09/1915
War Diary	Mazingaribe	28/09/1915	30/09/1915

Map	Line of Advance Made By 1st Northamptonshire Regt. on Sat Sep 25 And Position Held During The Following Night.		
Miscellaneous	Extract From field Returns A.F. B. 213.		
Heading	2nd Infantry Brigade. 1st Division. War Diary 1st Northamptonshire Regiment. October 1915		
War Diary	Loos	01/10/1915	01/10/1915
War Diary	Noeux Les Mines	02/10/1915	06/10/1915
War Diary	Mazingarbe	07/10/1915	07/10/1915
War Diary	German Captured Trenches	08/10/1915	13/10/1915
War Diary	Inaction	14/10/1915	14/10/1915
War Diary	Lillers	15/10/1915	31/10/1915
Heading	2nd Infantry Brigade. 1st Division. War Diary 1st Northamptonshire Regiment. December 1915		
Heading	2nd Infantry Brigade. 1st Division. War Diary 1st Northamptonshire Regiment. November 1915		
War Diary	Lillers	01/11/1915	13/11/1915
War Diary	Trenches in front Hulluck	14/11/1915	20/11/1915
War Diary	Mazingarbe	21/11/1915	21/11/1915
War Diary	In The Trenches	22/11/1915	26/11/1915
War Diary	Mazingarbe	27/11/1915	01/12/1915
War Diary	In The Trenches	02/12/1915	10/12/1915
War Diary	Philosophe	11/12/1915	11/12/1915
War Diary	In The Trenches	12/12/1915	14/12/1915
War Diary	Neoux-Les-Mines	15/12/1915	19/12/1915
War Diary	In The Trenches	20/12/1915	31/12/1915
Heading	1st Division 1st Battalion Northamptonshire Regt. Jan-Dec 1916		
Heading	2nd Brigade. 1st Division. 1st Battalion Northamptonshire Regiment January 1916		
Heading	1st Northampton Regt Jan Vol XVI 2nd Bde		
War Diary	In Support Trenches	01/01/1916	01/01/1916
War Diary	Noeux Les Mines	02/01/1916	07/01/1916
War Diary	A 2 From Line Trenches	07/01/1916	14/01/1916
War Diary	Lillers	15/01/1916	31/01/1916
Heading	2nd Brigade. 1st Division. 1st Battalion Northamptonshire Regiment February 1916.		
Heading	1 Northampton Regt. Feb 1916 Vol XVII		
War Diary	Lillers	01/02/1916	15/02/1916
War Diary	Les Brebis	16/02/1916	18/02/1916
War Diary	Maroc Section	19/02/1916	20/02/1916
War Diary	Mazingarbe	21/02/1916	26/02/1916
War Diary	Support Batt Loos	27/02/1916	29/02/1916
Heading	2nd Brigade. 1st Division. 1st Battalion Northamptonshire Regiment March 1916.		
Heading	1 Northampton Regt Vol XVIII March 1916		
War Diary	Right Batt Loos	01/03/1916	03/03/1916
War Diary	Les Brebis	04/03/1916	06/03/1916
War Diary	Right Batt Loos.	07/03/1916	09/03/1916
War Diary	Bracquemont.	10/03/1916	15/03/1916
War Diary	S. Maroc	16/03/1916	22/03/1916
War Diary	Right Sub Sector.	23/03/1916	24/03/1916
War Diary	S. Maroc	25/03/1916	27/03/1916
War Diary	Les Brebis	28/03/1916	31/03/1916
Heading	2nd Brigade. 1st Division. 1st Battalion Northamptonshire Regiment April 1916.		

Heading	To D.A.G. 3rd Echelon Base War Diary For Month Of April 1916		
War Diary	Les Brebis	01/04/1916	02/04/1916
War Diary	Left Sub-Section Loos.	03/04/1916	04/04/1916
War Diary	Left Batt Loos.	05/04/1916	05/04/1916
War Diary	Left Res. Batt	06/04/1916	08/04/1916
War Diary	Left Front Batt Loos	09/04/1916	11/04/1916
War Diary	Support Batt Loos.	12/04/1916	14/04/1916
War Diary	Les Brebis	15/04/1916	20/04/1916
War Diary	Right Sub-Sector Maroc	21/04/1916	23/04/1916
War Diary	Support Maroc	24/04/1916	26/04/1916
War Diary	Right Sub. Section Maroc	27/04/1916	28/04/1916
War Diary	Maroc Right Front Batt	28/04/1916	28/04/1916
War Diary	Right Support Batt Maroc	29/04/1916	30/04/1916
Heading	2nd Brigade. 1st Division. 1st Battalion Northamptonshire Regiment May 1916.		
War Diary	Right Reserve Batt Maroc.	01/05/1916	02/05/1916
War Diary	Les Brebis "B" Area	03/05/1916	07/05/1916
War Diary	Les Brebis	08/05/1916	08/05/1916
War Diary	N. Maroc.	09/05/1916	11/05/1916
War Diary	Rg, Front Batt Loos	12/05/1916	14/05/1916
War Diary	N. Maroc.	15/05/1916	18/05/1916
War Diary	Les Brebis	19/05/1916	25/05/1916
War Diary	Left Batt Maroc	26/05/1916	31/05/1916
War Diary		29/05/1916	29/05/1916
Heading	2nd Brigade. 1st Division. 1st Battalion Northampstonshire Regiment June 1916.		
Heading	War Diary 1st Bn Northamptonshire Regt. June 1916		
War Diary	N. Maroc.	01/06/1916	03/06/1916
War Diary	Maroc	04/06/1916	07/06/1916
War Diary	N. Maroc.	08/06/1916	09/06/1916
War Diary	Maroc	10/06/1916	10/06/1916
War Diary	Petit Sains	11/06/1916	16/06/1916
War Diary	Maroc	17/06/1916	21/06/1916
War Diary	N. Maroc	22/06/1916	25/06/1916
War Diary	S. Maroc Rg Front Batt.	25/06/1916	30/06/1916
Heading	2nd Bde. 1st Div. War Diary 1st Battalion Northampton Regiment. July 1916.		
Heading	1st Bn. Northamptonshire Regt. July 1916		
War Diary	Maroc Right Battn.	01/07/1916	04/07/1916
War Diary	Marles Les M	05/07/1916	07/07/1916
War Diary	Flesselles	08/07/1916	08/07/1916
War Diary	Frechencourt	09/07/1916	09/07/1916
War Diary	Bresles	10/07/1916	10/07/1916
War Diary	Becourt Wood	11/07/1916	17/07/1916
War Diary	N.E. of Contalmaison	18/07/1916	18/07/1916
War Diary	O.G. 112	19/07/1916	24/07/1916
War Diary	Albert	24/07/1916	26/07/1916
War Diary	Franvillers	27/07/1916	30/07/1916
War Diary	Henencourt	31/07/1916	31/07/1916
Miscellaneous	Cover For Branch Memoranda. Unregistered		
Heading	2nd Brigade. 1st Division. 1st Battalion Northamptonshire Regiment August 1916		
War Diary	Henencourt Wood	01/08/1916	13/08/1916
War Diary	Maroc's Redoubt	14/08/1916	14/08/1916
War Diary	Support Trenches in Left of High Wood	15/08/1916	15/08/1916

War Diary	Front Line Left of High Wood	16/08/1916	16/08/1916
War Diary	Front Line Captured on 16th	17/08/1916	18/08/1916
War Diary	Becourt Wood	21/08/1916	27/08/1916
War Diary	Lozenge Wood	28/08/1916	31/08/1916
War Diary	Becourt Wood	22/08/1916	22/08/1916
Heading	2nd Brigade. 1st Division. 1st Battalion Northamptonshire Regiment September 1916.		
Heading	1st B. Northamptonshire Regt War Diary September 1916		
War Diary	High Wood	01/09/1916	02/09/1916
War Diary	Albert	03/09/1916	05/09/1916
War Diary	Quadrangle	06/09/1916	09/09/1916
War Diary	High Wood	09/09/1916	11/09/1916
War Diary	Baizieux Wood	12/09/1916	13/09/1916
War Diary	Bresle	14/09/1916	19/09/1916
War Diary	Mametz Wd	20/09/1916	20/09/1916
War Diary	Albert	21/09/1916	25/09/1916
War Diary	Res. Position S of High Wood	26/09/1916	26/09/1916
War Diary	S. of High Wood	27/09/1916	28/09/1916
War Diary	Albert	29/09/1916	30/09/1916
Heading	2nd Brigade. 1st Division. 1st Battalion Northamptonshire Regiment October 1916.		
Heading	1st Northamptonshire Regt Vol 25 War Diary October 1916		
War Diary	Millencourt	01/10/1916	03/10/1916
War Diary	Acheux	04/10/1916	31/10/1916
Heading	2nd Brigade. 1st Division. 1st Battalion Northamptonshire Regiment November 1916.		
War Diary	Bresle	01/11/1916	04/11/1916
War Diary	Albert	05/11/1916	19/11/1916
War Diary	High Wood	20/11/1916	21/11/1916
War Diary	Eaucourt L'Abbaye	22/11/1916	27/11/1916
War Diary	Mametz Wood	28/11/1916	30/11/1916
Heading	2nd Brigade. 1st Division. 1st Battalion Northamptonshire Regiment December 1916.		
War Diary	Mametz Wood	01/12/1916	10/12/1916
War Diary	Hight Wood E Camp	11/12/1916	14/12/1916
War Diary	Flers Line	15/12/1916	18/12/1916
War Diary	Bazentin	19/12/1916	22/12/1916
War Diary	Factory Corner	23/12/1916	26/12/1916
War Diary	Bazentin Huts	27/12/1916	29/12/1916
War Diary	Albert	30/12/1916	30/12/1916
Heading	1st Division 2nd Infy Bde 1st Battalion Northamptonshire Regt Jan-Dec 1917		
Heading	War Diary 1st. Northamptonshire Regiment. 2nd. Infantry Brigade.1st. Division. January. 1917.		
Heading	1st Northamptonshire Regiment War Diary January 1917 Vol 28		
War Diary	Millencourt	01/01/1917	09/01/1917
War Diary	Albert	10/01/1917	22/01/1917
War Diary	Warloy	23/01/1917	23/01/1917
War Diary	Bresle	24/01/1917	31/01/1917
Heading	War Diary 1st. Northamptonshire Regiment. 2nd. Infantry Brigade. 1st. Division. February. 1917.		
War Diary	Bresle	01/02/1917	02/02/1917
War Diary	Mericourt. Sur Somme	03/02/1917	04/02/1917

War Diary	Chuignolles	05/02/1917	06/02/1917
War Diary	Front Line en Frond of Barleux	07/02/1917	10/02/1917
War Diary	Moved into Support in Luis De Boulogne	11/02/1917	13/02/1917
War Diary	Chuignes	14/02/1917	22/02/1917
War Diary	Front Line in front of Barleux	23/02/1917	25/02/1917
War Diary	Move into Support	26/02/1917	28/02/1917
Heading	War Diary (With Appendix). 1st. Northamptonshire Regiment. 2nd. Infantry Brigade. 1st Division. March. 1917.		
War Diary	In Support	01/03/1917	02/03/1917
War Diary	Front Line Barleux	03/03/1917	06/03/1917
War Diary	Becquincourt	06/03/1917	10/03/1917
War Diary	Chuignolles	11/03/1917	18/03/1917
War Diary	Brie	19/03/1917	31/03/1917
Miscellaneous	1st Division No. G. 277/14/17.	09/03/1917	09/03/1917
Heading	War Diary 1st. Northamptonshire Regiment. 2nd. Infantry Brigade. 1st. Division. April 1917.		
War Diary	Brie	01/04/1917	05/04/1917
War Diary	Chuignolles	06/04/1917	15/04/1917
War Diary	Morcourt	16/04/1917	30/04/1917
Heading	War Diary. 1st. Northamptonshire Regiment. 2nd Infantry Brigade. 1st Division. May. 1917.		
War Diary	Morcourt Sur Somme	01/05/1917	16/05/1917
War Diary	Morcourt	17/05/1917	18/05/1917
War Diary	Villers Bretonneux	19/05/1917	31/05/1917
Heading	War Diary. 1st. Northamptonshire Regiment. 2nd. Infantry Brigade. 1st. Division. June 1917		
War Diary	Meteren	01/06/1917	10/06/1917
War Diary	Nr. Cassel	11/06/1917	19/06/1917
War Diary	Wormhoudt	20/06/1917	20/06/1917
War Diary	Coudekerque	21/06/1917	23/06/1917
War Diary	Nr Coxyde Bains	23/06/1917	31/06/1917
Heading	War Diary (With Appendices). 1st. Northamptonshire Regiment. 2nd. Infantry Brigade. 1st. Division. July 1917		
War Diary	Camp be Hocue Oost-Dunkerque and Oost Donkerque Bains Front Line in Front of Nieuport Bains	01/07/1917	10/07/1917
War Diary	Rinck Camp On Road be Hocue Coxyde-Bains & Oust-D-Bains	11/07/1917	14/07/1917
War Diary	Ghyvelde	15/07/1917	15/07/1917
War Diary	Armbouts Capelle.	16/07/1917	18/07/1917
War Diary	St. Pol	19/07/1917	31/07/1917
Miscellaneous	2nd Infantry Brigade Intelligence Summary. Covering period 24 hours to 6 a.m. 9th July 1917.	09/07/1917	09/07/1917
Operation(al) Order(s)	Report on The Operations of July 10th, 1917. Reference Map-Secret Map attached.	14/07/1917	14/07/1917
Map	German Front Line		
Heading	War Diary. (With Appendices). 1st., Northamptonshire Regiment. 2nd Infantry Brigade. 1st. Division. August. 1917.		
War Diary	Le Clipon Camp	01/08/1917	31/08/1917
Miscellaneous	1st Battalion, The Northamptonshire Regiment. Appendix	25/08/1917	25/08/1917
Miscellaneous	Fourth Army No. G.s.843. 1st Division	25/08/1917	25/08/1917
War Diary	Le Clipon Camp	01/08/1917	31/08/1917

Miscellaneous	1st Battalion. The Northamptonshire Regiment. Appendix		25/08/1917	25/08/1917
Heading	War Diary 1st. Northamptonshire Regiment. 2nd. Infantry Brigade. 1st. Division. September. 1917.			
War Diary	Le Clipon		20/09/1917	30/09/1917
War Diary	Le Clipon Camp		01/09/1917	19/09/1917
Heading	War Diary 1st. Northamptonshire Regiment. 2nd. Infantry Brigade. 1st. Division. October.1917.			
War Diary	Le Clipon Camp		01/10/1917	17/10/1917
War Diary	Le Clipon		18/10/1917	21/10/1917
War Diary	Eringham		22/10/1917	23/10/1917
War Diary	Nouveau Monde		24/10/1917	24/10/1917
War Diary	Near Poperinghe		25/10/1917	31/10/1917
Heading	War Diary 1st. Northamptonshire Regiment. 2nd Infantry Brigade. 1st Division. November. 1917.			
War Diary	Schools Camp at St Janster Biezen		01/11/1917	02/11/1917
War Diary	W of Poperinghe		03/11/1917	05/11/1917
War Diary	Poperinghe		06/11/1917	07/11/1917
War Diary	Hilltop Farm		07/11/1917	11/11/1917
War Diary	Hilltop		12/11/1917	15/11/1917
War Diary	Dambre Camp.		16/11/1917	18/11/1917
War Diary	Hilltop		19/11/1917	23/11/1917
War Diary	Tunnelling Camp.		24/11/1917	26/11/1917
War Diary	Herzeele		27/11/1917	30/11/1917
Heading	War Diary 1st. Northamptonshire Regiment. 2nd. Infantry Brigade. 1st. Division. December. 1917.			
War Diary	Herzeele Area		01/12/1917	07/12/1917
War Diary	Waayemburg Ref. Map. Sheet 19.X.14.C.		08/12/1917	09/12/1917
War Diary	Woesten Camp		20/12/1917	20/12/1917
War Diary	Bn.H.Q.		21/12/1917	21/12/1917
War Diary	La Chavdiere		22/12/1917	22/12/1917
War Diary	U. 14. C. 6.6		23/12/1917	23/12/1917
War Diary	Ref. Map. Bixchoote 1/10,000		24/12/1917	24/12/1917
War Diary	Bn.H.Q.		25/12/1917	25/12/1917
War Diary	U.9.d. 4.6		26/12/1917	28/12/1917
War Diary	Woesten Camp		29/12/1917	29/12/1917
War Diary	Zuidhuis Camp		30/12/1917	31/12/1917
War Diary	Ref Belgium Sheet 20. S.28. a.		11/12/1917	13/12/1917
War Diary	Woesten Bn. H Q at T.25.d.6.4 (Sheet 20)		14/12/1917	19/12/1917
Heading	1st Division 2nd Brigade Northamptonshire Regt. 1918 From 1 January, To 31st 1919 May			
Heading	2nd Brigade. 1st Division. 1st Battalion Northamptonshire Regiment April 1918.			
War Diary	Zuidhuis Camp		01/01/1918	05/01/1918
War Diary	Camp at T.25.d.6.4		06/01/1918	11/01/1918
War Diary	Bn H.Q. at U.14.C.4.0		12/01/1918	14/01/1918
War Diary	Bixchoote 1/10,000		15/01/1918	16/01/1918
War Diary	H.Q. at U.q.d. 3.3.		17/01/1918	21/01/1918
War Diary	T. 25. d. 6.4.		22/01/1918	22/01/1918
War Diary	Zuidhuis Camp		23/01/1918	28/01/1918
War Diary	T.25.d 6.4		29/01/1918	31/01/1918
War Diary	Vandamme Camp		01/02/1918	01/02/1918
War Diary	Woesten		01/02/1918	08/02/1918
War Diary	Bn H Q. Hubner Fm. D.I.C.4.6 Peel 28 1/40,000		08/02/1918	09/02/1918
War Diary	Hubner Fm D. I. C. 4.6.		10/02/1918	10/02/1918
War Diary	H.Q at C 11.2.3.6 (Sheet 28 1/40,000)		11/02/1918	12/02/1918

War Diary	H.Q at Norfolk House	12/02/1918	12/02/1918
War Diary	V.19. a. 6.2 (Sheet 20 S.W & S.E) 1/20000	13/02/1918	16/02/1918
War Diary	H.Q. at C.11.b.3.6	17/02/1918	18/02/1918
War Diary	Hubner Fm (B.H.Q.)	19/02/1918	20/02/1918
War Diary	Hospital Camp	21/02/1918	21/02/1918
War Diary	Elverdinghe	22/02/1918	28/02/1918
War Diary	Hospital Farm	01/03/1918	01/03/1918
War Diary	Elverdinghe	02/03/1918	04/03/1918
War Diary	Hilltop Farm	05/03/1918	10/03/1918
War Diary	1st Northamptonshire Regt.	11/03/1918	11/03/1918
War Diary	Hilltop Farm	12/03/1918	16/03/1918
War Diary	Hugel Halles	16/03/1918	17/03/1918
War Diary	Hubner Farm D.I.C. 4.6	18/03/1918	22/03/1918
War Diary	Hugel Halles	23/03/1918	24/03/1918
War Diary	Norfolk House V19 a 6.2 (Sh. 20 S.W. & SE) 1/40,000	25/03/1918	28/03/1918
War Diary	Kempton Park	29/03/1918	04/04/1918
War Diary	Lapugnoy	05/04/1918	06/04/1918
War Diary	Cuinchy	07/04/1918	09/04/1918
War Diary	Ref Map Gorre 1/20,000	09/04/1918	13/04/1918
War Diary	Cambrin	14/04/1918	18/04/1918
War Diary	Ref Map. Gorre 1/20,000	18/04/1918	20/04/1918
War Diary	Givenchy Ref Map Gorre 1/20,000	20/04/1918	20/04/1918
War Diary	Bn. H.Q. A.14.a 5.5.	21/04/1918	22/04/1918
War Diary	La Bourse	23/04/1918	23/04/1918
War Diary	Cambrin	24/04/1918	25/04/1918
War Diary	Bn H.Q. A.20 d.5.3	26/04/1918	30/04/1918
War Diary	Ref Map Gorre 1/20,000 Bn H.Q. A.20.d.5.3.	01/05/1918	01/05/1918
War Diary	Noeux Les Mines	02/05/1918	12/05/1918
War Diary	Annequin	13/05/1918	16/05/1918
War Diary	Bn H.Q. at A.25.d.8.2	17/05/1918	18/05/1918
War Diary	Ref. Map Gorre 1/20,000	19/05/1918	23/05/1918
War Diary	Bn H.Q at A.25.d.8.2.	24/05/1918	25/05/1918
War Diary	Annequin	26/05/1918	28/05/1918
War Diary	Noeux Les Mines	29/05/1918	04/06/1918
War Diary	Bn H Q. A.20.d	05/06/1918	05/06/1918
War Diary	Ref Map. Gorre 1/20,000	06/06/1918	16/06/1918
War Diary	Bn H.Q. A.20.d	17/06/1918	18/06/1918
War Diary	Ref Map Gorre 1/20,000	19/06/1918	21/06/1918
War Diary	Noeux Les Mines	22/06/1918	02/07/1918
War Diary	Annequin	02/07/1918	06/07/1918
War Diary	Front Line Left Hohenzollern Sector.	07/07/1918	07/07/1918
War Diary	R D Martin Lt for Lt. Col. Comdg	08/07/1918	16/07/1918
War Diary	Annequin	17/07/1918	21/07/1918
War Diary	Noeux Les Mines.	22/07/1918	25/07/1918
War Diary	R D Martin Lt for Lt. Col. Comdg	26/07/1918	31/07/1918
War Diary	Cambrin	01/08/1918	21/08/1918
War Diary	Bours	22/08/1918	30/09/1918
War Diary	Arras	31/09/1918	31/09/1918
War Diary	Arras	01/09/1918	15/09/1918
War Diary	Caulaincourt	16/09/1918	23/09/1918
War Diary	Caulaincourt Wood Q 36 D 62 Q. 120000 SE	23/09/1918	30/09/1918
War Diary	Caulaincourt.	01/10/1918	01/10/1918
War Diary	Magny-La-Fosse.	10/10/1918	10/10/1918
War Diary	1 Kilm. N Of Bohain.	16/10/1918	23/10/1918
War Diary	La Vallee Mulatre	24/10/1918	30/10/1918
War Diary	Vaux Andigny	31/10/1918	02/11/1918

War Diary	Mazinghien	03/11/1918	04/11/1918
War Diary	La Justicex Roads	04/11/1918	04/11/1918
War Diary	Fesmy	04/11/1918	05/11/1918
War Diary	La Valee Mulatre & Fresnoy	06/11/1918	06/11/1918
War Diary	Fresnoy	07/11/1918	12/11/1918
War Diary	Fauril	13/11/1918	15/11/1918
War Diary	Sars Poteries	16/11/1918	18/11/1918
War Diary	Stree	19/11/1918	19/11/1918
War Diary	Pry	20/11/1918	22/11/1918
War Diary	Morialme	23/11/1918	23/11/1918
War Diary	Falaen	24/11/1918	30/11/1918
War Diary	Sommiere	01/12/1918	01/12/1918
War Diary	Miranda Chateau	02/12/1918	02/12/1918
War Diary	Villers Sur Lesse	03/12/1918	07/12/1918
War Diary	Chevetogne Abbey	08/12/1918	08/12/1918
War Diary	Sin Sin	09/12/1918	09/12/1918
War Diary	Hotton	10/12/1918	10/12/1918
War Diary	Erezee	11/12/1918	13/12/1918
War Diary	Malempre	14/12/1918	14/12/1918
War Diary	Sart	15/12/1918	15/12/1918
War Diary	Rogery	16/12/1918	16/12/1918
War Diary	Neidingen	17/12/1918	17/12/1918
War Diary	Manderfield	18/12/1918	18/12/1918
War Diary	Dahlem	19/12/1918	20/12/1918
War Diary	Blankenheimerdorf	21/12/1918	21/12/1918
War Diary	Munstereifel	22/12/1918	22/12/1918
War Diary	Odendorf	23/12/1918	23/12/1918
War Diary	Duisdorf	24/12/1918	04/03/1919
War Diary	Lengsdorf	05/03/1919	14/05/1919
War Diary	Antwerp	15/05/1919	20/05/1919

1ST DIVISION
2ND BRIGADE

1ST BATTALION
NORTHAMPTONSHIRE REGT.
AUG – DEC 1914

2nd Brigade
1st Division.

1st BATTALION

NORTHAMPTONSHIRE REGIMENT

AUGUST 1914.

Rearguard Section
ETREUX
27th Aug. 1914

G.O.C. 1st Division

1. The 1st (Guards) Bde formed the rearguard of 1st Division
   under Brig Gen F.J. Morse C.M.G. C.B. D.S.O. consisted
   [of troops?] DOMPIERRE, via [   ] and kept touch
   [with?] [ ] to FESMY [   ] CAMBRESIS and
   [ ] LAURETTE where it arrived a [   ] after
   after dark and billeted with B.H.Q.
   Headquarters at FESMY.   1 Motor Machine Gun Battery.
   11th Bde R.F.A.   1 Battery 43 Howitzer Bde
   23rd Field Co. R.E.   2 troops 15th Hussars and
   1st Guards Brigade. [   ] Finding was also
   No 1 Field Ambulance available only on 27th.

2. About 2.15 A.M on Aug 27th 1st Division orders
   were received to the following effect:—
   The 1st Div of Corps moving on our road
   will retire on GUISE covered by the troops
   under Brig Gen Morse who will occupy by
   6 A.M the line North edge FESMY connecting
   at [ ] Regiment the LE MAULCOURT
   NASSIGNY (exclusive) which was to be held
   by 2nd Infantry Brigade.
   The remainder of 1st Division was to
   move about 6 A.M from OISY, and the
   Trains of the 1st, 2nd, + 3rd Brigades were
   to collect south of OISY and then [   ],
   ready to follow 2nd Division main
   column.

3. At about 7 A.M Brig Gen Morse ordered his
   Hd Qrs to move to Canal Bridge N of [   ]

LE CAMBRESIS, as being more central, and just as he himself was moving out of FESMY Major Gen Lomax came to FESMY in a motor car and gave General Maxse, verbally, the situation of affairs as it was known. Major

6. Colonel, -[illegible], Major Gen Maxse was also present when the G.O.C. 1st Division spoke to General Maxse. The chief point insisted on by the G.O.C. 1st Division was the fact that two divisions were passing through ETREUX with their trains, and moreover that supplies were being stored in ETREUX. It would therefore be essential to hold on to the FESMY - WASSIGNY position in order to prevent ETREUX being shelled by the enemy. He also stated that a flank guard was being provided by the Welsh regiment on road FESMY - BERGUES - DIVE - DORENG, - IRON, & he left it to Brig: Gen Maxse's discretion to fix the hour for starting the retirement of both the rearguard and the 3rd Brigade at WASSIGNY.

4. Brig: Gen Maxse concluded from these instructions that the evacuation of ETREUX by 1st & 2nd Divisions would decide the hour for starting the retirement of the rearguard, and issued orders to the O.C. Black Watch & 23 Field Co R.E (in reserve) to reconnoitre and prepare an intermediate rearguard position about the Sc du Bois on mile North of ETREUX.

that the existing position while ETREUX
could be changed, but wrote out
his orders for the retirement 7th (day)
leaving out the time for subsequent
insertion. These orders were made
out to a mounted officer (one from
unit to headquarters) at about 12 noon
and they (including Major Davis) returned
to their battalions to explain the
retirement order to C.O.s. The same
written orders were subsequently sent
out to all units at 12.15 p.m. with the
time filled in as "retreat at once".
This was done immediately on receipt
of the following message from Lt.
Colonel Cameron of the 1st Division
Staff. "ETREUX is now clear of
infi. divisn. G.O.C. says you can
move to ETREUX now." Dated 12.20 p.m.
27th Aug. 1914 at ETREUX Station.

Br. Gen. Gosse's orders to his units
& to 2nd Brigade were sent out at
12.15 p.m. as shown in attached copy,
& the Black Watch took up its
allotted position.

c. Major Day (Royal Munster Fusiliers)
who started at about 12 noon from a
Petit CAMBRESIS with the verbal orders
reached Major Charrier in safety &
these retained to Bde. Hd. Qrs. but the
Munster cyclist who carried the same
orders in writing at 12.50 p.m. did not
reach his destination because he was
fired upon by Germans between CAMBRESIS

and FESMY. He delivered his written
message to Major Day whom he met
some hours afterwards.

5. Major H. J. F. de Fonblanque Kennett & Lieutenant
Walker M'pherson Hunter were each sent at
intervals, & when they arrived they were already
stopped by a force of the enemy.
But the at FESMY, under Major
Chamier's orders, were 1 troop 15th
Hussars & 1 section 118th Battery R.F.A.
The last message received from Major
Chamier reached Bde. Hd. Qrs. where
Major Day reported himself & stated
that he left Major Chamier at about
1.30 p.m. heavily engaged with the enemy.
Written messages from Major Chamier
despatched between 1.15 p.m. & 1.30 p.m.,
stated that he was fighting & killing
Germans & seemed to be opposed by 2
Regiments & some guns, that he had
taken prisoners from the 15th German
Regt. & was getting on very well,
these two ...

6. In order to extricate the Musketeers there
was a long delay in the retirement of
the whole rearguard & Major Day
again attempted to get through to
FESMY, but without success. Realising
that the safety of the whole force
would be jeopardised if the retirement
were further delayed & owing the
fact that a gap of many miles already
existed between the rearguard and
the main body Gen. Musse issued fresh orders

peremptory orders for the retirement
of the rearguard to be continued,
in spite of the inability of the
Royal Munster Fusiliers to extricate
themselves from the grip of superior
forces of the enemy. The officers
commanding the 1st Bn. Coldstream
Guards and the 1st Bn. Black Watch
delayed their retirement until
after 4 p.m. when they were still
south of ETREUX, endeavouring
to help out the Munster Fusiliers.
In fact they compromised the safety
of themselves and of the whole force
by their prolonged delay, but I
cannot for one moment blame them
in view of the fact that
they took this risk for the sole
purpose of succouring their comrades
of the Munster Fusiliers.
The rearguard was so soon clear
of ETREUX that is to say on the
level plateau south of it, than it
was attacked both in front and
on its eastern flank by dismounted
cavalry & horse artillery. Fighting
continued all the way from
ETREUX to LA M^{on} ROUGE without
intermission from about 3 p.m.
till after dark, and it is estimated
that the enemy's force comprised
of one cavalry division (employing
dismounted action) and two batteries
of horse artillery. This force appears

appears to have been supported
by infantry also, but the infantry
did not make itself felt before
our retirement commenced operations.
All infantry had been set on
at an early hour to ST GERMAINS,
south of GUISE, & thence through
GUISE to JONQUEUSE. The four
batteries of artillery were at
about 3 p.m. placed in favourable
positions near JERUSALEM HUB and
LA MAISON ROUGE where they did splendid
work by their accurate fire in
helping the infantry to retire unmolested
across the flat plain. Without going
into detail or describing the actions
of the units concerned, it will be
sufficient to record that a
brisk rearguard action ensued
on the ground already indicated.
It was executed with steadiness &
marked success by the three arms in
continual cooperation. I venture
to bring to the notice of the Major
General Commanding the 1st Division
the names of the following officers
for special mention:—

Lt Colonel Cunliffe-Owen — R.F.A.
Lt Colonel E. Forbes L.H.G. D.S.O. Scots Guards.
Lt Colonel A. Grant Ophin — Black Watch.
Major Greenwright — R.F.A.
Captain House — Grenadier Guards.
Capt Wilson — West Yorks Rgt. Corps.
Lieut. Hon. Hardinge — 15th Hussars.

I have the honour to be
Sir
Your obedient servant

(sd) L. J. Trevor Maj General.
Commanding 1st Guards Brigade.

Army Form C. 2118

WAR DIARY 1st Wiltshire from the Regt.
or
INTELLIGENCE SUMMARY.
(Erase heading not required.)

Hour, Date, Place	Summary of Events and Information	Remarks and references to Appendices
12 August 1914	Left BLACKDOWN and embarked at South-	
13th August "	-AMPTON on S.S. GALIRA	
	Disembarked at HAVRE and went into Rest	
	Camp. 2 interpreters joined Battalion.	
14th August "	HAVRE	
15th " "	Entrained at No.7 point for ETREUX	
16th " "	Detrained at ETREUX and went into billets	
17th "ESQUEHERIES"	Marched at 7 a.m. to ESQUEHERIES	
	Route March	
18th " "	Route March	
19th " "	Route March	
20th " "	Ordered to move North.	

I have the honour to be
Sir
Your obedient servant

(sd) L.J. Moncic Maj General.
Commanding 1st Guards Brigade.

ETREUX.

Army Form C. 2118

1st Bn. Connaught Rangers Regt.

WAR DIARY
or
INTELLIGENCE SUMMARY.
(Erase heading not required.)

Instructions regarding War Diaries and Intelligence Summaries are contained in F.S. Regs., Part II. and the Staff Manual respectively. Title pages will be prepared in manuscript.

Hour, Date, Place	Summary of Events and Information	Remarks and references to Appendices
12 August 1914	Left BLACKDOWN and embarked at SOUTH-AMPTON on S.S. GALIKA	
13th August "	Disembarked at HAVRE and went into Rest Camp. 2 interpreters joined Battalion.	
14th August "	HAVRE Entrained at No 7 point for ETREUX	
15th " "		
16 " "	Detrained at ETREUX and went into billets Marched at 7 a.m. to ESQUEHERIES	
17th "ESQUEHERIES"	Route March	
18th " "	Route March	
19th " "	Route March	
20th " "	Ordered to move North	

Army Form C. 2118

WAR DIARY 1st Bn. Hampshire Regt.

INTELLIGENCE SUMMARY.

(Erase heading not required.)

Instructions regarding War Diaries and Intelligence Summaries are contained in F.S. Regs., Part II. and the Staff Manual respectively. Title pages will be prepared in manuscript.

Hour, Date, Place	Summary of Events and Information	Remarks and references to Appendices
21/8/14 ETROEUNGT	Marched to ETROEUNGT (near AVESNES) + billeted	
22/8/14 "	Battalion order to move at 4:30 A.M. Marched N about 15 miles. Halted for 2 or 3 hours near BEAUFORT and then went into billets. Battalion was detailed as divisional troops	
23/8/14 GIVRET	Marched to GIVRET. In the evening ordered to reinforce the Berkshire Regt. Shelled. No casualties.	
24/8/14 "	6 A.M. ordered to retire to GIVRET from Rear Guard 5.1st Division retiring. Arrived in MAUBEUGE.	
25/8/14 MARBAIX	Marched to MARBAIX. Brigade in Rear Guard. Rifle fire stampeded A.S.C. transport. Our casualties 1 man killed 3 wounded. Due to false alarm.	
26/8/14 "	Marched to OISY. Battalion took up position to cover retirement of 3rd Brigade. Retirement safely accomplished.	

Army Form C. 2118

1st Battalion the Wilts

WAR DIARY
or
INTELLIGENCE SUMMARY.
(Erase heading not required.)

Instructions regarding War Diaries and Intelligence Summaries are contained in F. S. Regs., Part II. and the Staff Manual respectively. Title pages will be prepared in manuscript.

Hour, Date, Place	Summary of Events and Information	Remarks and references to Appendices
27/8/14	Brigade moved to WASSIGNY + took up position to cover rear of Division - The Battalion in position on right. 'C' Company captured German patrol. When division in clear we retire & go into Billets at HAUTVILLE	
28/8/14	Receive orders to move at 3.30 A.M. Brigade to take up Right Flank Guard position to cover main body of Division. The Battalion is detailed to 2nd line. Our position on high ground near LA FERE. Enemy's Cavalry appeared about 12.30 p.m. Enemy guns came into action about 1 p.m. No determined Infantry attack. Ordered to retire about 2 p.m. to village of TRIBEMONT. Battalion Marched off as Rear Guard to the Brigade and got to bivouac 12 Mile higher about 3 miles from LA FERE.	

Army Form C. 2118

WAR DIARY
INTELLIGENCE SUMMARY.
(Erase heading not required.)

Instructions regarding War Diaries and Intelligence Summaries are contained in F.S. Regs., Part II. and the Staff Manual respectively. Title pages will be prepared in manuscript.

Hour, Date, Place	Summary of Events and Information	Remarks and references to Appendices
29/8/14	Rested for the day. Machine Gun Section take up position at LA FERE	
30/8/14	Moved at 3.30 A.M. towards SOISSONS. Brigade bivo'd for the night at ANESEY-CHATEAU.	
31/8/14	Moved at 5.30 A.M. in a Southerly direction past SOISSONS about 20 miles and bivouac.	

2nd Brigade.
1st Division.

1st BATTALION

NORTHAMPTONSHIRE REGIMENT

SEPTEMBER 1914.

WAR DIARY
INTELLIGENCE SUMMARY.
(Erase heading not required.)

Army Form C. 2118.

Instructions regarding War Diaries and Intelligence Summaries are contained in F.S. Regs., Part II. and the Staff Manual respectively. Title pages will be prepared in manuscript.

Hour, Date, Place	Summary of Events and Information	Remarks and references to Appendices
1/9/14	Retire went continued	
2/9/14	Retirement continued. Billet - 8 horses about 4 mile N.g NEAUX	
3/9/14	Moved E end of River MARNE about 4 a.m. to LA FERTE. Burn the road & take up a position facing N + N.E. at 5½ a.m. West from MARNE and billet at ROMENY about 5 m S g LA FERTE	
4/9/14	at 3 a.m. marched to AULNOY. at 4 p.m. enemy attacked his Brigade did not come into action.	
5/9/14	at 2.30 a.m. marched to BONNAY & billeted. 1st Reinforcement (1 Officer 100 other ranks)	
6/9/14	Our army taken offensive. Brigade remained in Reserve & at 5 p.m. march N to VANDOY & bivouac.	
7/9/14	Continue advance to VOUAY and billet there.	
8/9/14	Marched to REBAIS - front. Jn. 2nd Reinforcement (1 officer & 60 men / Sqn.	

WAR DIARY
or
INTELLIGENCE SUMMARY.
(Erase heading not required.)

Army Form C. 2118.

Instructions regarding War Diaries and Intelligence Summaries are contained in F.S. Regs., Part II. and the Staff Manual respectively. Title pages will be prepared in manuscript.

Hour, Date, Place	Summary of Events and Information	Remarks and references to Appendices
Sept 9th	Advance cross River Marne, bivouac near Domurect (not in action)	
10th	Rôle advance guard to Division. Scouts report enemy holding high ground above village called Priers. advance halted. Capt Lloyd, Stephen & Jervoise wounded. Enemy retired after about two hours fighting.	
11th	advanced to Curry Wheeled from	
12th	advance N.E. to Paars.	
13th	Cross the R Aisne. What operation. Batt came into Action 3 mile N of Moulin 1st day of the Battle of the aisne	
14th	Two Companies of the Regiment attacked High Ground of Troyon village in Conjunction with rest of the Brigade. Capt White & Capt Paget killed. The Remaining Two Companies came up at night & entrenched to fill in Gap between Guards & R Lancs.	

WAR DIARY
or
INTELLIGENCE SUMMARY.
(Erase heading not required.)

Army Form C. 2118.

Hour, Date, Place	Summary of Events and Information	Remarks and references to Appendices
Sept 1st	What- An attack by the enemy heavy shelling by both sides. Capt Gordon Ralli getting some of the boys into advanced trenches. Very hot	
10th	Very hot. No attack	
17th	Sta verbal orders attacked us in two [places] about 1.30 P.M. order to charge them out of trenches. last three to own lines. Capt Parker killed leading the charge, which has succeeded — an ultimate included received in which 2 officers man & men were killed. The enemy showed the white flag — have been surrounded by 2 [?] a van when for him. We trusted they put white over of the flag	

WAR DIARY
or
INTELLIGENCE SUMMARY.
(Erase heading not required.)

Army Form C. 2118.

Instructions regarding War Diaries and Intelligence Summaries are contained in F.S. Regs., Part II. and the Staff Manual respectively. Title pages will be prepared in manuscript.

Hour, Date, Place	Summary of Events and Information	Remarks and references to Appendices
Sept 18th	Night attack but heavily repulsed	
19th	relieved by the 18th Bde got to Pargnan all reserve	
20th	- at Pargnan	
21st	Move to Paissy	
22nd	at Paissy in reserve	
23rd	Genl Sir John French visits the Bde - at Paissy	
24th	at Paissy	
25th	return to the Trenches at Troyon taken over from the 18th Batt	
26th	in the Trenches at Troyon	

Army Form C. 2118.

WAR DIARY
or
INTELLIGENCE SUMMARY.
(Erase heading not required.)

Instructions regarding War Diaries and Intelligence Summaries are contained in F.S. Regs., Part II. and the Staff Manual respectively. Title pages will be prepared in manuscript.

Hour, Date, Place	Summary of Events and Information	Remarks and references to Appendices
Sept 27th	attacked at Dawn in the town but repulsed. It tomette bounded by a stell shilishe.	
28th	all quiet	
29th	—	
30th	—	
Oct 1st	—	
2	slight attack at night easily repulsed	
3	h—attack	
4th		
5		

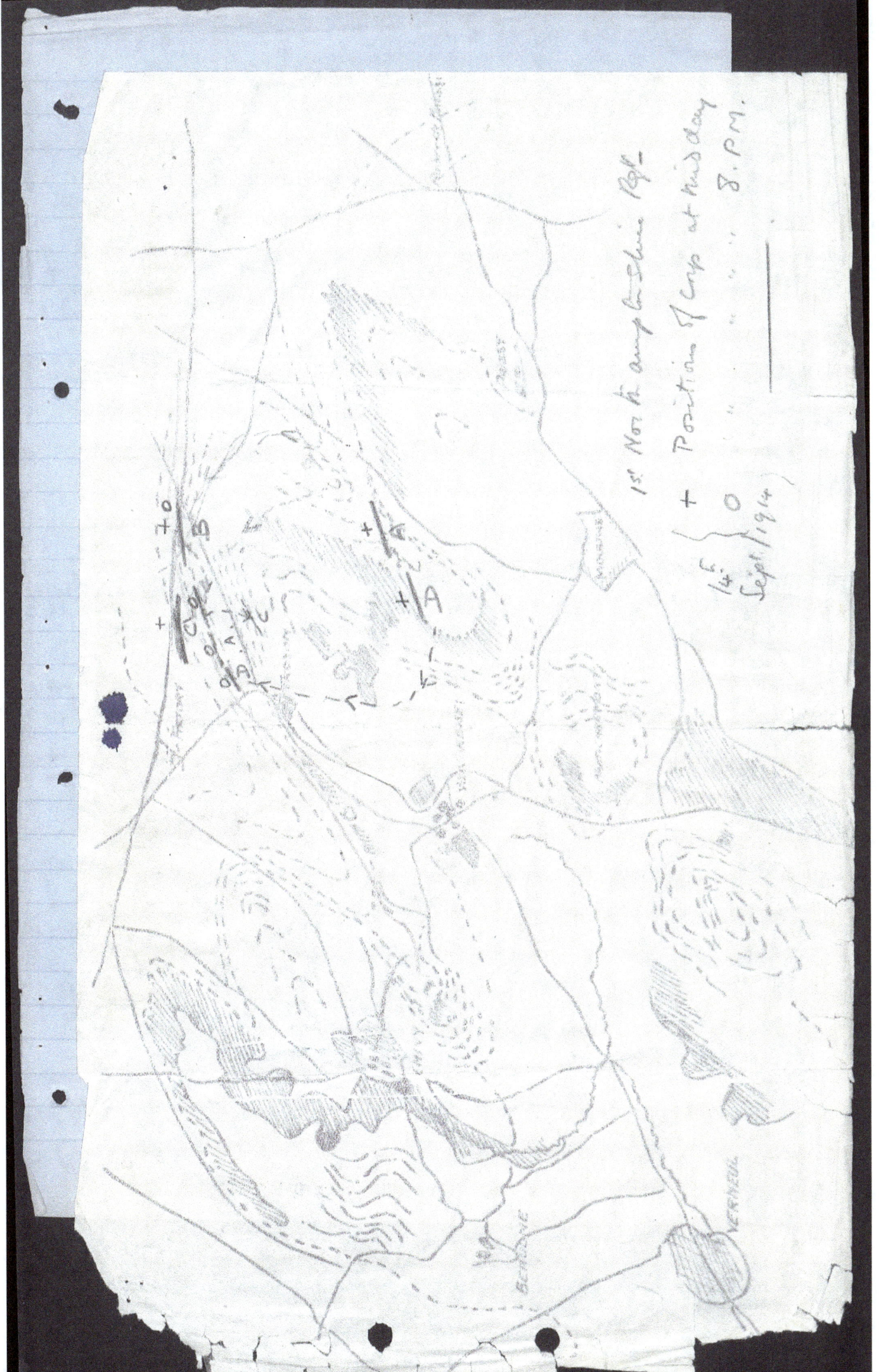

Head Quarters
2nd Infantry Brigade

Part taken by 1st Batt. Northamptonshire
Regiment in fighting of 14th instant.

The positions of the battalion is shown
on attached plan at 12·0 m.d. - day and 8·0 p.m.
"B" & "C" Companies took part in the fighting on our
right flank with the Queens and other Regiments.
"A" & "D" Companies remaining in reserve as marked.—
About 8·0 p.m the Battalion occupied the Trenches
as marked in relief of the 2nd Bn Kings Royal
Rifles, one company being in reserve.

Rentoul Smyth
Lieut Colonel
Commg 1st Bn Northamptonshire Regiment

29/9/14

1st [illegible]

[signature]
2/4/15

This Narrative was received fighting on
at 7·30 pm traced up by pen [illegible]
drawings put in and forwarded with reference

47

2nd Brigade.

1st Division.

1st BATTALION

NORTHAMPTONSHIRE REGIMENT

OCTOBER 1 9 1 4

WAR DIARY

Copied from last page of War Diry for September, 1914

Oct. 1st   All quiet
2nd   Slight attack at night easily repulsed.
3rd   No attack.
4th   "
5th   "

WAR DIARY
or
INTELLIGENCE SUMMARY.
(Erase heading not required.)

Army Form C.

Instructions regarding War Diaries and Intelligence Summaries are contained in F.S. Regs., Part II. and the Staff Manual respectively. Title pages will be prepared in manuscript.

Hour, Date, Place	Summary of Events and Information	Remarks and references to Appendices
15th		
7th		
8th		
9th to 14th	no notices of any intention — heavy shelling but dies not harm	
15th		
16th	Rule to be relieved by 115 French — relief commenced at 10.30 PM finished at 2.30 AM next day.	
17th	Go S. to Vaudere	
18th	return at Fresnes	

WAR DIARY
or
INTELLIGENCE SUMMARY.
(Erase heading not required.)

Army Form C. 2118.

Instructions regarding War Diaries and Intelligence Summaries are contained in F.S. Regs., Part II. and the Staff Manual respectively. Title pages will be prepared in manuscript.

Hour, Date, Place	Summary of Events and Information	Remarks and references to Appendices
Sept 19th	Arrive Cassel —	
20th	Move at 5 A.M. to Elverdinghe	
21st	Advance to Pilken - Boe & Crps reserve	
22nd	ordered up to help Camerons due N of Pilken, about 2 A.M. on Von Corps to relieve to attack on turn in the Bixschote - Langemark Rd. It was not successful but Russell was killed in the attempt	
23rd	allies had also Bill again a very vigorous attack in the evening but it was repulsed —	

Army Form C. 2118.

WAR DIARY
or
INTELLIGENCE SUMMARY.
(Erase heading not required.)

Instructions regarding War Diaries and Intelligence Summaries are contained in F.S. Regs., Part II. and the Staff Manual respectively. Title pages will be prepared in manuscript.

Hour, Date, Place	Summary of Events and Information	Remarks and references to Appendices
Oct 24th	Relieved by the French in the trenches after a fairly quiet day.	
Oct 25th	Rested — men rested during the three days we were out. Casualties for the three days were Captain Russell, Rentin, Fothrin RAMC killed, Captain Powell, Pope & Lt. L. Robinson Lt. Needham. Been wounded. Marched to Ypres — in reserve —	
Oct 26th to Nov 15th	The Regiment has heavily engaged most of this time in (act) or about 14th this was only Two officers left — about 300 men —	
Nov 16th	Marched to Westoutre from Ypres	
17th	To Strazeele to refit — 15th division has been brought back in the future	

2nd Brigade.
1st Division.

1st BATTALION

NORTHAMPTONSHIRE REGIMENT

NOVEMBER 1 9 1 4

WAR DIARY

Copied from last page of War Diary for October.

Oct 26th to)
November 15th)   Diary lost.   The Regiment was heavily engaged most of the time in fact on November 14th there were only two officers left – about 300 men –

Nov 16th   Marched to WESTOUTRE from YPRES,

" 17th   to STRAZEELE for refit. 1st Division has been brought back for this purpose

* Army Form C. 2118.

WAR DIARY
or
INTELLIGENCE SUMMARY.
(Erase heading not required.)

Instructions regarding War Diaries and Intelligence Summaries are contained in F. S. Regs., Part II. and the Staff Manual respectively. Title pages will be prepared in manuscript.

Hour, Date, Place	Summary of Events and Information	Remarks and references to Appendices
Nov 18th	at Shapele	
Nov 19th	at Hazebruck	
Nov 20	at Hazebruck	
21		
22		
23		
24		
25		
Nov 26 1914 to Dec 20th 1914	Battalion was resting at Hazebruck.	

2nd Brigade.
1st Division.

1st BATTALION

NORTHAMPTONSHIRE REGIMENT

DECEMBER 1 9 1 4

1st Division
2nd Inf. Bde.

WAR DIARY

1st Battalion NORTHAMPTON REGIMENT

December

1914

(26.11.14 — 31.12.14)

1st Northamptonshire Regt.

Army Form C. 2118.

WAR DIARY
or
INTELLIGENCE SUMMARY
(Erase heading not required.)

Hour, Date, Place	Summary of Events and Information	Remarks and references to Appendices
Nov. 26th 1914 to Dec 20th 1914.	The Battalion was resting at Hazebrouck.	
Dec 21st 1914.	The Battalion left Hazebrouck at 7 A.M. in Motors. Arrived at Zelobes close to Vieille Chapelle at 12 Noon. After filling both Rations & Ammunition, the Battalion was ordered to move to Le Touret. Orders here sometime about 4 P.M. orders were received that the Battalion in conjunction with 1st Royal North Lancashire Regt. was to make a night attack to recover trenches about ½ a miles East of Rue de l'Epinette ½ mile South of Rue de Bois, which had been lost the previous night. — The Two Battalions moved to the attack about 7. P.M. The Battalion had Two Companies in the front line Two in support.	

1st Northamptonshire Regt.

WAR DIARY
or
INTELLIGENCE SUMMARY.
(Erase heading not required.)

Army Form C. 2118.

Instructions regarding War Diaries and Intelligence Summaries are contained in F.S. Regs., Part II and the Staff Manual respectively. Title pages will be prepared in manuscript.

Hour, Date, Place	Summary of Events and Information	Remarks and references to Appendices
Dec 21st. 1914.	1st Northamptonshire R. was on the north of L.N.L. on South. By 10 P.M. the position in front of us had been taken with slight loss. Most of our casualties coming from Artillery fire. Total Casualties Killed + wounded. Three officers - about 60 men. — Wounded. According to previous orders when the position had been retaken the Battalion was to withdraw the line to be held by the 1st L.N.L. Regt. We had however to leave one Company D. in the line. The Rest of the Battalion withdrew back about 2 miles to Gillets reaching him about 1 A.M. - on Dec 22nd.	+ 2/Lieut Pasfield 2/Lieut Wainwright Killed. Capt O.B. Reem wounded.
Dec 22nd. 1914.	Received news about 9 A.M. that the enemy had attacked & broken through our three companies (B.C.A.) were at once ordered up to support. It was found that a much larger force however than the (second?) 300 yards.	

WAR DIARY
or
INTELLIGENCE SUMMARY

Army Form C. 2118.

Hour, Date, Place	Summary of Events and Information	Remarks and references to Appendices
Dec 22 1914	line held the previous night was intimately to a line taken up about 300 yards in rear. Our D. Coy was very highly congratulated on its resistance by the Brigadier General Commanding 2nd Inf. Bde. This line was held by the Battalion during the day with no difficulty.	Major Coulthy received the D.S.O. for the great work he did this day and 2/Lt. Puttin his Military Cross. Two N.C.M's were also given to men.
Dec 23rd 1914	The Battalion still in the trenches as on 22nd inst. We were relieved at night by the 4th Guard Bde. – Go to billets at Essars. –	
Dec 24th 1914	In billets at Essars.	

Army Form C. 2118.

WAR DIARY
or
INTELLIGENCE SUMMARY.
(Erase heading not required.)

Instructions regarding War Diaries and Intelligence Summaries are contained in F.S. Regs., Part II. and the Staff Manual respectively. Title pages will be prepared in manuscript.

Hour, Date, Place	Summary of Events and Information	Remarks and references to Appendices
Dec 25 1914.	In billets at Essars. Gifts received from Princess Mary.	
Dec 26. 1914.	March to Cambrin arriving about 2 P.M. The Battalion relieved the Royal Berkshire Regt. (1st Bde) from the trenches just N.E. of Givenchy - relief carried out with no difficulty. Two Companies go into the firing line. Two in reserve. The trenches were very wet, weather cold.	
Dec 27.	In trenches at Givenchy. Quiet day.	
28th	In trenches at Givenchy. Quiet day.	

(73989) W4141—463. 400,000. 9/14. H.&J.Ltd. Forms/C. 2118/10.

Army Form C. 2118.

WAR DIARY
or
INTELLIGENCE SUMMARY.
(Erase heading not required.)

Instructions regarding War Diaries and Intelligence Summaries are contained in F.S. Regs., Part II. and the Staff Manual respectively. Title pages will be prepared in manuscript.

Hour, Date, Place	Summary of Events and Information	Remarks and references to Appendices
Dec 29th. 1914.	In Trenches at Givenchy all Quiet. Walkin had.	
30th.	"	
31st.	"	Capt Humphrey 31st to King into to Hospital

1ST DIVISION
2ND BRIGADE

1ST BATTALION

NORTHAMPTONSHIRE REGT.

JAN - DEC 1915

2nd Infantry Brigade.
1st Division.

WAR DIARY

1st NORTHAMPTONSHIRE REGIMENT.

J A N U A R Y

1 9 1 5

1/ Northamptonshire Regt.

January 1915.

	1915.		
Jan	1st	"	(In trenches at Guinchy (see quite water bed))
		1.1.15 N.Y. to hospital sick 2/1/15	
Jan	2nd	"	The Battalion is relieved from the trenches at Guinchy by 1st Batt Coldstream Guards. — Go into billets at Annequin.

(73989) W4141—463. 400,000. 9/14. H.&J.Ltd. Forms/C. 2118/10.

WAR DIARY
or
INTELLIGENCE SUMMARY.
(Erase heading not required.)

Army Form C. 2118.

Hour, Date, Place	Summary of Events and Information	Remarks and references to Appendices
Jan 3rd 1915.	Move from Annequin to Villers to Cambrin. Orders received that the Battalion is to relieve the 2nd K.R.R. from the trenches first East of Cuinchy	
4th 1915.	Relieve 60th Rm trenches East of Cuinchy. These trenches are much drier than the Givenchy section. The Communicating trenches are being lost. These trenches are in front of the Railway triangle in front of the Brewery	
5th	in trenches at Cuinchy. Quiet day. Weather better.	
6th	Quiet day. Our Artillery shell heavily. Results appear to be very effective.	

1st Northamptonshire Regt.   Army Form C. 2118.

WAR DIARY
or
INTELLIGENCE SUMMARY.
(Erase heading not required.)

Instructions regarding War Diaries and Intelligence
Summaries are contained in F.S. Regs., Part II.
and the Staff Manual respectively. Title pages
will be prepared in manuscript.

Hour, Date, Place	Summary of Events and Information	Remarks and references to Appendices
Jan 9th 1915	Battn in trenches at Cuinchy. Quiet day	Capt Renny to hospital
" 8th	Heavy shelling by our Artillery.	Capt Jackson joined the Regiment.
" 9th	In trenches at Cuinchy. Heavy shelling by our guns	2/Lt Nye wounded (from trouble)
" 10th	The 60th Rifles were ordered to attack a spot on the Railway Embankment. The Battalion was in support of the attack. The Germans counter-attacked in the evening. Our C Coy was sent up to support the 60th	Lieut At Airy killed Casualties slight
" 11th	The Battalion was relieved at night by 2 R. Sussex. Moved to billets in Cambrin	

WAR DIARY
or
INTELLIGENCE SUMMARY.
(Erase heading not required.)

Army Form C. 2118.

Hour, Date, Place	Summary of Events and Information	Remarks and references to Appendices
Jan 12th 1915	in billets at Cambrin	
Jan 13th		
Jan 14th 1915	Relieve 60th Rif[le]s in trenches at Cuinchy	
Jan 15th	Quiet day	
Jan 16th	Relieved by 60th 95 billets in Cambrin	
Jan 17th	in Cambrin	
Jan 18th	Relieve 60th at Cuinchy	28th
Jan 19th		

Army Form C. 2118.

WAR DIARY
or
INTELLIGENCE SUMMARY.

(Erase heading not required.)

Instructions regarding War Diaries and Intelligence Summaries are contained in F.S. Regs., Part II. and the Staff Manual respectively. Title pages will be prepared in manuscript.

Hour, Date, Place	Summary of Events and Information	Remarks and references to Appendices
Jan 20th 1915	Quiet day	At Champion 65 Hospital —
21st 1915	Quiet day. Brigade relieved 6/15 1st Bde — 90 into billets at Bethune	
22nd to 24th 1915	In billets at Bethune	22nd Capt Mylne rejoined the Regiment
25 1915	Battalion is ordered to move to Beuvry. The 1st Bde having had a night review. Stay in Beuvry 1st day	Major Mowatt joined the Battalion. 2/Lt Bunyan sick to hospital
26th 1915	Leave Beuvry about 4.30 P.m. go into billets at Cambrin	

Army Form C. 2118.

WAR DIARY
or
INTELLIGENCE SUMMARY.
(Erase heading not required.)

Instructions regarding War Diaries and Intelligence Summaries are contained in F.S. Regs., Part II. and the Staff Manual respectively. Title pages will be prepared in manuscript.

Hour, Date, Place	Summary of Events and Information	Remarks and references to Appendices
Jan 27th 1915	Relieve 60th Regt Trenches at Cuinchy - Trench dug during the night to connect up with French - all quiet.	2/Lt Campling wounded
28th	In trenches at Cuinchy. Quiet day.	
Jan 29th 1915	The Enemy attacked our line in force about 9.30 AM after 1/2 an hours very severe fight. The Enemy were driven off. Our losses were slight. About 25 men killed & wounded. 2 Officers. A few prisoners - about 30 were taken - a great number of the enemy were killed during the attack.	2/Lt Orelho killed 2/Lt Pillins wounded

WAR DIARY
or
INTELLIGENCE SUMMARY.
(Erase heading not required.)

Instructions regarding War Diaries and Intelligence Summaries are contained in F. S. Regs., Part II. and the Staff Manual respectively. Title pages will be prepared in manuscript.

Hour, Date, Place	Summary of Events and Information
Jan 30th 1915.	Quiet day. Brigade relieved by 1th 4th Bde and go into billets in Bethune.

Jan 31st to Feb. 4th } 1915 in Billets in Bethune.

2nd Infantry Brigade.
1st Division.

WAR DIARY

1st NORTHAMPTONSHIRE REGIMENT.

FEBRUARY

1915

1/Northamptonshire Regt.
February 1915.

		Remarks and references to Appendices
Jan. 31st to Feb 4th	1915	in billets in Bethune. 17th 2/15 Lt. Champion rejoined. 15th 2/2/Lt Phipps to Hospital.
Feb 5th to Feb 28th	1915	in billets in Allouagne. 5th 2/15 Col E. O. Smith rejoined as Regiment and assumed Command. 8th 2/15 2/Lt Whits) joined 05 21st Thompson) Regiment. 9th 2/15 Col E O Smith to Hospital sick. 15 2/15 Capt Sir F Robinson rejoined the Regt.

2nd Infantry Brigade.
1st Division.

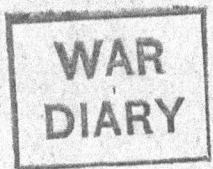

1st NORTHAMPTONSHIRE REGIMENT.

M A R C H

1 9 1 5

1/ Northamptonshire Regt.

March 1915.

March 1st } 1915. in billets in OBLINGHEM.
to
March 5th

A/Adjt. 1st Northamptonshire Regt.
Capt.
P. St Farrar

1st Northamptonshire Regt.

WAR DIARY
or
INTELLIGENCE SUMMARY.
(Erase heading not required.)

Army Form C. 2118.

Instructions regarding War Diaries and Intelligence Summaries are contained in F.S. Regs., Part II. and the Staff Manual respectively. Title pages will be prepared in manuscript.

Hour, Date, Place	Summary of Events and Information	Remarks and references to Appendices
March 9th 1915 OBLINGHEM	Orders Received that the Battalion is to move to LoCon as Army Reserve	
10th	March to LoCon. The Brigade is army reserve We are however not used	
11th	at LoCon	
12th	March from LoCon to Le Touret Bivouac for the night ready to move off at short notice to support any part of the 1st Division front.	
13th	Return to LoCon	

WAR DIARY
or
INTELLIGENCE SUMMARY.
(Erase heading not required.)

Army Form C. 2118.

Instructions regarding War Diaries and Intelligence Summaries are contained in F.S. Regs., Part II. and the Staff Manual respectively. Title pages will be prepared in manuscript.

Hour, Date, Place	Summary of Events and Information	Remarks and references to Appendices
March 14th 1915	Relieved the 3rd Bde in the Festubert section	16/3/15 Major Morvault Capt Jackson left to join the 2nd Batt—
March 15th	In the trenches at FESTUBERT. Quiet day	
16th–17th	"	
18th	Relieved by the 2 K.R.R. & go back into billets at LA TOURING FNS (N° GORRE)	
19th 20th 21st	In billets	
22nd	Relieve the 1st Bde in the Quinque Rue – Chocolat Menier Corner Section. The Battalion has a long line to hold, but Enemy fire is very quiet here	

WAR DIARY
or
INTELLIGENCE SUMMARY.
(Erase heading not required.)

Army Form C. 2118.

Hour, Date, Place	Summary of Events and Information	Remarks and references to Appendices
March 23rd, 24th, 25th	In the trenches in the La Quinque Rue Chateau Menier Crier. Section. Everything quiet.	
26th	Relieved by the 60th & 90th into billets in the Rue de l'Epinette – one Coy is left in the front line	
27th 28th 29th	In billets in the Rue de l'Epinette	
30th	Relieved by Knden 50th & 9th into trenches at Canet le Malo.	
31st	In billets at Cornet le Malo.	

A.A.A.9. /1st Batt Northamptonshire Regt.
H. Fawcett Capt
1st Batt Northamptonshire Regt.

2nd Infantry Brigade.
1st Division.

WAR DIARY

1st NORTHAMPTONSHIRE REGIMENT.

A P R I L

1 9 1 5

1/NORTHAMPTONSHIRE. REGT.

WAR DIARY
or
INTELLIGENCE SUMMARY.

(Erase heading not required.)

Army Form C. 2118.

Instructions regarding War Diaries and Intelligence
Summaries are contained in F. S. Regs., Part II.
and the Staff Manual respectively. Title pages
will be prepared in manuscript.

Hour, Date, Place	Summary of Events and Information	Remarks and references to Appendices
April 1st Billets (CORNET-LE-MALO)	In Billets all day. Reorganization, re-equipment & general cleaning of the Battalion —	A/- 2/Lt K.E. MONRO joined Bn from 3rd R.B.R.
2nd "	"	2/Lt C.H. BACON rejoined from sick leave (May 23)
3rd "	"	
4th "	"	
5th "	"	
6th "	"	
7th (Trenches)	The Battalion relieves the Pl Black Regt in line just South of NEUVE CHAPELLE & front of BOIS DU BIEZ. Relief commenced at 11 P.M. Completed at 3 A.M. — Quiet night no casualties. Trenches held by our right & centre coys. Three companies in front line with three platoons of 9th Kings Liverpool Regt. attached in support at PORT ARTHUR. Bn. H.Q. also at PORT ARTHUR.	

Army Form C. 2118.

WAR DIARY
or
INTELLIGENCE SUMMARY.
(Erase heading not required.)

Instructions regarding War Diaries and Intelligence Summaries are contained in F. S. Regs., Part II. and the Staff Manual respectively. Title pages will be prepared in manuscript.

Hour, Date, Place	Summary of Events and Information	Remarks and references to Appendices
April 9th Trenches (CM)	Quiet day, 1 man killed —	8/ 2/Lieut C.K. WAUCHOPE rejoined Battalion from Base leave (invalid) — took over Machine Gun Section —
9th	Quiet day. 9th hostile shells of about size of pins Companies pine in at present hasn't attended to Repairs trench & the trenches for practice.	9/ Lieut R.H. MARSHALL (3rd) rejoined the Battalion from sick leave (wounded) —
10th	all quiet —	10/ 2/Lt 2nd Lieut joined the Battalion
11th	Quiet Shelling, seven men wounded —
12th	Quiet day, 2 wounded — Relieved in the evening by 1st Lafalla & 3rd Gurkhas & to billets at LES FACONS Les Facons in Billets
13th (LES FACONS)	
14th	Leave LES FACONS & march to LES HARISOIRES & Billet Here — Corps reserve — new Sisters
15th BILLETS (LES HARISOIRES)	W.B. BETHUNE —

Army Form C. 2118.

WAR DIARY
or
INTELLIGENCE SUMMARY.
(Erase heading not required.)

Instructions regarding War Diaries and Intelligence Summaries are contained in F.S. Regs., Part II. and the Staff Manual respectively. Title pages will be prepared in manuscript.

Hour, Date, Place	Summary of Events and Information	Remarks and references to Appendices
April 16th Billets (LES HARRISOIRES (Sm.))	Battalion parade daily for Route marching & General Training & specials, ie Machine Gunners Lewis & "V.B" gunners & Bomb Throwers under R.L. Cowey	COMPLIMENTARY ORDER
17th	"	
18th	"	
19th	Capt. S.R.G. Robinson rejoined the Battalion from S.B.S. (2nd B.S.) who are now ARMENTIERS (Lieut S.) Took over duties of adjutant from Capt. J.H. THOMAS.	Boxing Tournament
20th	are held having etc —	
21st	Draft of 1 Officer & 5 men for the Battalion (Lieut F. C. POWELL)	
22nd	Continued fine weather Battalion Route marching training etc — A successful Boxing Tournament held at 11.30 & 1.30 with —	

(73089) W4141—463. 400,000. 9/14. H.&J.Ltd. Forms/C. 2118/10.

WAR DIARY or INTELLIGENCE SUMMARY

Army Form C. 2118.

Hour, Date, Place	Summary of Events and Information	Remarks and references to Appendices
April 23rd Brielen	Bn. first known to football match & afternoon	
LES HARISOIRES (n)	Went Les Harisoires & march to Richebourg - St. Vaast	
24th Rièges (Richebourg)	taking new trenches from 24th to 9 — R.E. & Plenish B.M. night near Factory in Rue du Bois — 1 man wounded —	24/ Major W.O. COURTNEY D.S.O. refund from Hospital —
25th "	Bn. first Battalion in working parties each night	27/ 7 km reports from Hospital 2/ Lieut R.H. DAVISON - refund —
26th "	Bn. first 1 wounded & 4 lightwounds —	WOUNDED
27th Support Trenches	Received orders to move to Support trenches and Richebourg by Windy Corner & about 1500' taken first line trenches here & at 7.30 P.M.	27/ Lieut C.K. WAUCHOPE accidentally wounded by a trek not to hit a practice bomb thrown by men. He was killed, his face & arm upper chest cut badly injured
28th "	Bn. first first weather, the battalion & coyd. holding support trenches —	
29th & 30th "	Bn. first working parties — first working the trenches	
	Bn. first Supt. Shelling —	

2nd Infantry Brigade.
1st Division.

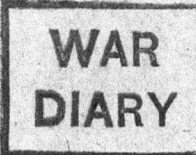

1st NORTHAMPTONSHIRE REGIMENT.

M A Y

1 9 1 5

1/Northamptonshire Regt.

WAR DIARY
or
INTELLIGENCE SUMMARY.

Army Form C. 2118.

Hour, Date, Place	Summary of Events and Information	Remarks and references to Appendices
MAY 1st In Support trenches in front of RICHEBOURG- St VAAST	About 4. a.m. the enemy heavily bombarded our trenches toward NEUVE CHAPELLE & PORT ARTHUR & a certain amount at the FACTORY - RUE DU BOIS - Battalion stood to arms. No attack was made by the enemy - the Bombardment continued from one to two hours —	
MAY 2nd "	About 4 p.m. weather bad - In the evening the Battalion is relieved by the Coldstream Guards about 9 p.m. marches & reaches billets at OBINGHAM where we are to remain in reserve [?] ready for the next of ESSAIRS about 11 p.m. & at intervals at 1 a.m.] a draft of 81. men joined the Battalion. Strength about 1000 approximately all ranks + Depot strength of 800 -	

Army Form C. 2118.

WAR DIARY
or
INTELLIGENCE SUMMARY.
(Erase heading not required.)

Instructions regarding War Diaries and Intelligence Summaries are contained in F.S. Regs., Part II. and the Staff Manual respectively. Title pages will be prepared in manuscript.

Hour, Date, Place	Summary of Events and Information	Remarks and references to Appendices
May 3rd (ORLINGHAM) BILLETS	All quiet, day spent cleaning up billets.	
4th "	Rifle cleaning, kit etc.	
5th "	Fell-ollen to be ready to move at short notice & fall in two hours.	
6th (LE TOURET) BILLS	Received orders to proceed to LE TOURET where we arrive about 6 p.m. Billet there for the night.	
7th "	Orders & instructions issued regarding an attack & assault of the Enemy Trenches preceded by an artillery bombardment. This is to be carried out at 5 am tomorrow.	
8th "	Assault postponed to 24 hours. Battalion remain in billets at LE TOURET until 8 p.m. when we marched up RUE DU BOIS & took up positions for attack with movement. The battalion are in the first line with 2/Sussex on our left but taken over by further [illegible]	

(73989) W4141—463. 400,000. 9/14. H.&J.Ltd. Forms/C. 2118/10.

Army Form C. 2118.

WAR DIARY
or
INTELLIGENCE SUMMARY.
(Erase heading not required.)

Instructions regarding War Diaries and Intelligence Summaries are contained in F.S. Regs., Part II. and the Staff Manual respectively. Title pages will be prepared in manuscript.

Hour, Date, Place	Summary of Events and Information	Remarks and references to Appendices
May 8th (cn)	The Black Watch stood [illegible] in [illegible] South of the RUE DU BOIS, about 1½ miles S.E. of RICHEBOURG ST VAAST. The Battalion with the 1st [illegible] have been chosen to make [illegible] the honour of making the initial assault on the Bosche trenches by the 8d & 7th Divisions. The 9th Rifles, Munsters & [illegible] Line to [illegible] Battalion being in reserve [illegible] Kings, [illegible] to attack on the right — to battalion being [illegible] The 2nd R.B. was to attack on the right — the battalion being in [illegible] right of the advance — the [illegible] on [illegible]. The [illegible] but advanced under our assault & [illegible] the 2nd Division on right. The 2nd Division [illegible] accepted — The 3rd Brigade on [illegible]. The 1st King's Shropshire [illegible] are in reserve behind the 1st Army [illegible] & follows up [illegible] as we [illegible] enemy's trenches. Our [illegible] in the trenches this night on 26 Officers & about 763 men. All ranks in [illegible] & eager for the coming fight. —	

WAR DIARY
or
INTELLIGENCE SUMMARY.
(Erase heading not required.)

Army Form C. 2118.

Instructions regarding War Diaries and Intelligence Summaries are contained in F.S. Regs., Part II. and the Staff Manual respectively. Title pages will be prepared in manuscript.

Hour, Date, Place	Summary of Events and Information	Remarks and references to Appendices
May 9th	Everyone was up & ready at daybreak expecting last details & arrangements. We had a cup about 5 oclock. Being such a lovely morning however, little flags for showing progress etc. The morning was fine & very clear & the Battalion forgot it was attached for the day & the Battalion. At 5.0 am sharp perfect morning for Artillery. The Bombardment of the enemy lines & the trenches managed for ten minutes behind — 13 pounders — 15" and 9. 9.2 inch howitzers. The wire was on top. The Bombardment continued until 5.30 when they shifted the fire onto [places] in the various trenches. Batteries & field(?) howes & was of the line. From 5.30 until 5.40 everyone from our trench on the evening trenches (not have the Durstey Brindle) the 18th from the field from playing in the Bands was instruments & our popps to no infantry	

Forms/C. 2118/10.

WAR DIARY or INTELLIGENCE SUMMARY

Army Form C. 2118.

Hour, Date, Place	Summary of Events and Information	Remarks and references to Appendices
May 9th (cont)	assault. During this 10 minutes the men of No two leading companies B under Capt Dickens & D under Capt Parnis got over the parapet preceded by the Bombers in company behind it. These companies advanced a close approach to about 100 y enemy parapet. While they were met by Bombardment and again at the same time the companies in the support trenches "A" & "C" under Capt Hughes & Capt Eu Roberts & Bn H.Q. moved from the support trenches to the front trenches & these now occupied the support B & D. At 5.40. a.m. presenting the Brigadiers orders of the Battalion into a Rifle Force rushes to the assault. Now that Major Parnis rushed up to the German Barbed wire & Capt Dickens + about 20 men reached a top made by our guns in the wire dug. Here this Force all that then Capt Dickens being killed at wire & also Capt Parnis the latter & about 2 leavg wife & mother from fire	

Army Form C. 2118.

WAR DIARY
or
INTELLIGENCE SUMMARY.
(Erase heading not required.)

Instructions regarding War Diaries and Intelligence Summaries are contained in F. S. Regs., Part II. and the Staff Manual respectively. Title pages will be prepared in manuscript.

Hour, Date, Place	Summary of Events and Information	Remarks and references to Appendices
May 9th (cont)	Men ran trenches before we were told for our trench & we were moved down. It was impossible to take the position & the assault had failed. Our artillery appeared to have done little damage to the enemy's parapets either the parapet was so wide themselves to even touch the bombardment — themselves to even touch the bombardment — The trenches rifle shots & machine gun fire was directed on our men so they came out on far guns. By this time we were exposed fire into his guns and heavy shells on parapets . trench hurdles & RUE DU BOIS. — Mr Bellasis was being hit between his two trenches, unable to advance. & retire to our lines became short, about fired on. Throughout the day the men lay out absolutely exposed to the rifle, machine gun & shell fire from the German line. A few who managed to return	

WAR DIARY or INTELLIGENCE SUMMARY

Army Form C. 2118.

(Erase heading not required.)

Hour, Date, Place	Summary of Events and Information	Remarks and references to Appendices

May 9th (con)	On the roller being given - skirmishers collected behind the line & support trenches & Fire trenches manned for the remainder of the day - at 3 A.M. another Bombardment & assault was ordered, the 1st R.B. undertaking the time, with no better result. Roughly a few men of the Black Watch got into the German trenches but were found of water - when returning came the hurricane of shells (having been) not so to the German trench, having landed his head cased for 14½ hours - He wounded the had cased he got to; were brought back, the wanted officers went Battalion that being volunteer work in the way - The Commanding Officer & Adjutant brought out the remainder of the Battalion (150 odd) to LE TOURET when rations were served to built then the night - The 2nd Devon having taken over the trenches of the firing line at 7P.M.	CASUALTIES
		
		2nd in Command
		Major W. O. Cantley D.S.O. KILLED S.
		
		A/Cpt F.B. Dickson
		2/Lt H. Thompson
		   R. Davies
		C.Q. M. Sgt C.S. Conisby
		2nd Lt J.M. Parker
		      T.G. Powell
		2/Lt W.E. Munro Disappeared
		
		WOUNDED
		Capt. E.G. Myhre
		HE N.H. Attwater
		     R.G. Champion
		HE T.C. Fulton
		Capt J. R.M. Robertson
		2/Lt N.H. Fraser
		     Kye
		     Harman
		     Lister

Army Form C. 2118.

WAR DIARY
or
INTELLIGENCE SUMMARY.
(Erase heading not required.)

Hour, Date, Place	Summary of Events and Information	Remarks and references to Appendices
May 9th (con)	Our losses were approximately 8 Officers killed, killed 9, 9 wounded & 521 men killed wounded & missing. Of the 17 Company Officers that had not up to date returned in hurt —	SPECIAL ORDER. *[handwritten notes illegible]*
May 10. LE TOUSET (Billets)	Day spent in reorganising the battalion & collecting a certain number of men who had been away — Brewis & others & ??????? to march back to OBLINGHEM when we arrive about 9.30 P.M.	
May 11. OBLINGHEM (Billets)	Day spent reorganising the emergency companies	
May 12. BETHUNE (Billets)	Brewis orders to march to BETHUNE where we billet	
" 13 "	In BETHUNE billets — wet day —	

Army Form C. 2118.

WAR DIARY
or
INTELLIGENCE SUMMARY.
(Erase heading not required.)

Instructions regarding War Diaries and Intelligence Summaries are contained in F.S. Regs., Part II. and the Staff Manual respectively. Title pages will be prepared in manuscript.

Hour, Date, Place	Summary of Events and Information	Remarks and references to Appendices
May 14th (BETHUNE) Billets	Bethune Shelled in North side, little damage done.	To G.O.C 2nd Bde. [illegible handwritten notes]
May 15th GORRE BRIDGE (Billets)	Received orders to proceed to GORRE BRIDGE about 3 miles E. of BETHUNE - Regt in in Bde Reserve (1st Div) was attached to Pernie't Bahn. Bde, 1st Bde. 2nd & 3rd Bde. Division who were to [illegible] opposite FESTUBERT, We relieve 6th Irish Rif at GORRE E. The 2nd & 3rd Divisions are attacking from [illegible] [illegible] on 14/5. 7 [illegible] - we say - Battalion [illegible] ready attack. Billets to left ready Brinn at short notice.	
May 16th "	Attack by 2nd + 3rd Div proceeds with considerable success but with [illegible] losses. In 2nd Div. 6th Bde. is reserve at GORRE [illegible] down at short notice.	
May 17th "	[illegible] attack [illegible] some 650 prisoners and [illegible] guns [illegible] but few large points. Draft for B's arrives of 61 [illegible] and 2/Lt A.W. Tuckey. Jnr 2nd Bn.	

(73989) W4141—463. 400,000. 9/14. H.&J.Ltd. Forms/C. 2118/10.

Army Form C. 2118.

WAR DIARY
or
INTELLIGENCE SUMMARY.
(Erase heading not required.)

Instructions regarding War Diaries and Intelligence Summaries are contained in F.S. Regs., Part II. and the Staff Manual respectively. Title pages will be prepared in manuscript.

Hour, Date, Place	Summary of Events and Information	Remarks and references to Appendices
May 18th (GORRE BRIDGE Billets)	No further attack to our troops. We are holding the line consolidating position taken. The following Officers joined the Bn:- 2/Lt RICE. 2/Lt HAMBLETON. 2/Lt VARNELL - both Hampshire Regt.	The 2n Hampshires state that the casualties when received from the hour in the line of the bombardment — 52/R Hants wounded — 15 May 1915 now 9th Division — 2 — The Brigadier General has had phones & temperature and is also unable to the actions. I am of G, R to S.O.C. 1st Division — S.H. steers hope upper says Sept R 2.
May 19th BETHUNE (Billets)	Weather for last few days: wet & windy but on whole favourable. The afternoon rather an anxious and wounds back to our old Billets in BETHUNE — When he arrived at 6 P.M. 1st Divn bus Coys attached to 5th & 6th BRIGADE Front —	
May 20th	The 2nd Bn'tts above the 3rd Bde in trenches S. of CUINCHY — GIVENCHY. Such have been taken over by Battns from his 4th — new disposition tops in this afternoon — Battalion 4 4th Bn Reserve at ANNEQUIN — 2/Eden, 2/hanson & 2/thompson taking into trenches — Relief completed by 7.p.m.	

WAR DIARY or INTELLIGENCE SUMMARY

Army Form C. 2118.

(Erase heading not required.)

Instructions regarding War Diaries and Intelligence Summaries are contained in F.S. Regs., Part II. and the Staff Manual respectively. Title pages will be prepared in manuscript.

Hour, Date, Place	Summary of Events and Information	Remarks and references to Appendices
May 21st ANNEQUIN (Billets)	all spent in examining O.C. Companies to go & trenches & reconnoitre ways of approach. In afternoon & evening men stitch on breast & to complete 1 & 2/K w/R S/amplets prior to Battalion —	
" 22 "	About 5.30 a.m. & 7.30 a.m. a violent Bombardment on our left Battalion Front & during & long & an attack by enemy. We however cleared and same off & all quiet rest of day. The following Officers joined the Battalion: Major C. ROYSTON-PIGOTT, Capt. E.C. WARR, 2/Lieut. E.I. HUGHES and W.V. JERVOIS — also draft of 5-8 men —	
" 23 "	Killed in the evening but no damage done — 2/Lt. Melton took [?] the Battalion into trenches in relief of 2/K.R.R. just S. of LA BASSEE ROAD. Three trenches in Fort & lachrymatists trenches. a big way back to that relief can be done by daylight — Enemy close at 40' away. Relief complete by 6 p.m. A.D.D. & front line C. & support.	
" 24 " TRENCHES.		

Army Form C. 2118.

WAR DIARY
or
INTELLIGENCE SUMMARY.
(Erase heading not required.)

Instructions regarding War Diaries and Intelligence Summaries are contained in F.S. Regs., Part II. and the Staff Manual respectively. Title pages will be prepared in manuscript.

Hour, Date, Place		Summary of Events and Information	Remarks and references to Appendices
May 25th	TRENCHES	All quiet. Germans threw bombs & hissed verlains into proposal. Did little damage done - [Rest taken start on our right & hour division on our left -] 1 man killed -	
May 26th	"	Mine exploded just outside our lines by the enemy, no damage done - Enemy active with Bombs & Rifle Grenades. Stand-to arranged - 1 killed - 2 wounded -	
" 27th	"	All quiet. Bombs after previous & trench mortars west of hill. Relieved	
" 28th	ANNEQUIN Billets	Relieved by 2/K.R.R. at 12 p.m. & march back to our Billets in ANNEQUIN. Relief completed 2.6 am -	
" 29th	TRENCHES	Redistribution of time. 2.30 p.m. Orders recd to kneps hit Battalion ready if tdmpo lost in attack on 6 Trenches at CUINCHY hit N. LA BASSEE ROAD where B Coy was in December operations - Take over from Welch Reg. Relief carried out in daylight simples by 6 p.m. Communication trenches from the trenches not to find way. Close of previous to road J.B.Coy - A.B.C. Coys informing lines. "D" coy in Support. Capt A.M. READ rejoined Bn from Royal Flying Corps.	

WAR DIARY
or
INTELLIGENCE SUMMARY.
(Erase heading not required.)

Army Form C. 2118.

Hour, Date, Place	Summary of Events and Information	Remarks and references to Appendices
May 30th Trenches	All quiet. Enemy active with Rifle Grenades - 3 men killed & 5 wounded. Slight Shelling during day - Draft consisting of following officers joined the Battalion 2nd Lt METCALFE, 2/Lt CLARKE } from 3rd Battalion 2/Lt ROBYNS 2/Lt WOODS } from Depot 19th - Also 81 other ranks - Strength of Battalion was 19 Officers & 520 men	
May 31st	All quiet. Battalion H.Q. heavily shelled from 10.30 - 11 a.m. About 12 H.E. Shells dropping within a few yards - no casualties. Weather continues fine for the week.	

2nd Infantry Brigade.
1st Division.

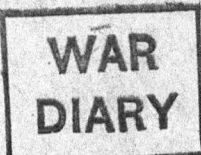

1st NORTHAMPTONSHIRE REGIMENT.

J U N E

1 9 1 5

1/NORTHAMPTONSHIRE REGT.

WAR DIARY
or
INTELLIGENCE SUMMARY.
(Erase heading not required.)

Army Form C. 2118.

Instructions regarding War Diaries and Intelligence Summaries are contained in F.S. Regs., Part II and the Staff Manual respectively. Title pages will be prepared in manuscript.

Hour, Date, Place	Summary of Events and Information	Remarks and references to Appendices
June 1st. In trenches (Cuinchy Section)	The Battalion is relieved by the 1/Royal Sussex in afternoon & retire to Brigade reserve in Billets at CAMBRIN —	Capt E.C. Walk (sick to Hospital)
" 2nd. Billets in CAMBRIN	All that portion of Band not by B.Bn before relief was blown to by a hostile mine —	
" 3rd. "	all quiet —	
" 4th. "	Relieved by the Placestershire Regt (3rd Bs) & march to back trenches of LA BEUVRIÈRE & there placed in about 10 mile behind the firing line —	
" 5th. Billets at LA BEUVRIÈRE	Cleaning up of Equipment, billets etc. —	2/Lt P. Chown (sick to Hospital)
" 6th. "	Drill training of recruits from new drafts etc —	

Army Form C. 2118.

WAR DIARY
or
INTELLIGENCE SUMMARY.
(Erase heading not required.)

Instructions regarding War Diaries and Intelligence Summaries are contained in F.S. Regs., Part II. and the Staff Manual respectively. Title pages will be prepared in manuscript.

Hour, Date, Place	Summary of Events and Information	Remarks and references to Appendices
June 7th Billets at LABEUVRIERE	Drill musketry in trench warfare near Tannay etc —	7/. Following officers join Capt C.G. Bickell 2/Lt F.E.M. Prinsep " J.C.O. Marriott " R.H.C. Bolton " A.T.L. March " C.V. Kipps " C.F.T. East
" 8th	The Battalion is inspected by Genl Sir Charles Monro G.O.C. 1st Corps. He expressed himself entirely satisfied with everything, hoped that the Battalion would shortly be brought up to strength.	
" 9th	Training etc continued. Weather very hot & dry	
" 10th	Receive orders to proceed to ALLOUAGNE - 3 mile W. of LABEUVRIERE. Relief Nil —	2/Lt WOODS sick (to Hospital)
" 11th Billets at ALLOUAGNE	Commence training Battalion drill close & extended order, machine gun, bombers etc. —	
" 12th	"	Draft joins B. 2/Lt. T.R. Price & 10 O.R.
" 13th	" — Battalion concert	

WAR DIARY
or
INTELLIGENCE SUMMARY.

(Erase heading not required.)

Army Form C. 2118.

Instructions regarding War Diaries and Intelligence Summaries are contained in F. S. Regs., Part II. and the Staff Manual respectively. Title pages will be prepared in manuscript.

Hour, Date, Place	Summary of Events and Information	Remarks and references to Appendices
June 14th Billets at ALLOUAGNE	Training etc —	2nd Lieut R. Marriage to R.F.C. on probation —
15th "	Boxing tournament —	
16th "	Received orders to move up into trenches in 'A' Section, Vist Sector A.3. CUINCHY area — Leave ALLOUAGNE at 9.30 a.m. a halt for dinner on the way distance about 11 & 12 miles — Reach CAMBRIN at 5 P.M. & take over trenches when the Battalion had before from Black watch — Relief completed at 7 P.M. Canadians & 7th Division attacked on our left — but were not very successful —	
17th Trenches in Cuinchy area	Alle [?] quiet. A bombardment of our left took place during the night but little result —	
18th "	Alle [?] quiet. No Lewis Contact any —	

Army Form C. 2118.

WAR DIARY
or
INTELLIGENCE SUMMARY.
(Erase heading not required.)

Instructions regarding War Diaries and Intelligence Summaries are contained in F.S. Regs., Part II. and the Staff Manual respectively. Title pages will be prepared in manuscript.

Hour, Date, Place	Summary of Events and Information	Remarks and references to Appendices
From 19th Trenches in Cuinchy area	Received orders to the effect that the Battalion will be relieved in the morning by the Royal Berkshire Regt. — The 2nd W.R. by the 6th Bn. — The 1st Devons to the 2nd — Battalion after relief marches back to former Billets in BETHUNE —	Draft of 7 officers joined the Battalion
20th Billets at BETHUNE	Received orders that the ready troops at short notice to the present trench —	
21st "	Still in Billets at BETHUNE — awaiting relief, during which time companies cannot adequately parade for exercise etc — Baths a & clothes in time, great strain is laid on their branch of training — Trench warfare having proved to necessitate a always parade of —	
22nd "		
23rd "	No orders yet received —	

Army Form C. 2118.

WAR DIARY
or
INTELLIGENCE SUMMARY.
(Erase heading not required.)

Instructions regarding War Diaries and Intelligence Summaries are contained in F.S. Regs., Part II. and the Staff Manual respectively. Title pages will be prepared in manuscript.

Hour, Date, Place	Summary of Events and Information	Remarks and references to Appendices
June 24th BETHUNE	Receive orders to march to ALLOUAGNE. The whole Bde are instructed to do the place - we got into Billets about 2 P.M.	
" 25th ALLOUAGNE	hot day having tea -	
" 26th "	Quiet day - Bde in [billets].	
" 27th "	Orders received that 2nd Bde will move up to Trenches S. of LA BASSÉE Road - The Battalion is there in support 2 companies at CAM B an APS + H.Q. + 2 companies C.P.D. at BUNZOUIN. have a long march of our 15 miles - which the men arrive in first style taking no [consideration] to fact that Rue is little marching done during this kind of warfare - arrived in ANNEZUIN + CAMBRIN about 8.P.M. taking over from 4th Guards Bde.	Draft of 1 Sergt + 5-3 B. Ranks joined the Bn.

(73989) W4141—463. 400,000. 9/14. H.&J.Ltd. Forms/C. 2118/10.

WAR DIARY
or
INTELLIGENCE SUMMARY.
(Erase heading not required.)

Army Form C. 2118.

Instructions regarding War Diaries and Intelligence Summaries are contained in F. S. Regs., Part II. and the Staff Manual respectively. Title pages will be prepared in manuscript.

Hour, Date, Place	Summary of Events and Information	Remarks and references to Appendices
June 28th CAMBRIN to ANNEQUIN	all quiet -	
29th	Bn H.Q. move up to Bn H.Q. in CAMBRIN, huts raining -	
30th	not training - Trenches muddy, working parties at clearing communication trenches so far as possible -	

2nd Infantry Brigade.
1st Division.

WAR DIARY

1st NORTHAMPTONSHIRE REGIMENT.

J U L Y

1 9 1 5

Army Form C. 2118.

WAR DIARY
or
INTELLIGENCE SUMMARY.
(Erase heading not required.)

Instructions regarding War Diaries and Intelligence Summaries are contained in F.S. Regs., Part II. and the Staff Manual respectively. Title pages will be prepared in manuscript.

Hour, Date, Place	Summary of Events and Information	Remarks and references to Appendices
July 1st ("Relief" at CAMBRIN & ANNEQUIN.)	All quiet during the day - working parties are employed clearing up trenches after yesterday's attack. 2nd - Slight shelling round CAMBRIN in evening. At 2.30 p.m. the Battalion relieves the [illegible] Vacates left & 2nd Relief Coys & sent support to [illegible] Germans are front & left flank - no 600[?] away from German lines - Enemy have a strong [illegible] [illegible] salient opposite scale Company which is bounded HOHENZOLLERN FORT. Have imposed were [illegible] & a Brigade from Cuthay & [illegible] section the trenches - Rifles are [illegible] [illegible] fire.	
July 2nd		

(73989) W4141—463. 400,000. 9/14. H.&J.Ltd. Forms/C. 2118/10.

WAR DIARY
or
INTELLIGENCE SUMMARY.

(Erase heading not required.)

Army Form C. 2118.

Hour, Date, Place	Summary of Events and Information	Remarks and references to Appendices
July 3rd (Junction)	All quiet except that owing to a working party showing themselves by day got shelled in the morning & lost 1 sergt & 1 man killed & 3 wounded. Parties working at improving trenches from cellars & clearing up.	
July 4th	Our front trench shelling. Battn working party active & no preventing night – 1 man killed & Enemies sniper —	
July 5th	All quiet. French active near SOUCHEZ	
July 6th	Sniper shelling behind our lines –	

Army Form C. 2118.

WAR DIARY
or
INTELLIGENCE SUMMARY.
(Erase heading not required.)

Instructions regarding War Diaries and Intelligence Summaries are contained in F. S. Regs., Part II. and the Staff Manual respectively. Title pages will be prepared in manuscript.

Hour, Date, Place	Summary of Events and Information	Remarks and references to Appendices
July 7th (Sailly)	Battalion relieved by 2/K.R.R.C at 3.30 P.M. 85 ORs killed & Sailly-La-Bourse sent to reinf killed & 3 wounded in rest - less a Brigade Reserve	
July 8th (Sailly-La-Bourse)	Enemy active not in 2" or support lines. Shortage of water & vegetables. Reconnaissance of 25 hrs line of defence & approaches to them	
" 9th	Working parties of 300 in 2" —	
" 10th		
" 11th	2/Lieut S.G.S. made into dept of 61. Oak Ranks found Battalion. Reconnaissance of 3rd line of defence between VERMELLES & CAMBRIN. Training. Coy parade &c. —	
" 12th		

Army Form C. 2118.

WAR DIARY
or
INTELLIGENCE SUMMARY.
(Erase heading not required.)

Instructions regarding War Diaries and Intelligence Summaries are contained in F. S. Regs., Part II. and the Staff Manual respectively. Title pages will be prepared in manuscript.

Hour, Date, Place	Summary of Events and Information	Remarks and references to Appendices
July 13. Billets (LABOURSE)	The Battalion came into billets at LABOURSE about 1 mile from SAILLY-LA-BOURSE. B⁴ hours from a Divisional Reserve at 2 hrs notice —	
July 14. "	Billets at LABOURSE. B⁴ hours - Broken march	
July 15. "	Promoters Special course x⁴	
July 16. "		
July 17. "		
July 18. "		
July 19. (Trenches)	Battalion relieved Yorkshire Prints in trenches at Y'Kaolin opposite VERMELLES — Leave Billets at 8 P.M. Relief completed by 11 P.M.	

(73989) W4141—463. 400,000. 9/14. H.&J.Ltd. Forms/C. 2118/10.

Army Form C. 2118.

WAR DIARY
or
INTELLIGENCE SUMMARY.
(Erase heading not required.)

Instructions regarding War Diaries and Intelligence Summaries are contained in F.S. Regs., Part II. and the Staff Manual respectively. Title pages will be prepared in manuscript.

Hour, Date, Place	Summary of Events and Information	Remarks and references to Appendices
July 20th (Trenches)	Our front trenches have been shewn 500x to 600x yesterday. B*: Head Quarters on to LE RUTOIRE (a few minutes). Howard J Offirces V N L Sc. of Kees Army are attached Regt. for two days at a time for instructional purposes. There is a great dearth of work to be done on the trenches, improving defensive posts & dropping a new hire —	
July 21st "	Our front w Cavalier rolling routine not of sight. Slight shelling during day — Capt B 1st Officer (Capt A. M. HENNIKER (? 754) + 105 other Ranks 'in the Regt.	
July 22nd "	Our front rolling routine as usual — a few trenches henry dug from a RED FLAG —	

WAR DIARY
or
INTELLIGENCE SUMMARY.
(Erase heading not required.)

Army Form C. 2118.

Hour, Date, Place	Summary of Events and Information	Remarks and references to Appendices
July 23rd (Fenderson)	Our front improving trenches & defence works — DAY'S KEEP & LE RUTOIRE KEEP —	
July 24th	Our front — we have had L.O.S. attached & N.C.O's of 9th Fr. was army (15th Division) attached to our coy for instruction. Valofette MAYER — Reserve no troops & New Army units	
July 25th	Relieved at 9 P.M. by to troops to take barracks Rd NOYELLES. Battalion in relief billets in NOYELLES. H.Q. & "A" Coys & Coys of 1st Division — 1st Division (Scottish & 1st Divn) (New army) 47th Division	
July 26th Billets (NOYELLES)	Our front 600 men a day on at digging new line of defence in 2nd round VERMELLES — Strong points round the place for defence —	

Army Form C. 2118.

WAR DIARY
or
INTELLIGENCE SUMMARY.
(Erase heading not required.)

Instructions regarding War Diaries and Intelligence Summaries are contained in F.S. Regs., Part II. and the Staff Manual respectively. Title pages will be prepared in manuscript.

Hour, Date, Place	Summary of Events and Information	Remarks and references to Appendices
July 27th (Billets) (MOYENNES)	Our front looking parties stopped throughout the day.	
July 28th "	Enemy shelled our Billets from 5 P.M. – 6 A.M. especially round church & little hamlet close to ground H.J. HAMBLETON (Shown no men killed. Buying bombers & bomb specials – Bombing parties as usual – see front –	
July 29th "	"	
July 30th "	Relieved at 9.30 P.M. by the 42nd Welch Fusiliers – Relief the Battalion was clear both of ANNEZIN & on their way to BETHUNE when the relief was known – W. of BETHUNE – Divisional Reserve at 12 hours notice –	
July 31st "		

2nd Infantry Brigade.

1st Division.

WAR DIARY

1st NORTHAMPTONSHIRE REGIMENT.

A U G U S T

1 9 1 5

1/NORTHAMPTONSHIRE REGT

Army Form C. 2118.

WAR DIARY
or
INTELLIGENCE SUMMARY.
(Erase heading not required.)

Instructions regarding War Diaries and Intelligence Summaries are contained in F.S. Regs., Part II. and the Staff Manual respectively. Title pages will be prepared in manuscript.

Hour, Date, Place	Summary of Events and Information	Remarks and references to Appendices
August 1st Billets ANNEZIN.	General cleaning up — Inspection of Equipment &c &c.	
August 2nd "	"	
August 3rd "	Inspection of Right Half Battalion by Commanding Officer. Marched in column of companies — musketry &c &c.	
August 4th "	Inspection of Left Half Battalion by Commanding Officer. Musketry. Also visit by O.C. companies — Brigade Hdqrs. pt/o & General " BETHUNE —	
August 5th "	Musketry, drill &c. Brigade lines close to BETHUNE Spa — French —	
August 6th "	The Battalion moves up into Support at CAMBRIN & MAISON ROUGE. "B" Coy being in Rt Support. "B" Coy takes over P.L. "Z". "B" when known (later) Posted — 11 P.M. —	
August 7th CAMBRIN (Billets + dugouts)	"	
" 8th "	All quiet - working parties employed in the trenches	

WAR DIARY or INTELLIGENCE SUMMARY

Army Form C. 2118.

(Erase heading not required.)

Hour, Date, Place	Summary of Events and Information	Remarks and references to Appendices
August 9th Pollet CAM/13 RIM	Bee Quiet, working parties employed on the trenches	
August 10th "	Capt E.L. HUGHES to IVth Corps H.Q. for instruction in staff duties	
" 11th "	" working parties to work	
" 12th TRENCHES Z2	Relief 2/K.R.R. & extra 2nd junt (i.e. of 2/13 MIDX Regt.) During the night the enemy were active with trench mortars, rifle grenades were retaliated & also had our Heavy & Rifle Batteries on the German trenches – three men were wounded & considerable portion of trenches were blown in –	WOUNDED 11th/Capt A.M. HENNIKER 12th/ 2/Lieut STANFIELD Returns from hospital
" 13th "	Quite front. Slight shelling in the evening from French mortar shelling went on – Enemy night mortar 5.30 – 6.30. a.m. Enemy started with their trench mortar very early on Bouting – They were silenced by our after an hour. The pine line also asked them on – Casualties 1 men killed & 2 wounded –	

Army Form C. 2118.

WAR DIARY
or
INTELLIGENCE SUMMARY.
(Erase heading not required.)

Instructions regarding War Diaries and Intelligence Summaries are contained in F.S. Regs., Part II. and the Staff Manual respectively. Title pages will be prepared in manuscript.

Hour, Date, Place	Summary of Events and Information	Remarks and references to Appendices
August 14th Trenches 2nd	Quiet except for the usual trench mortar shelling — Enemy air has been active. Three fellows B. took our position — a German was shot by a man of J.B's Coy.	
August 15th "	At 4 a.m. an attempt was made towards a bombardment of the enemy trenches in which our French mortars rifle grenades & bombs were employed. A sniping party for Brant Storming party was formed & the most effort — The enemy replied vigorously with trench mortars — Casualties 7 men wounded. Battalion was relieved at 5 p.m. by 1st Leicestershire Regt. at 5.30 p.m. to Relief Bn. went back B.13 to reserve in SAILLY LA BOURSE.	
August 16th "	Weather had raining, all Bn. employed in fatigue cleaning of trenches etc.	
" 17th "	All quiet, continued bad weather, the Bn. still employed in cleaning of trenches —	

Army Form C. 2118.

WAR DIARY
or
INTELLIGENCE SUMMARY.
(Erase heading not required.)

Instructions regarding War Diaries and Intelligence Summaries are contained in F. S. Regs., Part II. and the Staff Manual respectively. Title pages will be prepared in manuscript.

Hour, Date, Place	Summary of Events and Information	Remarks and references to Appendices
August 18th Billets ANNEZIN	Relieved in afternoon by South Wales Borderers in relief from back to Billets in ANNEZIN. Batt in Divisional Reserve – An enemy aeroplane dropped bomb in BETHUNE & ANNEZIN –	
August 19th "	Half Battalion employed on fatigue at mine near VERQUIN – General cleaning up & equipment to be made – latter machin –	
" 20th "	Bombing at Bois des MONTAGNES near BETHUNE, route march & bathing –	
" 21st "	1 man killed & 1 wounded while bombing. ring & premature explosion of a bomb – Pioneers to repair of Battalion by G.O.C. 2nd Infantry Bde. (General THESIGER)	
" 22nd "	Relieved the 1st Worcestershire Regt in VERMELLES at 6 p.m. Batt attached 5th Bde for a few days –	

WAR DIARY or INTELLIGENCE SUMMARY.

(Erase heading not required.)

Army Form C. 2118.

Hour, Date, Place	Summary of Events and Information	Remarks and references to Appendices
August 23rd Billets VERMELLES	The Battalion & Scots Guards have been withdrawn from L.t B.de & Prince's division is to be pressed - All quiet - no shelling - Battalion employed on fatigues under RE.	
" "		
24th TRENCHES "Y"	Relieve Black Watch in "Y" sector at LE RUTOIRE. Situation to prepare our left to push forward. Our 20 x by legs - this has been tried front -	
" 26th "	All quiet. Slight shelling in evening.	
" 26th "	1 man killed & 2 wounded by those fire to support but situation front. Enemy working party active at night.	
" 27th "	Quiet during day, at night wounded relieve to work on parapets extending sap no: 303 from our front line. C Company were sharply opposed by German party but - three Germans part of them killed our patrol. Ridge on the sap without much hindrance. (B) > C were employed throughout the night on Rue - 1 Officer wounded 1 man killed & 5 wounded.	27/ WOUNDED. CAPT. C.G. BUCKLE.

Army Form C. 2118.

WAR DIARY
or
INTELLIGENCE SUMMARY.
(Erase heading not required.)

Instructions regarding War Diaries and Intelligence Summaries are contained in F. S. Regs., Part II. and the Staff Manual respectively. Title pages will be prepared in manuscript.

Hour, Date, Place	Summary of Events and Information	Remarks and references to Appendices
August 28th VERMELLES	Relieved at 5 P.M. by 2/R.B.R. & returned to billets in VERMELLES — Fatigue parties under R.E.	
August 29th TRESNES	At 3 P.M. received sudden orders to return to the trenches — Party of about D. Coy. & Bomber 'Y' & two Platoons 'X' Coy — 2 Lewis Sections Y² Y¹ B² were hurriedly absorbed into 6 Y's 'Bolluhei employed) up again at 5.30 P.M. Enemy kept dropping heavy hyper & artillery steady teaching men — a venture in being found 300ˣ in front of present line — Casualties 1 killed & wounded —	
August 30th TRESNES	Continued work on front line & Windposts keeping a left hand sap. Enemy began active against our bombing & covering parties — Casualties 2 wounded —	

Army Form C. 2118.

WAR DIARY
or
INTELLIGENCE SUMMARY.
(Erase heading not required.)

Instructions regarding War Diaries and Intelligence Summaries are contained in F. S. Regs., Part II. and the Staff Manual respectively. Title pages will be prepared in manuscript.

Hour, Date, Place	Summary of Events and Information	Remarks and references to Appendices
August 31st (Trenches)	Work continued & improved - 4 Coys. have been under heavy shell was heefo heavily shelled. While at mr. J. McStephens - known 1 wounded - Evening fairly Quiet during day -	KILLED. 2/Lt A.J. L. NEISH.

1st Division
2d Brigade.

W A R   D I A R Y

O F

1st Northampton

S E P T E M B E R

1 9 1 5

1/Northamptonshire Regt.

Army Form C. 2118.

WAR DIARY
or
INTELLIGENCE SUMMARY.
(Erase heading not required.)

Instructions regarding War Diaries and Intelligence Summaries are contained in F.S. Regs., Part II. and the Staff Manual respectively. Title pages will be prepared in manuscript.

Hour, Date, Place	Summary of Events and Information	Remarks and references to Appendices
September 1st Trenches in front of VERMELLES	Work on digging new trenches continued during the night. Saphead's being pushed out towards up - enemy quite active with rifle fire & machine guns, but no serious effort was made to interfere with the work – Casualties 2 killed & 6 wounded —	
September 2nd	Relieved in trenches by 2/ Queens Regt. Capt B. W. Reed & A & D Coys march back to VERQUIN where they went to be billeted – Head Quarters & B & C Coys remain in VERMELLES in WATER TOWER Redoubt as conformable & satisfactory no Coys being very uncomfortable & weather being wet – H.Q. in MINES available & weather being wet up to trenches if for dusk. KEEP – B & C Coys for up to trenches in front line & continue digging into Premier & Cavallion "Saps" – Casualties 2 wounded	

WAR DIARY
or
INTELLIGENCE SUMMARY.

(Erase heading not required.)

Army Form C. 2118.

Instructions regarding War Diaries and Intelligence Summaries are contained in F.S. Regs., Part II. and the Staff Manual respectively. Title pages will be prepared in manuscript.

Place	Hour, Date	Summary of Events and Information	Remarks and references to Appendices
VERMELLES & BURBURE	September 3rd	Orders received for "A" & "D" Coys to march back to the Brigade less 2 Bns to BURBURE, which is about 15 miles west (beyond AUCHEL) — being met half way, arriving the whole line – the two Coys arriving "D" & "A" in motor lorries. These have a bad time & naturally have to move into a few limbers annexed horses in VERMELLES — supping is unusual. The enlist to Cavalries.	
	September 4th		
	5"	2 Coys arrive in VERMELLES supping in hut lines after dark	
	6"	" BURBURE. Cleaning up & personal reorganization	
	7"	2 W. Bde relieved by 3rd Bn H.R. & B.C. Coys march back to billets near VAUDRICOURT for the night	

Army Form C. 2118.

WAR DIARY
or
INTELLIGENCE SUMMARY.
(Erase heading not required.)

Instructions regarding War Diaries and Intelligence Summaries are contained in F.S. Regs., Part II. and the Staff Manual respectively. Title pages will be prepared in manuscript.

Hour, Date, Place	Summary of Events and Information	Remarks and references to Appendices
September 8th (BURBURE)	Leave Burbure at 6.30 a.m. & march to BURBURE & join up with remainder of Battalion - all Bttns here - Billets here -	8th Lieut RICE (Walter) Army to England - medically unfit - Th Stamfd -
" 9th "	Training, cleaning & inspection of equipment - Brigadier training recruits from training at Billets -	9th Lieut ESSAM joins Battalion - Draft of 37 arrived -
" 10th "	"	
" 11th "	Rest - Church Parade - inspection of Billets -	17th Draft of 28 arrived -
" 12th "	Training etc -	
" 13th "	"	Battalion is now up to Establishment
" 14th "	Route march - concert in evening -	
" 15th "	Training etc -	
" 16th "	"	
" 17th "	Field days - attack practice -	

Army Form C. 2118.

WAR DIARY
or
INTELLIGENCE SUMMARY.
(Erase heading not required.)

Instructions regarding War Diaries and Intelligence Summaries are contained in F. S. Regs., Part II. and the Staff Manual respectively. Title pages will be prepared in manuscript.

Hour, Date, Place		Summary of Events and Information	Remarks and references to Appendices
September	18th BURBURE	Equipment inspection etc —	
"	19th "	Rest — Church Parade —	
"	20th "	Training etc — leave BURBURE + move up to Billets in LAPUGNOY —	
"	21st LAPUGNOY	Completing arrangements as regards preliminary Concentration of troops. Brigade conference — Drawing	
"	22nd "	Experiments in use of Smoke Bombs & candles —	
"	23rd "	Battalion moves from Billets at 8.P.M. & Bivouacs at Railway Cutting area K — near NOEUX LES MINES — 2/R.R.F. & kept into trenches near up to Tranches & Y. Cellar in front of VERMELLES — Battalion leaves LA AUG NOY 8 P.M. & Arrives Bivouac 2 A.M. Heavy wet night —	

Army Form C. 2118.

WAR DIARY
or
INTELLIGENCE SUMMARY.
(Erase heading not required.)

Instructions regarding War Diaries and Intelligence Summaries are contained in F.S. Regs., Part II. and the Staff Manual respectively. Title pages will be prepared in manuscript.

Hour, Date, Place	Summary of Events and Information	Remarks and references to Appendices
September 24th (Bomey)	A general attack is about to take place see along line - Recce & Butts & for inspection day saw him continually & heavily bombarding & enemy position & trenches - Gas equipment issued & the men & all preparation complete - At 3 p.m. "A" Coy moved up to the trenches into the fire trench in Y. opposite trenches they were attacked & R.E. for digging & installing - At 9.20 p.m. the Battalion Claims position was - "A" Coy in the ground immediately in rear & support trenches in Y. Putting into the fire & support trenches about 2 a.m. - Battle position about 2 a.m. -	General Idea - 7th Division moves on Sept 1 & 15 Bays & on Repts - 11th Division attacks on 1st Sept 9 1200 & 1st & 2nd 1200 Bays assembling & 3rd Bn in reserve - objective - 1st Div LOOS & HILL 70 - 2nd Bde BOIS HUGO - CHALK PIT & 2nd line & parallel - 1st Bde HULLUCH & trenches & S.E. of it -
September 25th (Trenches)	Day broke showed promise of fine day with very little wind & what there was B. to favourable to us for the trap & support & fire - The 60th Rifles & the Royal Scots to Lancashire are in the front line 656's to right. The 4/trench are in support to the Battalion in reserve - The first two	

Army Form C. 2118.

WAR DIARY
or
INTELLIGENCE SUMMARY.
(Erase heading not required.)

Hour, Date, Place	Summary of Events and Information	Remarks and references to Appendices
Sp Cinders 25/7/(16)	are to carry out the assault at 21.5.50 a.m. The gas is turned on + Enemy's rear position heavily shelled by Four B.M. Calibre. The few cylinders of previously been placed in attack are almost broken - there was importantly very little wind. However owing to the fact that no portion has a salient the fire being in an awkward + pool. About 2 companies of the 6/L + a portion away 100 of R.A.G. who were to have kept hammering at the 40 mins. G.S. for the top assaulting Battalion after the attack had been unable to have had not the Enemy trenches owing to the fact of a pocket in the Enemy trenches between the two lines - The Company in hardly between was Entirely in gassed. 2/ Prince armed forward + moved + their Platoon + the Battalion however forward in front of lancashire were unable to get in to the forward trench trenches were knocked + got to an advanced rifle positions + hold line after withdrawn.	

WAR DIARY
or
INTELLIGENCE SUMMARY.
(Erase heading not required.)

Army Form C. 2118.

Instructions regarding War Diaries and Intelligence Summaries are contained in F.S. Regs., Part II. and the Staff Manual respectively. Title pages will be prepared in manuscript.

Hour, Date, Place	Summary of Events and Information	Remarks and references to Appendices
September 25th 1915	Loos attack. A third attack was then ordered. The Regpes [Regiment] taking place on the left circle on the line – the Battalion and "A" Coy. & party of "B" who have now (for company purposes called the right) – This attack commenced about 9 a.m. The men went forward well – On our side were kept close [illegible] and belonging men were found the next. "C" having a share which was [illegible] to havenes [illegible] were unable Open ground & [illegible] to havenes were unable to get to the forward & [illegible] heavy casualties. Lieut Jackson being instantly wounded – The line was unable to advance close enough to cut the wire & [illegible] lying out for 2 hours [illegible] on the left being in some [illegible]. Both knowing no our front we were held up both our flanks (10–25 on right & 26th Bde on left) had made good their line	

WAR DIARY or INTELLIGENCE SUMMARY

Army Form C. 2118.

Hour, Date, Place	Summary of Events and Information	Remarks and references to Appendices
September 25th (Cont.)	I hear advancing hotly hyd the furthermost 1st line - [About 12 non came back news that 15th Division on our right had captured LOOS & that 14th Bde had passed S. end of HULLUCH] The enemy from front trenches about 3 P.m. the flanks threatened surrendered in masses. Some 300 prisoners were falling into our hands. All Battalions of the Brigade were advanced & ordered to push on to capture if possible the objective which was BOIS HUGO & then objective which was BOIS HUGO & then objective at Pail 14 Bis - The Battalion was pushed forward on right making forward A & B in front line & C & D in support. The LOOS - HULLUCH Road was crossed & CHALK PIT WOOD occupied without opposition. As night was now falling it was decided to dig in on line (running) from Pail 14 bis going along BOIS HUGO and faced now SW but swing along Bois Hugo to East with STANDS on our right.	

WAR DIARY or INTELLIGENCE SUMMARY

Army Form C. 2118.

Hour, Date, Place	Summary of Events and Information	Remarks and references to Appendices
September 25th (cont.)	The 46th B.C. (15th Division) being on their Right, staff statements the remainder of the Brigade arrived & extended on their left & took over the left flank trenches back to the KENS - HULLUCH ROAD - Hill 70 was on our right & it was unknown if it was held by our troops or those of the enemy - on the evening of the 25th the advance was not a distance of some 2 miles - The night was very quiet & the men without greatcoats or supper spent disheartful night - C.O. Macleurii finer did the front line & "C.O.Ds" him to support. no serious opposition was encountered except for a slight shelling & snipers all was quiet. Bn. H.Q. were in huts in Posts 14 Bush, the right Bn. H.Q. were by Chalk Pit -	

WAR DIARY or INTELLIGENCE SUMMARY

Army Form C. 2118.

Hour, Date, Place	Summary of Events and Information	Remarks and references to Appendices
September 26	At 5 a.m. rain was reported that the Bde would be relieved at 5.45 a.m. - At about that hour enemy counter attacked weakly along edge of wood & were cut up by our machine gun fire which was most effective & stopped the attack. The Battalion was relieved soon after by the 2nd Yorkshires of the 21st Division who occupied the trenches we had dug - Several casualties occurred getting away from Hills & Shell-trenches but eventually we retired to our own lines & rested where he remained until dark. Returns, relief, casualties etc. being handed up. During the day it was seen that the 21st Division were retiring from positions west of Bois 8 & there was received that Boys. Hugo & Hill 70 were also in Enemy hands about R.R. In we were relieved up & infantry	

Army Form C. 2118.

WAR DIARY
or
INTELLIGENCE SUMMARY.
(Erase heading not required.)

Instructions regarding War Diaries and Intelligence Summaries are contained in F.S. Regs., Part II. and the Staff Manual respectively. Title pages will be prepared in manuscript.

Hour, Date, Place	Summary of Events and Information	Remarks and references to Appendices
September 27th	German trenches a ridge N.W. of LOOS. The Guards Division came up during the night & 2 Rfl came into our trenches — all were put during night the General trenches being consolidated — Royal North Lancashires were on our right — Received orders to move back to British front line trenches but S. of HULLUCH ROAD to rest - further orders went forward that attack on Guards Division to relate from had Bois HUGO & HILL 70. An attack also took place by 21st Division on HULLUCH — Casualties heavy on our left in HULLUCH — shelling front night —	

Army Form C. 2118.

WAR DIARY
or
INTELLIGENCE SUMMARY.
(Erase heading not required.)

Instructions regarding War Diaries and Intelligence Summaries are contained in F.S. Regs., Part II. and the Staff Manual respectively. Title pages will be prepared in manuscript.

Hour, Date, Place	Summary of Events and Information	Remarks and references to Appendices
September 28th (MAZINGARBE)	Received orders to fall back to MAZINGARBE for the day & recompense & to engage in the opposite trenches. Casual lists up to date. Are 10 officers & 279 o.r. Ranks. Remaining fighting strength 8 officers & 380 o.r. Ranks. Draft of 30 arrived.	Casualties — KILLED — Capt. A. MOUTRAY READ. Lieut. A. W. TUCKEY. — WOUNDED 2/Lieut. A.H.G. CLARKE. " C.E. EAST. " W.B. STANFIELD " T.R. PRICE. accidentally wounded Lieut. S.H. LEWIS — R. West Kent Rgt. Suffering from Gas poisoning Temp Capt. G.H.D. METCALFE. 2/Lt. C.V. KERPEN. " J.L. ELSTON
September 29th	Capt Read had very fallen to fire not really a party of about 60 men of different units who were retiring disorganised owing to the gas drifting back — He himself was led forward again by him & took up a position S. of LONE TREE. When very man (and?) New Colours (for true knew —) Capt Read was mortally wounded during the time.	

Army Form C. 2118.

WAR DIARY
or
INTELLIGENCE SUMMARY.
(Erase heading not required.)

Hour, Date, Place	Summary of Events and Information	Remarks and references to Appendices
September 29th (cont)	About 9.30 p.m. Batt. took over the defence of Loos captured last night by the Brigade with 25th — A very wet night & all troops & the trenches he took over from 2nd Cavalry Division — they had been relieved up to a hurry to stop the retirement which had set in by the falling back of the 21st Division on 26th Sept. the trenches of this line were taken up (app) 1000 — Rough entrenchments were also (taken) by him N + E. of Loos — It was nine trenches that the Batt. took over — The Battalion with nine trenches stretched from its left I have to Crown Henry, on the right C company in support — Enemy entrenched, shelled the town — which is in Ruins — German snipers many. There I all Battns —	SPECIAL ORDER. The Brigadier has issued pleasure in making known that the O.C. 1st Division has personally expressed to Lieut Colonel the conduct of the 2nd Battn in the present operations & has attributed & the way which he has in the face of heavy losses & the difficulty of Captains come 800 or 900 missing afterwards (killed) in the trenches which he has occupied — The Brigadier feel inspired that the Brigade will continue to meet his praise by sticking without flinching together when every yet be reported the (C.O.C. the more heavier gave risks —
Brig: Fuel Pollard.

Army Form C. 2118.

WAR DIARY
or
INTELLIGENCE SUMMARY.
(Erase heading not required.)

Instructions regarding War Diaries and Intelligence Summaries are contained in F.S. Regs., Part II. and the Staff Manual respectively. Title pages will be prepared in manuscript.

Hour, Date, Place	Summary of Events and Information	Remarks and references to Appendices
September 30th	Buzy informing Trenches – French's division are holding line in front of us but have not gained Hill 70 – Enemy shelled LOOS off & on. Some casualties. A Coy Coy 6 men by a shell in one of their houses –	Extract from Routine orders by Major General Holland, C.B. M.V.O. D.S.O. Comdg. I/Division – 29th Sept/15. SD2, Special order – The Corps Commander has expressed his appreciation of the gallantry & dash displayed by the 1st Division in taking & holding HULLUCH VILLAGE. We fully realize the difficult circumstances under which the attack of HULLUCH was delivered & the difficulties since confronted this 2nd Bde in attacking the front line

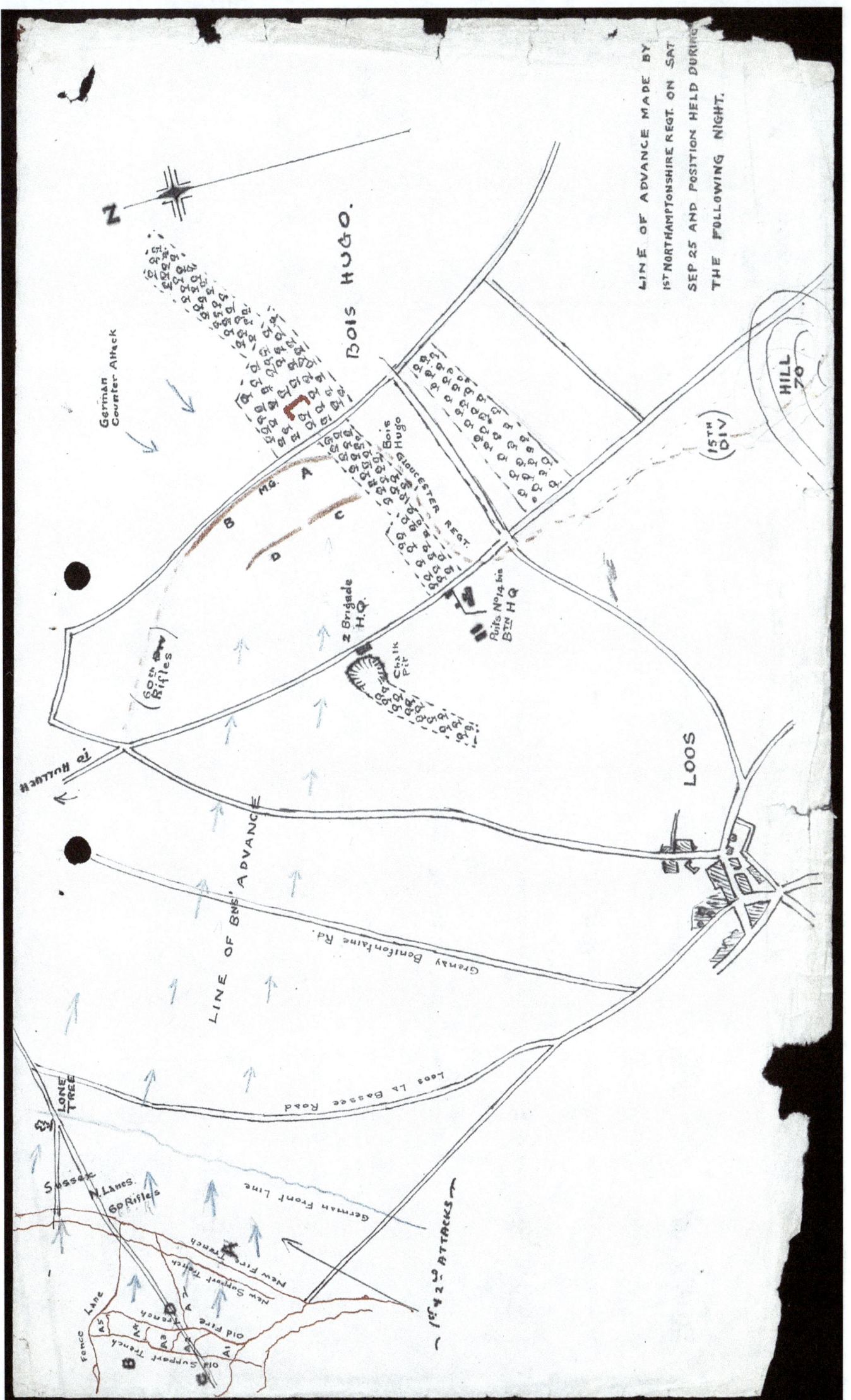

Extract from Field Returns. A.F. B.213. of 18th September 1915. and 3rd October. 1915.

Total strength of Battalion. 16. 9. 15.
Officers. 24.
Other Ranks. 986.

Total strength of Battalion 3. 10. 15.
Officers 14.
Other Ranks. 659.

Total casualties during Operations from 25. 9. 15. to 1. 10. 15.
10 Officers.
289. Other Ranks.

2nd Infantry Brigade.
1st Division.

WAR
DIARY

1st NORTHAMPTONSHIRE REGIMENT.

O C T O B E R

1 9 1 5

Army Form C. 2118.

WAR DIARY
or
INTELLIGENCE SUMMARY.
(Erase heading not required.)

Instructions regarding War Diaries and Intelligence Summaries are contained in F.S. Regs., Part II. and the Staff Manual respectively. Title pages will be prepared in manuscript.

Hour, Date, Place	Summary of Events and Information	Remarks and references to Appendices
6 am 1st Oct 1915 LOOS	Orders recd. that LOOS is to be taken over by French who wish to use it as a jumping off place to attack LENS from the N. Enemy shelling town heavily all day. About 11 pm the French came & took over lines. Two Battalions 800 strong actually in & around LOOS and a third Bn in reserve. A most unfortunate occurrence during relief was that a shell exploded in cellar occupied by 13th H.Q. & killed the Brigade Major (Major Terry). Shortly thereafter Brigadier Genl Pollard & killed the French General & his Staff Officer. The remainder of the relief was carried out in quietness. the Battalion moving back to billets in NOEUX les MINES. It was fortunately a moonlit night. 5 Dublin Officers arrived. *	2/L F.W. WRIGHT " G.G. ROBINSON " E.L. BURDIE " D.V. EVANS " J.G. CLAYTON *
2nd Oct NOEUX les MINES	Arrived in billets at 3 am very bad & crowded. very busy reorganizing & outfitting.	
3rd Oct "	Reorganization continues Battalion Re-Sebastian Officer arrived @	@ 2/L D.C. CHISHOLM
4th Oct "	Reorganization continues Draft of 198 men and 10 Officers joined the Battalion.	

Army Form C. 2118.

WAR DIARY
or
INTELLIGENCE SUMMARY.
(Erase heading not required.)

Instructions regarding War Diaries and Intelligence Summaries are contained in F.S. Regs., Part II. and the Staff Manual respectively. Title pages will be prepared in manuscript.

Hour, Date, Place	Summary of Events and Information	Remarks and references to Appendices
Noeux les Mines Oct 5th	Wet day reorganising &c. Two Officers joined Battalion ⓪	⓪ Major H.R.H. DREW 2/Lt. L.H.M. MCKENZIE. Major Drew took over Command from Major (Capt t/c) Moysten Regt. who has been in Command since July 11th. 2/Lt. J. CLARK Enjoined.
Oct 6th	Battalion moves to billets in MASINGARBE - now in Divnron Reserve. Btn. to be used for working parties at night digging new trenches - 2/ Battn. to hospital sick.	
MAZINGARBE Oct 7th	Battalion moves up to trenches in Old German lines near POSEN STREET with 2/ Sussex Regt. on our left; 1st and 3rd Brigades are holding front line near HULLUCK and 9th Lifeguards are lent to 3rd Brigade.	
GERMAN CAPTURED TRENCHES Oct 8th	Heavily bombarded by enemy all front line trenches (1st and 3rd Bdy) have a very bad time. About 3:30 p.m. Germans attacked in mass but were everywhere beaten back; fighting continued until evening. Battalion stood to & were ready to reinforce but were not required.	
Oct 9th Oct 10th	All quiet, busy digging new trenches all night. Carrying parties after dark bringing up 250 gas Cylinders otherwise quiet which were stored in Old German Lines & the "Quarry". Otherwise quiet.	

(73989) W4141—463. 400,000. 9/14. H.&J.Ltd. Forms/C. 2118/10.

Army Form C. 2118.

WAR DIARY
or
INTELLIGENCE SUMMARY.
(Erase heading not required.)

Instructions regarding War Diaries and Intelligence Summaries are contained in F. S. Regs., Part II. and the Staff Manual respectively. Title pages will be prepared in manuscript.

Hour, Date, Place	Summary of Events and Information	Remarks and references to Appendices
GERMAN Captured TRENCHES MAZINGARBE		Lt Col. L.G.W. Dobbin Reformed Battalion from Sick Leave.
Oct 11th	Still in Old German Lines and digging trenches new Assembly trenches.	
Oct 12th	Busy completing arrangements & issuing stores for new attack tomorrow. Carry gas cylinders into front trenches.	
Oct 13th	The 2nd Sussex and ourselves are lent to 1st Brigade (Br Genl Reddy) to act in support. They move forward though 1st Brigade and capture the S.W. end of Hulluck if attack is successful. The Battalion began filing out of Old German trenches near POSEN STREET about 1am and moved forward into battle stations in new assembly trenches. These trenches and Battalion H.Q. dug out at H.18 (Central) also advanced Bn H.Q. about ½ mile nearer enemy, were only roughly completed an hour before we occupied them. Reassembly trenches were about 5ft deep and 2ft broad, slightly serpentine. Those to the South being dug in soft loamy soil, the remainder in hard chalk. Lt Col Dew was ordered to remain in Command of the Battalion	

(73989) W4141—463. 400,000. 9/14. H.&J.,Ltd. Forms/C. 2118/10.

Army Form C. 2118.

WAR DIARY
or
INTELLIGENCE SUMMARY.
(Erase heading not required.)

Hour, Date, Place	Summary of Events and Information	Remarks and references to Appendices
Oct 13th (cont.)	As Lieut Col Gothin was attached to 2nd Bde H.Q. so observing. So "Zero" was timed for 1p.m. when our own intense bombardment started; but the bombardment of Fosse 8 (11th Corps) began at noon. Our gas and smoke appeared to go very well and at 2pm the 1st Brigade began to advance into it and reports came back saying all was well. It appears however that the gas had little effect and the German line was practically uncut. In consequence only a small portion of the German line was penetrated (by Black Watch). Our own trenches were heavily shelled by the enemy: the Assembly trench occupied by "B" Company had three absolutely direct hits with coal boxes about a dozen men being killed or buried × and some of the Officers having narrow escapes × being knocked about. Before the advance started Captain Jervois was hit in the arm + handed over to Lt Purdue. The latter officer had only joined a few days.	

Army Form C. 2118.

WAR DIARY
or
INTELLIGENCE SUMMARY.
(Erase heading not required.)

Instructions regarding War Diaries and Intelligence Summaries are contained in F.S. Regs., Part II. and the Staff Manual respectively. Title pages will be prepared in manuscript.

Hour, Date, Place	Summary of Events and Information	Remarks and references to Appendices
13th Oct Cont.	"A" Company of ours and "A" Company 2/Sussex were detailed as two strong patrols to advance across our line & on into HULLUCH being supported by bombers on their outer flanks. They never got over our front line, being severely handled by the Germans as they advanced up to & in the open from the rear. The German trench being about 200" distant. Lt Bundey was badly hit in the shoulder and practically half the Company either killed or wounded in the space of a few minutes. The survivors advanced as quickly as they could & took cover in our front line. "A" Company 2/Sussex also suffered heavy losses Captain Burgess who was in Command being killed. Each man in the Battalion was issued with two MILLS Bombs and grenadiers carried 8 each. Most of these were sent to help the Black Watch in their attempt to dislodge the Germans from the trench in which we (Black Watch) had gained a footing. As the afternoon wore on the Battalion was moved up into trenches nearer the front & 9th Loyal North Lancs & KRR pushed in in support	

WAR DIARY or INTELLIGENCE SUMMARY

Army Form C. 2118.

Hour, Date, Place	Summary of Events and Information	Remarks and references to Appendices
Oct 13th Cont'd	The trenches became very much blocked & movement was most difficult: all sorts of rumours were in circulation but nobody was able positively to say how the attack had fared – Our "A" and "C" companies were by this time both mixed up with the Black Watch & 10th Gloucesters in the front trenches, whilst "B" and "D" were more or less together in some of the old German communicating trenches further back. As it got dark companies were able to shake themselves free and reorganize to some extent.	
About 7 p.m.	It had now become evident that there was a hitch somewhere & orders were received to report exactly the position of all units. Ourselves and the 2/Sussex again coming under the orders of our own Brigadier. Bn H.Q. were (temporarily) established at point 18 (our Dressing Station). 2/Lot Dean & Lt Clarke (acting Adjt) were called away to a Brigade Conference at Quesnoy leaving Major Morstan Pigott in charge.	

Army Form C. 2118.

WAR DIARY
or
INTELLIGENCE SUMMARY.
(Erase heading not required.)

Hour, Date, Place	Summary of Events and Information	Remarks and references to Appendices
Oct 14th 3.30 am Inaction.	Lt Col Oare returned from Conference about 3.30 am with orders to form up as the leading battalion of 2nd Brigade which was to deliver an attack in mass at 4 am 'break through at all costs'. The attack was to be delivered on about a two hundred yards front at a point almost due W of HULLUCH in the following order: 1st Northamptonshire 2/Sussex 2/KRR 9th Liverpools. The latter two battalions being much weaker than the two former.	
5.20 am	Battalions were so mixed in the dark that it was finally 5.20 am instead of 4 am when the Brigade heading to advance, lying down outside the trenches were present, and all arrangements were carried out direct as between C.O.s. Lieut Col Ramsay 9th Liverpool who happened to be the Senior present moved up into the front fire trench. Broad daylight was rapidly approaching, but a heavy mist hung over the trenches and it was owing to this fact that we were able to get into position	

WAR DIARY or INTELLIGENCE SUMMARY

Army Form C. 2118.

Hour, Date, Place	Summary of Events and Information	Remarks and references to Appendices
Oct 14th Continued 5.30 am	About 5.30 am our patrols who had been sent out scouting came back & reported all quiet but enemy were practically in sight. About 5.40 am our men began advancing from our front trench parapet. At this moment an order arrived cancelling attack. Brigade was withdrawn (Casualties very slight, two men killed & a few wounded. Capt McClure was hit in the temple by a stone 15mm up by a ricochet & became a casualty). The whole Brigade ordered into neighbouring trenches which were in consequence once more choc a bloc - men most uncomfortable and a good many dead & wounded lying in our trench which was shelled persistently. Tel communication broken & spying by the enemy. Brigade remained in position until dark & was finally relieved by 15th & 8th London (47th Divn) about midnight.	

Army Form C. 2118.

WAR DIARY
or
INTELLIGENCE SUMMARY.
(Erase heading not required.)

Instructions regarding War Diaries and Intelligence Summaries are contained in F.S. Regs., Part II. and the Staff Manual respectively. Title pages will be prepared in manuscript.

Hour, Date, Place	Summary of Events and Information	Remarks and references to Appendices
Oct 15. LILLERS	Arrived LILLERS about 5 am having entrained at NOEUX Les MINES abt 3 am. "A" and "D" Companies who had been in support having gone on ahead, remaining Companies were led out of trenches via LONE TREE by Maj Loyston-Pigott. Officers and men were dog tired on arrival in billets & slept in billets afternoon, the men being rather crowded.	2/Lt DW Evans to H.Q. Staff 15.10.15 2/Lt Bedcock reported to duty 15.10.15
Oct 16 LILLERS	Resting and cleaning up. The Q.M. to issuing practically whole Battalion with new Clothing. A draft of 69 other ranks also Lt Buckingham arrived —	
Oct 17.		
Oct 18.	Resting & cleaning up duties.	
Oct 19.	Names of 6 Officers & 20 men submitted for leave. Battalion march to rifle ranges near Lefarnine & came in x how very weak in officers a "Bn" is × have been taken for	× Lt Yarnell (bombing) Wright (machine g.) Maj R. Pigott (OC S APM) Lt McKenzie (trench mortar) Lt Buckingham (scouting)
Oct 20.	Battalion training.	

Army Form C. 2118.

WAR DIARY
or
INTELLIGENCE SUMMARY.
(Erase heading not required.)

Instructions regarding War Diaries and Intelligence Summaries are contained in F.S. Regs., Part II. and the Staff Manual respectively. Title pages will be prepared in manuscript.

Hour, Date, Place	Summary of Events and Information	Remarks and references to Appendices
Oct 21st LILLERS	Bde Genl inspected billets — Div Genl visited Battalion in training Area.	
Oct 22nd	Battalion route march — town very busy, extremely 28th Divl artillery in process.	
Oct 23rd	Companies march to range at PSYNON and carry out firing at new temporary range in wood.	
Oct 24th	Church parade under Brigade arrangements	
Oct 25th	Very wet — Inspection by G.O.C. 28th postponed.	
Oct 26th	Battalion training as usual	
Oct 27th	Battalion route march	
Oct 28th	200 selected men from a Company of Brigade Comptd Battalion march to LAMBERS for King's Review — a wet day.	Draft of 20 other ranks arrive
Oct 29th	Lt Col Bothan in command of the Bn. Bn training — firing on temporary range	
Oct 30th	do	
Oct 31st	Church Parade.	

2nd Infantry Brigade.
1st Division.

WAR DIARY

1st NORTHAMPTONSHIRE REGIMENT.

DECEMBER

1915

2nd Infantry Brigade.

1st Division.

WAR DIARY

1st NORTHAMPTONSHIRE REGIMENT.

NOVEMBER

1915

WAR DIARY or INTELLIGENCE SUMMARY.

Army Form C. 2118.

Hour, Date, Place	Summary of Events and Information	Remarks and references to Appendices
November 1st Lillers	Inspection of N.C.O.'s & Buglers. Cancelled owing to inclement weather. Company Training carried on. Coy comdrs. reports re. inclement weather.	
" 2nd	Company training in Coy Range at Rumilles - nights operation.	
" 3rd	Musketry and Company Training	
" 4th	"	
" 5th	Church parade cancelled owing to sickness of Chaplain. Company Training	
" 6th	Companies at Bus for musketry bayonet fighting and bomb throwing.	
" 7th	Inspection by G.O.C. Brigade.	
" 8th	Field Training. Coy. companies at Rumilly range.	
" 9th	Bn. route marched in preparation for possible future.	
" 10th	March by Bn. to NŒUX-LES-MINES and then moved to MAZINGARBE arriving about 11am previous to trenches in front of HULLUCH taking up support position at "I am 19" & a fire occurred in a dug out occupied by the Mess Cpl. Lcpl Craik and R.S. Metzger who were severely burnt. It is not known as a great many uses been used as the would have lost — more ammunition that it would have two foot.	

[signatures] |

Army Form C. 2118.

WAR DIARY
or
INTELLIGENCE SUMMARY.
(Erase heading not required.)

Instructions regarding War Diaries and Intelligence Summaries are contained in F.S. Regs., Part II. and the Staff Manual respectively. Title pages will be prepared in manuscript.

Hour, Date, Place	Summary of Events and Information	Remarks and references to Appendices
Nov 14th Studio in fort Mullick	Company Commanders reconnoitring line trench and approaches to fort Trencher - all quiet	
Nov 15th	Front up to Jenny Lane trench was taken over from 2nd KRRC at 5.30 p.m.	
Nov 16th	Very quiet during night — enemy shelled to us the line trench	
Nov 17th	Very quiet during night 16/17 at about 7 am 19th enemy reported cutting wire in front of trench trench. Company prepared for attack but nothing ensued	
Nov 18th	Very quiet to front and enemy afterwards struck and passed word all along with all unsh[—] word.	
Nov 19th	Heavy bombardment of Enemy trenches by our artillery which was replied to by enemy 6" guns & whizz bang shell bursts about the our H.Q. dugouts and by short bursts from the signallers dugout, the artillery Lyr[.] started at 1.30 a.m. an 8" shrapnel bursting shell which had a strong fuse it had answered its way into the earth and had practically burst at a depth of about 25 ft. It was of the signallers dug-out and three wounded. Am relieved by the Royal Sussex Regt at about 10 pm marched back to billets at MAZINGARBE arriving about 10 pm	
Nov 20th	Spent the day in billets - Coys and Platoon up to Pt 19 This (next) inspected and precautions taken against	

[Signed] 1/Scots Guards

Army Form C. 2118.

WAR DIARY
or
INTELLIGENCE SUMMARY.
(Erase heading not required.)

Instructions regarding War Diaries and Intelligence Summaries are contained in F.S. Regs., Part II. and the Staff Manual respectively. Title pages will be prepared in manuscript.

Hour, Date, Place	Summary of Events and Information	Remarks and references to Appendices
Nov 21 MAZINGARBE	My object in clearing Rat-Trap Communication Trench at 4:40 p.m. and started to finish taking up position in Support of Bde orders one Coy of HULLUCK men in digging and improving Communication Trenches until 3 am 22nd	
Nov 22nd In the Trenches	Clearing up and improving support trenches men kept on this work to protect footfall. Very quiet, 10th and Rushy in crossing my left artillery fire. – No1 man wounded – 1 Off and 1 man wounded.	
Nov 23rd	From HAVRE Relieved 6th Camerons on Being Relieved by Hullock relief Completed at 6.30 a.m. Trenches, dug outs and latrines in very dirty condition men employed all day clearing up and making the Trenches sanitary. Nil man killed — two men wounded — during this night 24th/25 and 25/26 attempts to recover wounded between trenches to 80 & 90 left front. However found ten British and three German dead which were recovered and brought to vegetation. This Trench were lying in the open between 50+ of a German Sapa. He was repeatedly sniped during the performance of this duty.	[signatures]

Army Form C. 2118.

WAR DIARY
or
INTELLIGENCE SUMMARY.
(Erase heading not required.)

Instructions regarding War Diaries and Intelligence Summaries are contained in F.S. Regs., Part II. and the Staff Manual respectively. Title pages will be prepared in manuscript.

Hour, Date, Place	Summary of Events and Information	Remarks and references to Appendices
November 25th In the Trenches	All quiet during day — At about 8 p.m. the enemy commenced firing part flank trench. The Germans succeeded in temporarily getting the upper hand after persistent and heavy bombing, and the Stokes Trench & their work shelter and two Troop Cpl Sharpe whose section was occupying that part of the trench, then (in his own initiative) threw three Cylinder and improvised petrol-bombs to this German dug-outs and flung trench mortars at different places silencing and dislodging the Germans.	
Nov 26 — " —	All quiet during day — The Battalion was relieved about 7 p.m. by the 1st Cameron Highlanders and marched to billets in	
Nov 27th MAZINGARBE	Companies employed in cleaning up and refitting — needs felt, inspected and precautions taken against trench feet.	
Nov 28th — " —	Church present and inspection of billets	
Nov 29th — " —	Parades under Company Commanders.	
Nov 30th — " —	Parades and inspections of all Company Armaments. 1 draft arrived of 1 Officer 2 Sgts 3 Cpls L/Cpls 75 men	

(1)

First Battalion Northamptonshire Regt.

Army Form C. 2118.

WAR DIARY
or
INTELLIGENCE SUMMARY.
(Erase heading not required.)

Instructions regarding War Diaries and Intelligence Summaries are contained in F.S. Regs., Part II. and the Staff Manual respectively. Title pages will be prepared in manuscript.

Hour, Date, Place	Summary of Events and Information	Remarks and references to Appendices
1st Dec. 1915. MAZINGARBE.	"D" Coys headquarters struck by H.E. pipsqueak. 2nd Lt. E.S. Stevenson buried in the debris, he was eventually rescued, wounded and very much shaken.	
2nd " In the trenches.	Relieved 1st S.W.B. in A.1. sector, support line N.N.E. of LOOS. Relief completed by 8.30.p.m. no casualties.	
3rd " "	Night of 2nd/3rd all quiet. All quiet.	
4th " "		
5th " "	Enemy shelled our trenches, one shell landed in the trench wounding 9 men (one man died later from wounds). Two men wounded on working party.	
6th " "	All quiet — relieved Royal Sussex Regt. in A.1. sector. firing line on our right, we are in touch with the French 32nd Division.	
7th " "	All quiet.	
8th " "	All quiet — 3 men wounded. — Companies employed cleaning out trenches and laying trench boards — Trenches falling in owing to rain — men kept at work and by the men to avoid trench foot.	
9th " "	All quiet — 2 no men wounded.	
10th " "	Enemy bombarded our trenches, three men 2/Lt R.R.C. Killed and three men wounded in a machine gun emplacement in our line. Our casualties were two men wounded. — Relieved by 1st L.N. Lancs at 4.P.M.	

(2)

Army Form C. 2118.

WAR DIARY
or
INTELLIGENCE SUMMARY.
(Erase heading not required.)

Instructions regarding War Diaries and Intelligence Summaries are contained in F.S. Regs., Part II. and the Staff Manual respectively. Title pages will be prepared in manuscript.

Hour, Date, Place	Summary of Events and Information	Remarks and references to Appendices
11th Dec. 1915. Philosophe.	Men fairly comfortable — Billets have been repaired by Brigade Pioneers and permanent sanitary arrangement erected, also room allotted and fires kept going to enable men to dry their clothing — Companies employed washing feet and rifles — Anti frostbite grease — Enemy bombarding TUIT at PHILOSOPHE, one man killed from fragment of shell which struck TUIT 200x away	
12th. "In the trenches"	Relieved Royal Sussex Regt in A.2 sector support trenches.	
13th " "	In A.2 support all quiet	
14th " "	All quiet — Relieved at 4 P.M. by 10th Gloster Regt and rode in motor buses to billets at NOEUX-LES-MINES.	
15th. "NOEUX-LES-MINES."	A draft of ninety men joined from LE HAVRE — Companies employed cleaning up and removing traces of the trenches	
16th. " "	Companies render company commanders cleaning billets and refitting — 4 our officers and three hundred men proceeded to PHILOSOPHE in buses and from there marched to the trenches, employed at digging communicating trenches and improving light railway.	Lt Col 2th W Dutton Crossed to England for home service Major J.A. Bethell ? Home OC Command 16.12.15

Army Form C. 2118.

WAR DIARY
or
INTELLIGENCE SUMMARY.
(Erase heading not required.)

Instructions regarding War Diaries and Intelligence Summaries are contained in F.S. Regs., Part II. and the Staff Manual respectively. Title pages will be prepared in manuscript.

Hour, Date, Place	Summary of Events and Information	Remarks and references to Appendices
14. Dec. 1915. NOUX-LES-MINES.	Battalion taking in parties of thirty-five every half hour — "A" and "B" companies inspected by bombing officer.	
18th. " "	Company training under company officers — Smoke helmet drill.	
19th. " "	Preparation for the trenches — Less well rested men. Anti frostbite grease.	
20th. " In the trenches	Relieve 6 1st S.W.B. in B.2. sector, outpost — Enemy rather noisy in front of 15th Division who occupy QUARRIES north of HULLUCH	
21st. " "	Rather heavy bombardment by the enemy, some shells probably 5.9 fell into our trenches killing four men and wounding three men of "B" company.	
22nd. " "	A draft of twenty two men arrived from L.H. HAVRE — all guns & four officers and three hundred men employed carrying barbed wire, screw pickets, two men wounded by astray bullets	
23rd. " "	Very quiet — one man killed one man wounded.	
24th. " "	Relieved 2nd/60th R.R.C. in B.2. sector, firing line, three men wounded by rifle grenades.	

WAR DIARY
or
INTELLIGENCE SUMMARY.

(Erase heading not required.)

Army Form C. 2118.

Hour, Date, Place	Summary of Events and Information	Remarks and references to Appendices
25". Dec. 1915. In the trenches	Fairly quiet. Our guns reminding enemy that we have no desire for peace - a miniature locomotive was observed running on a track immediately behind the German trenches between BRECON SAP and MERTHYR SAP - Enemy were observed throwing mud and water from his trench. Two bombers from there threw seven bombs into the enemy trench. There was no retaliation - An enemy sniper was shot by one of our men - During the night 25/26th our patrols rushed the enemy wire and reported that a working party was digging in their trench, about twelve rifle grenades were fired into the trench. A draft of twenty-one men arrived from LA HAVRE - During the night 26/27th our patrols again visited the German wire and reported that their wire was in a very poor condition -	
26th " "	All quiet - No casualties	
27th " "		

(5)

WAR DIARY
or
INTELLIGENCE SUMMARY.

(Erase heading not required.)

Army Form C. 2118.

Instructions regarding War Diaries and Intelligence Summaries are contained in F.S. Regs., Part II. and the Staff Manual respectively. Title pages will be prepared in manuscript.

Hour, Date, Place	Summary of Events and Information	Remarks and references to Appendices
28th Dec. 1915. In the trenches	Between 11.30 am and 12.30 pm enemy trench mortars very active. A shell probably an 8" struck our parapet destroying the two bays (casualties four men killed and four men wounded.) Relieved by 1/5th Kings Own Lancs who are only 182 trench strength and two companies 2/4 Lancs. Companies employed clearing up Kit and getting fit clean and nilled with Anti frostbite Guard.	
29th " " PHILOSOPHE	Relieved 2nd/60th K.R.R.C. in support trenches B1.	
30th " " ————	During relief of the 47th Division (on our left) in front of 30/31st the Germans exploded two mines. Night of 30/31st very quiet.	
31st " " ————	All quiet. 2nd/21 K.O.Y.L.I. Shells intended for S.W.B.	

1ST DIVISION

1ST BATTALION
NORTHAMPTONSHIRE REGT.
JAN - DEC 1916

2nd Brigade.

1st Division.

1st BATTALION

NORTHAMPTONSHIRE REGIMENT

JANUARY 1916.

1st Northampton Regt
Jan
Vol XVI

2nd Bde

Army Form C. 2118.

WAR DIARY
or
INTELLIGENCE SUMMARY.
(Erase heading not required.)

Instructions regarding War Diaries and Intelligence Summaries are contained in F. S. Regs., Part II. and the Staff Manual respectively. Title pages will be prepared in manuscript.

Hour, Date, Place	Summary of Events and Information	Remarks and references to Appendices
In Support Trenches Jan 1st 1916.	In the trenches. Relieved by 8th Bn. Bedfordshires — Very stormy night. Late relief. Arrived Noeux les Mines about midnight where we billet. 2nd Lieut Neal died of wounds during the night from wounds received the day before.	
Jan 2nd Noeux les Mines	Cleaning up & inspection of Battalion. Church Parade in afternoon.	
Jan 3rd	Inspection of rifles and equipment. Heavy fatigues of 300 men during afternoon and evening repairing light railway to Bosen Sg and laying wires for telephones.	
Jan 4th	Company Parades. Conference at Bn H.Q. re training where we go back into Corps Reserve. Machine Gun detachments inspected.	
Jan 5th	Cleaning up billets — Company parades — Baths and change of clothing for men.	
Jan 6th	Inspection of Companies at Drill & iron rations inspected.	
Jan 7th Front line trenches	Battalion moves into front line trenches and relieves 6th Bt Welch (3rd Brigade). The trenches are on the whole in excellent order. Two companies occupy firing line about 1100 and one Company back in support Reserve. In addition B company (The Dublin Pals) hold a small post of

WAR DIARY
or
INTELLIGENCE SUMMARY.

(Erase heading not required.)

Army Form C. 2118.

Instructions regarding War Diaries and Intelligence Summaries are contained in F. S. Regs., Part II. and the Staff Manual respectively. Title pages will be prepared in manuscript.

Hour, Date, Place	Summary of Events and Information	Remarks and references to Appendices
Jan 8th	Quiet night on fatigue laying trench boards & repairing parapets &c. The "Dublins" Coy which are attached for instruction want a lot of help and supervision they have very sketchy ideas as regards Sentries	
9th	Large digging fatigues on New Support trench during night. Fairly quiet. One of our transport horses shot by a stray just outside our Bn. H.Q.	1 wounded
10th	Heavy bombardments of Putts IQ R's during the evening in conjunction with cutting out enterprise organized by 2KRR on our right near C.H. + K. Pif. Bennano retaliated heavily on our Support and Communication trenches, killing 5 of the Dublin Ino's and blowing in a machine gun emplacement & portions of The Trenches. An unpleasant night as there are no dugouts & The men are practically now sleeping in open trenches. A good deal of hostile trench mortaring on our front trenches which are shelved by our Hows. but charge position & return fire.	1 wounded (Two teams of mortars were called in different trenches) {6 killed {12 wounded
11th	During the night Corporal Norman D Coy went out with a small patrol and did	

Army Form C. 2118.

WAR DIARY
or
INTELLIGENCE SUMMARY.
(Erase heading not required.)

Instructions regarding War Diaries and Intelligence Summaries are contained in F.S. Regs., Part II. and the Staff Manual respectively. Title pages will be prepared in manuscript.

Hour, Date, Place	Summary of Events and Information	Remarks and references to Appendices
Jan 11th (continued) A 2 Front line	did some excellent work passing over our own and the German wire. They came to a dug out in the enemy front line which had a light burning in it (This dugout had been cleaned two nights previously but was then empty) Voices were heard inside and several grenades were thrown in by the patrol. Screams & groans followed - patrol withdrew without casualties, no very light were fired and very few rifle shots - See Cyphentel patrol report & work.	
Jan 12th	15th Division sent round Officers to inspect our trenches with view to take over on 14th Jan. Our How in chalk pit very active daily, & firing with great accuracy on trenches W of Hulluck. Most interesting to watch shells can be picked up with the naked eye guide easily followed for about 1000 — Germans open a sudden rather heavy strafe at dusk chiefly on front line & support trenches. A considerable number of casualties and damage to trenches - fatigue emploine on new support line	5 killed 1 wounded
Jan 13th	Repair work to regiment all day. A good deal of intermittent shelling and hostile trench	

Army Form C. 2118.

WAR DIARY
or
INTELLIGENCE SUMMARY.
(Erase heading not required.)

Hour, Date, Place	Summary of Events and Information	Remarks and references to Appendices
Jan 13th (Cont.) A 2 Front Line	Trench mortaring. Our trench mortar ammunition ran out & one of the heavy mortars blew up. Several casualties both morning & afternoon. Two apparently new big and powerful German Biplanes very active and apparently having matters very much their own way. Two of our machines (?) were unable to drive them off & had a rough time. Scarcely any anti aircraft guns fired on the Germans. During the night Cpl Norman's patrol again brought in useful information. Hand over to 10th Bordons after seven days in front trenches during which time our casualties averaged nearly 5 killed & wounded daily. Great improvements have been made to communication trenches, and new support trench almost finished ready for occupation. Two billeting parties sent on to Noeux les Mines and Lillers respectively, to take over our quarters for the night, and there for our months "Rest". (The Camerons billets very clean, & 8th L Scots the exact opposite.)	The shell case of one of our anti aircraft fell on one of our men in Loren alley & pierced 2 killed & 1 wounded 7 wounded
Jan 12th.		1 wounded

WAR DIARY
or
INTELLIGENCE SUMMARY.
(Erase heading not required.)

Army Form C. 2118.

Hour, Date, Place	Summary of Events and Information	Remarks and references to Appendices
Jan 15th Lillers	Battalion entrained at Nœux les Mines and arrive LILLERS about 11:30 am & settle down in billets which are on the whole good.	
16th	Clean up billets & redistribute men where necessary.	
17th	Kit inspection, inspection of quarters, and care of feet, clothing began. Our pioneers very busy glazing broken windows and generally doing repairs to billets. Armourer Sgt. begins a careful inspection of all arms. Companies carry out training according to programme	Draft of 39 other ranks.
18th	Company training & usual routine in 1st afternoon. The 2nd Brigade & Div mounted to have a practice ceremonial parade in fields near Ch. Philomel.	
19th	Very bitter weather. Company training in morning - Ceremonial inspection by General JOFFRE in afternoon. "The occasion was of some note being the first time on which British troops were inspected by Gen. Joffre in his capacity as the Allied C-in-C." Sir Douglas Haig, Sir Harry Rawlinson & Gen Wilson were all invited & decorated with	
20th	High Orders on the parade ground by the Allied C-in-C.	

WAR DIARY
or
INTELLIGENCE SUMMARY.

(Erase heading not required.)

Army Form C. 2118.

Instructions regarding War Diaries and Intelligence Summaries are contained in F. S. Regs., Part II. and the Staff Manual respectively. Title pages will be prepared in manuscript.

Hour, Date, Place	Summary of Events and Information	Remarks and references to Appendices
Letters 21st Jan	Company to Summary in Battalion Diary. Regimental B?	
22nd	of E.F.C. opened. In afternoon each Company sent a platoon to dig & prepare fire trenches on the range S. of BURBURE. 4 Lewis guns drawn from Ordnance.	
23rd	Snipers & Lewis guns fire on range. Companies carry out Platoon & Section bty training.	
24th	Church parade. —	
	Right half Battalion began firing on range. 1 too rounds has been allotted per man. End	
	this to being expended in 4 days. as far as possible under present Service Conditions is close range, Smoke helmets to fixed bayonets & night firing being especially insisted on	
25th	Left half B? have a baths.	
	Right half B? fire on range, remainder continue Company training, bombing &c	
26th	Right half B? fourth day firing on range.	
27th	Left half B? begin firing on range.	
	Company training, bombing &c remainder continue	
28th	Mosketry cancelled owing to Division being put on 2 hrs notice for trenches. Usual Company training continues	Draft 32 other ranks chiefly Specialists
29th		
30th	Left half B? recommence range firing. B? is now on 4 hours notice — according 9GCM Army No.6801 Decision promulgated	

Army Form C. 2118.

WAR DIARY
or
INTELLIGENCE SUMMARY.
(Erase heading not required.)

Instructions regarding War Diaries and Intelligence Summaries are contained in F. S. Regs., Part II. and the Staff Manual respectively. Title pages will be prepared in manuscript.

Hour, Date, Place	Summary of Events and Information	Remarks and references to Appendices
Lillers 30th Jan	Sentries on 26 Dennis thirty carried out at 7.10 a.m. by a firing party of 10 men of the Battalion. Musketry continued by Left half Bn on range. Surprise visit by C in C Sir D. Haig who inspected & complimented Regimental guard, and had a conversation with CO before leaving. Left half Bn firing on range but again delayed owing to 3 hrs notice for trenches. The enemy guns have been very audible the last two days.	This is believed to be the first case in the Regiment since Peninsula days.
3.1.16.	H.G.H. [signed]	
	[signed] Lieut Col Comdg 1/Northamptonshire Regt	

2nd Brigade.

1st Division.

1st BATTALION

NORTHAMPTONSHIRE REGIMENT

FEBRUARY 1916.

1st Northampton Regt.
Feb 1916
Vol XVII

Army Form C. 2118.

WAR DIARY
or
INTELLIGENCE SUMMARY.   1st Northamptonshire Regt.

(Erase heading not required.)

Hour, Date, Place	Summary of Events and Information	Remarks and references to Appendices
1916. February. 1st LILLERS.	Final of Platoon Competition.	J.P.T. Mennach Capt.
2nd "	Right half B. Coy. night firing in smoke helmets and with very lights	
3rd "	Coy. Bombing Practice - Left half Batt night firing.	
4th "	C.O. inspected Loos section. Bn exercise in night firing, bombing & Lewis guns.	
5th "	Cleaning of billets - inspection by C.O. & M.O. 2/Lt E.R.C. AYLETT joined for duty	
6th "	Bde Manoeuvres.	
7th "	Church Parade.	
8th "	Divl route march. 12 miles via AUCHY AU BOIS. Lecture on bombing by Lt YARNELL	
9th "	Battn inspected in bombing. (17 miles)	
10th "	Battn Field day and route march via NEDON and HERIONVILLE & 2 men fell out	
11th "	Coy. Bombing - very wet day.	
12th "	Bombing and Musketry - draft of 22 O.R. arrived.	
13th "	Physical Drill and inspection of Kits - preparatory to move. Church Parade - Coy Comdrs reconnoitre Trenches in LOOS - MAROC section: Lecture to officers of the 1st Divn by Lt Gen: Sir Henry Wilson - Cmdg IVth Corps. Capt HUMPHREY and Lt SPREY SMITH join the Batt. No 14 Platoon formed under Capt HUMPHREY is formed, and attached for duty to 1st S.W. Borderers as part of LOOS garrison.	
14th "	Packing and cleaning up before leaving LILLERS for LES BREBIS.	

Army Form C. 2118.

WAR DIARY
INTELLIGENCE SUMMARY. 1st Northamptonshire Regt.
(Erase heading not required.)

Instructions regarding War Diaries and Intelligence Summaries are contained in F. S. Regs., Part II and the Staff Manual respectively. Title pages will be prepared in manuscript.

Hour, Date, Place		Summary of Events and Information	Remarks and references to Appendices
February 15th	LILLERS	Major G.H. ROYSTON PIGOTT leaves Bn. to take Comd. of 10th Worcestershire Regt. Capt. Hon. D.P. TOLLEMACHE. 7th Hussars joins Battn. as 2nd in Comd. Lieut. ATTWATER and 2/Lieut. MARSHALL join Battn. Battn. parade 3.P.M. entrain 4.P.M. for NOEUX LES MINES arriving 5.P.M. march to billets at LES BREBIS - in Bde. reserve, MAROC section - reach billets 6.30.P.M	D.P. Tollemache Capt.
16th	LES BREBIS	Coy. Parade. Foot inspection. Smoke Helmet Practice. Handling of Arms. C.O. inspects billets. 2nd in Comd. visits Support Battn. in MAROC.	
17th	"	Coy. Parade. The Brig. Genl. the C.O., 2nd in Comd. and Coy. officers reconnoitred the line to be taken over - night Battn. MAROC sector.	
18th	"	Coy parades - inspection of smoke helmet, and of men's feet - application of anti-frostbite grease. at 6.P.M. Battn. marched, order A.C.B.D. coys, at 10 mins. interval, followed by Transport to MAROC and took over left half of MAROC section from 2nd K.R.R.C. Relief completed by 9.P.M.	
19th	MAROC Section	Night quiet. Trenches very wet - Wind variable - N.E. to S.E. - C.O. inspected the line from 12. min. to 7.A.M. - 2nd in Comd from 10 A.M. - 3 P.M. Dispositions C coy, plus 1 platoon of D (employed on carting away sandbag from mine) from LIVERPOOL STREET (excl) to SEVENTH AVENUE - A coy from latter point to KING STREET (excl) plus 1 Platoon of D. Coy. MG. B. Coy + D coy less 2 Platoons, in support, in MIDDLE ALLEY to SOUTH STREET. O.G.I. from	

3.

Army Form C. 2118.

WAR DIARY
or
INTELLIGENCE SUMMARY. 1st Northamptonshire Regt

(Erase heading not required.)

Instructions regarding War Diaries and Intelligence Summaries are contained in F.S. Regs., Part II. and the Staff Manual respectively. Title pages will be prepared in manuscript.

Hour, Date, Place	Summary of Events and Information	Remarks and references to Appendices
Feb. 19th (cont d) MAROC Section	All Coys hard at work cleaning Trenches. Draft of 2 sergts & 38. O.R. joined Battn	J.P. Tollemache. Capt.
" 20th " "	Quiet night. Wire reconnaissance carried out by Coy officers along whole Battn front. Sapt J. improved and more wire put out. C.O. inspected line at morning Stand To. At 2.30.P.M. our Trench Mortars 2" opened on wire at apex of German Triangle, in front of A coy. Several rounds fell short. At 4.30.P.M. our Howitzers opened on same objective making very good shooting. Firing ceased 5.30.P.M. At 7.P.M. relief of Battn by 1st Royal Highlanders commenced, completed 9.30.P.M. Battn marched via LES BREBIS to MAZINGARBE. To billets – last coy arriving 12.30.A.M.	
Feb. 21st MAZINGARBE	9.A.M. – Coy Parades; inspection of feet – cleaning of billets. 3.P.M. Orders recd To stand To, owing to attack by enemy on the right near GIVENCHY. 5.P.M. Troops fall out for tea, ready to fall in at 10. min notice. 8.30.P.M. Orders recd To be ready to move at ½ hours notice.	
" 22nd "	10.30 A.M. Orders recd " " Coy Parades and inspections – Fall of Snow. 4.P.M. inspection of billets and kits. Working Party of 4 offrs 16. N.C.O.s 200 men to the refort to O.C. Trench Maintenance Coy at St PANCRAS KEEP at 6.P.M. Party found by A and B Coys under Captain CHISHOLM	

4.

Army Form C. 2118.

Instructions regarding War Diaries and Intelligence Summaries are contained in F.S. Regs., Part II. and the Staff Manual respectively. Title pages will be prepared in manuscript.

WAR DIARY
or
INTELLIGENCE SUMMARY.
(Erase heading not required.)

1916.

1st Northamptonshire Regt.

Hour, Date, Place	Summary of Events and Information	Remarks and references to Appendices
February 23rd MAZINGARBE	Coy Parades and inspections. Weather frosty and cold. Working Party of 4 Offrs, 8 N.C.Os and 100 men of A. and D. Coys under Capt. MARTIN report to O.C. 173rd Mining Coy at MAROC at 7.P.M.	J.P. Tollemache Capt.
" 24th "	Coy Parades. Weather cold and frosty. Some snow. Baths arranged for men at the Brewery. C.O. lectured to Officers at 4.P.M.	
" 25th "	Coy Parades. Ground still covered with thin coating of snow. Coy officers reconnoitred the positions of the outpost Battn LOOS sector. Working Party of 4 Offrs 8 N.C.Os & 200 men of C & D. Coys under 2/Lt CLAYTON report to O.C. Trench Maintenance Coy at ST PANCRAS KEEP at 6.P.M. 2/Lt R. Farrell joins for duty. O.C. sees Coy Cmdrs at 5.30.P.M.	
" 26th "	Inspection of Feet and application of anti-frostbite grease. Cleaning of billets. Battn Bugle & P.M. take off [crossed out] to relieve R. Munster Fusiliers as support Battn LOOS SECTOR. – D. Coy starting 6.30.P.M. via PHILOSOPHE and LENS road to E.WAY. – B. Coy at 7.P.M. by same route to ENCLOSURE – C. Coy at 7.45.P.M. via LES BREBIS to O.G.1. (N. of PICCADILLY) A. Coy at 8.P.M. via LES BREBIS to MAROC – Battn H.Q. Fatigues 1. Offr. 75 men carrying M.G. material from R.E. Store LOOS to front line. 1 Offr. 100 men cleaning HAY HILL from ENCLOSURE to front line. 2 Offrs 200 men deepening PICCADILLY from WREXHAM TUNNEL to front line.	

Army Form C. 2118.

WAR DIARY
INTELLIGENCE SUMMARY.
(Erase heading not required.)

1st Northamptonshire Regt

Hour, Date, Place	Summary of Events and Information	Remarks and references to Appendices
Feb. 27th Support Bttn LOOS	Fine day. C.O. inspected each Cᵒʸ's position. At 6 P.M. we sprung small mine near HART'S crater in Left Battⁿ's sub. sector. No crater formed, but German mine gallery destroyed. Two Lewis guns placed at disposal of O.C. Left Battⁿ until operation concluded. Fatigues 1 off. 108 O.R. deepening and cleaning HAY HILL. 1 off. 108 O.R. deepening PICCADILLY near front line. B. Cᵒʸ improving cellars and approaches in ENCLOSURE. D. Cᵒʸ found various carrying parties at disposal of O.C. Left Battⁿ.	D.P. to Menache Captⁿ
" 28th "	Quiet night. Fine Day. Fatigues. 1 off. 60 men working on HARRISON'S CRATER. 1 off. 60 men on HART'S CRATER. 1 off. 80 men on ENCLOSURE AVENUE.	
" 29th "	Quiet day. Slight rain and thaw. At 6 P.M. Cᵒʸs moved to relieve Cᵒʸs of 2nd K.R.R.C. in Right Sub-Section. Relief completed 8.40 P.M. Dispositions D. Cᵒʸ from junction with 1st R. Highlanders, to HAYMARKET. B. Cᵒʸ HAYMARKET to the D, just W. of LENS road, with one patrol W. edge of HARRISON'S CRATER. A. Cᵒʸ in support, in SOUTH STREET with crater party in close support trench. C. Cᵒʸ in Reserve, in cellars in LOOS. Battⁿ H.Q. Fatigues - Both front line Cᵒʸs rebuilding parapets and fire steps and cleaning floors of trench. Support Cᵒʸ cleaning and laying trench boards in HAYMARKET. Reserve Cᵒʸ carrying rations.	

2nd Brigade.
1st Division.

1st BATTALION NORTHAMPTONSHIRE REGIMENT

MARCH 1916.

1 Northampton Regt
Vol XVIII

March 1916

Army Form C. 2118.

WAR DIARY
or
INTELLIGENCE SUMMARY.
(Erase heading not required.)

1st Northamptonshire Regt.

Hour, Date, Place	Summary of Events and Information	Remarks and references to Appendices
March 1916.		
March 1st Right Batt: LOOS.	Some rifle grenades into front trench, badly wounding a sergeant - otherwise quiet. Warmer with sunshine - Work - Both front line Coys rebuilding parapet and fire-steps, and cleaning floor of trench - Support Coy cleaning and laying trench-boards in HAYMARKET.	J.P. Le Mesurier Capt.
2nd "	Quiet night. 2 Germans shot while trying to put up loop hole plate just W. of LEWS road. About 4.P.M. small party of enemy approached our sap W. of HARRISON'S Crater, and threw bombs. Our bomber at sap head retaliated and drove enemy off. 4 Germans were seen dead - enemy removed bodies. Our 4.5 Howitzers were firing at this line on German line, just opposite our sap, and several shells fell very close to sap. At night 2 patrols went out from each Coy in front line, and discovered a listening post, unoccupied, just in front of German wire.	
3rd "	Quiet day. At 7.P.M. relief by 2nd K.R.R.C. commenced - relief completed 9.40.P.M. Battn marched to billets in LES BREBIS, in Bde reserve.	
4th LES BREBIS.	Coy Parade - Inspection of feet and of rifles and, at H.P.M. of Kits. Fatigues 1 off: 105 men carrying material for Trench Mortar Battery.	
5th "	Fatigues, 3 off: 200 men under R.E. for work on HARRISON'S Crater.	

2. March 1916.

Army Form C. 2118.

WAR DIARY
or
INTELLIGENCE SUMMARY.
(Erase heading not required.)

1st Northamptonshire Regt.

Instructions regarding War Diaries and Intelligence Summaries are contained in F.S. Regs., Part II and the Staff Manual respectively. Title pages will be prepared in manuscript.

Hour, Date, Place	Summary of Events and Information	Remarks and references to Appendices
March 6th LES BREBIS	Inspection of feet - application of whale oil - Weather cold and wintry. 6.P.M. - 6.30.P.M. Battn moves by Coy at 10 min interval. To relieve 2nd K.R.R.C. as Right Battn - LOOS sector. Relief complete 8.30.P.M. A patrol of 1/1 Corpl and 2 men went out and did not return. Night very foggy.	D.P. To Menache Capt
7th Right Battn LOOS.	2 Coy in front line - right Coy from M.S.C.4.b, in touch with left of 6th Welch. To HAYMARKET. Left Coy from latter point to M.6.d.1.6. each just W. of HARRISON'S Crater with crater party in close support trench. 1 Coy in support in SOUTH Str. 1 Coy in reserve in cellars in LOOS. Some hostile shelling of front line.	
8th " "	Quiet night. A strong officer's patrol went out from each Coy in front line - no enemy encountered. The trench at our junction with 6th Welch is frequently damaged by hostile shell fire. Our trench mortar (2") firing on ens. trench close to LENS road put a bomb into our sap W. of HARRISON'S Crater. Draft of 15. O.R. joined.	
9th " "	Patrols went out, saw no enemy. About 3.A.M. enemy were heard working on the wire in front of right Coy. A Lewis gun opened on them - cries were heard. Some hostile shelling of left Coy's trench in afternoon. The 116th Battery retaliated. Commencing 7.30 P.M. Battn relieved by 8th Royal Berks relief completed 9.30.P.M. Battn em-bussed at LES BREBIS, less 2 Coys which marched, Billets at BRACQUEMONT.	
10th BRACQUEMONT.	Coys inspections of feet, billets, kit, rifles etc. C.O. inspects each Coy in marching order. Permanent fatigue of 2.N.C.O. and 20 men at Div H.Q.	
11th " "	Cleaning of billets and roads.	

(73989) W4141—463. 400,000. 9/14. H.&J.Ltd. Forms/C. 2118/10.

WAR DIARY or INTELLIGENCE SUMMARY

Army Form C. 2118.

1st Northamptonshire Regt.

March 1916.

Hour, Date, Place	Summary of Events and Information	Remarks and references to Appendices
12th BRACQUEMONT	Parade service in MOEUX LES MINES. 11 A.M. Corps and Divl Commanders present. 5. P.M. Working party of 6 offs 24 N.C.O.s 300 men went by bus to LES BREBIS. vig: 4 offs 216 O.R. to report to O.C. Trench Maintenance Coy. 2 offs 108 O.R. to 173rd Coy R.E.	
13th "	A.M. Inspection of billets. Draft of 2 offs - 80 O.R. joined. Capt TREFUSIS and Lt CRAWFORD. P.M. C.O. held conference of Coy. Comdrs and directed to reorganize Coys. in 3 Platoons.	
14th "	Coys. Parade. Handling of arms. C.O. inspects Coys as reorganized. Fatigue 6 offs 324 O.R. left 3 P.M. by motor bus to LES BREBIS for work under Trench Maintenance Coy. C.O. attended conference at Bde H.Q.	D.P. Tollemache Maj.
15th "	Coys inspections of rifles and of billets. 6.15 P.M. Battn marched to BULLY - GRENAY - Thence by Coy at 10 min interval to S. MAROC in relief of 1st G. Gordons as support Battn in cellars. Work. Wiring support line. Cleaning WALL AVENUE, New Trench and QUARREY ROAD.	
16th S. MAROC	Work. 1 Coy wiring support line. 1 Coy deepening WALL AVENUE and new Trench N.E. to the Wall. 1 Coy continuing new Trench from the Wall to Quarry Road. 1 Coy cutting new Comn Trench round front of Dump to O.B. 3 - all forming front of new reserve line.	
17th "	Work. 1 Coy wiring support line. 1 Coy making T. heads in CHIMNEY ALLEY. 2 Coys continuing work on new Trench and Comn Trench as above	

4.

March 1916.

Army Form C. 2118.

WAR DIARY
or
INTELLIGENCE SUMMARY.
(Erase heading not required.)

1st Northamptonshire Regt

Instructions regarding War Diaries and Intelligence Summaries are contained in F.S. Regs., Part II and the Staff Manual respectively. Title pages will be prepared in manuscript.

Hour, Date, Place	Summary of Events and Information	Remarks and references to Appendices
Sat. 18th S. MAROC.	6-15 P.M. Relieved 2nd K.R.R.C. in right sub sector. Relief completed 8 P.M. Dispositions 1 Coy (A) from 50x S. of EDGEWARE ROAD to BOYAU 8. incl. 1 Coy (D) from latter front to Sap F. incl. 1 Coy (B) from latter to LIVERPOOL St. 1 Coy (C) in support – in cellars in S. MAROC. Batt. H.Q. in cellars M. 3. c. 3. 2.	
19th —	A & D Coys relieved by 3 Coys of the 8th R.G. Fus. and return to cellars in S. MAROC. Work – 1 Coy wiring support line. 1 Coy Fire-stepping EDGEWARE ROAD. 1 Coy deepening WALL AVENUE. B. Coy, a till in front line, have to strong patrol reconnoitring under S. arm of CRASSIER. 2/Lt PHIPPS reconnoitred German Sap.	
20th — "	6 offrs attend lecture at LES BREBIS on Mining. Work 1 Coy on new trench from WALL to QUARRY ROAD. 1 Coy carrying Trench Mortar Amn. at 7.24 P.M. Germans blast a small mine on S. arm of Crassier. No damage to us. B. Coy again sent out large patrol. Corpl. NORMAN met 3 Germans and pursued them, firing his revolver. They got back into their Sap-head.	
21st "	D. Coy relieve B in front line at 4.A.M. — and sent out strong patrol – no signs of enemy. Work. 1 Coy Wiring support line. 1 Coy deepening new Comn. Trench from Quarry Road to O.B.3. B & C. Coys relieve R.G. Fus. in front line. A. Coy in support.	
22nd — "	D. Coy remains in front line, B & C. Coys relieve R.G. Fus. in front line. A. Coy in support. Capt. OLIVER, 2/4th LEICESTER Regt. attd. for instruction – and join D. Coy in front line.	

5. March 1916.

Army Form C. 2118.

WAR DIARY
or
INTELLIGENCE SUMMARY.
(Erase heading not required.)

1st Northamptonshire Regt.

Instructions regarding War Diaries and Intelligence Summaries are contained in F.S. Regs., Part II. and the Staff Manual respectively. Title pages will be prepared in manuscript.

Hour, Date, Place	Summary of Events and Information	Remarks and references to Appendices
Thurs 23rd Right Sub-sector	Heavy fall of Snow. Each Coy sent out patrol. No enemy met.	
24th "	Col. OLIVER. 2/Lt Leic. Regt leaves for England. Capt HUMPHREY goes sick.	
25th S. MAROC	Battn relieved by 2nd K.R.R.C. and returns to cellars in S. MAROC, as support Battn. Relief completed 9. P.M. Work: 1 Coy wiring. 1 Coy filling in Trenches. 1 Coy digging new Trench. 2/Lt PHIPPS acting as Adjt vice Capt MARRIOTT of 2nd Coy.	
26th "	Work. 1 Coy wiring support line. 1 Coy filling in QUARRY Road. 1 Coy on O.B.3. 1 Coy on new Trench at M.q.b.3.7.	
27th "	Quiet day. Work continued as above.	
28th LES BREBIS	Brig. visits Battn 10.30 A.M. Battn relieved by 1st Cameron and moves to LES BREBIS. Fatigue party of 300 men including the permanent fatigue of 100 men.	D.P. Tollemache
29th "	Fatigue as above - 200 men digging new Trench - 100 (permanent) laying a cable.	
30th "	" " " C.O. inspected NOYELLES reserve line.	Maj
31st "	Fatigue of 100 men as above - German aeroplane active. Concert in Div.l Club at 6.30. P.M. Draft of 13 men arrived - C.O. visits reserve line.	

2nd Brigade.

1st Division.

1st BATTALION

NORTHAMPTONSHIRE REGIMENT

APRIL 1916.

Confidential.

1 Northampton Regt
Vol XIX

To D.A.G.
   3rd Echelon.
      Base.

War Diary
for
Month of
April.
1916.

1/ April 1916.

Army Form C. 2118.

WAR DIARY
—or—
INTELLIGENCE SUMMARY.
(Erase heading not required.)

1st Northamptonshire Regt.

Instructions regarding War Diaries and Intelligence Summaries are contained in F.S. Regs., Part II. and the Staff Manual respectively. Title pages will be prepared in manuscript.

Hour, Date, Place	Summary of Events and Information	Remarks and references to Appendices
Sat 1st LES BREBIS.	Working Party of 100 men. Considerable hostile shelling of LES BREBIS between 11 A.M. and 3 P.M. Very inadequate retaliation by our artillery.	J.P. Tollemache Major
2nd " "	Battn relieves 1st S.W. Borderers in left sub. sector LOOS. C.oys move off at 10 min interval, commencing 6.30. P.M. Relief completed 9.10. P.M. The right C.oy line had been heavily shelled during the afternoon. Parts of front line trench and saps on to HART'S CRATER damaged, and C.oy H.Q. blown in, burying 10 O.R. and 4 men (killed) Our night C.oy assisted by party from support C.oy restored front line trench during the night. Party from Left Support Batt n. under direction of R.E. restored the Saps to Crater. Dispositions. 1 C.oy ("D") SCRUB LANE (incl.) to PICCADILLY (excl.) 1 C.oy ("C") from latter point to BLACK WATCH ALLEY (incl.) 1 C.oy ("B") from latter point to GORDON ALLEY excl. 1 C.oy ("A") in cellars in Enclosure Avenue. Batt n. H.Q. at junction of Enclosure Avenue and Standen Road. D. and B. coys each find a Crater Party. Patrol from each C.oy examined every sap.	
3rd Left Sub Section LOOS.	Quiet Day. Some hostile activity with rifle grenades, causing a few casualties. Patrols went out at night and saw no enemy in front of the trenches. Work of improving trench and parapet continued. Much fresh sand-bag revetting required.	
4th " "	Night passed quietly. Day fine and bright.	

2/ April. 1916.

WAR DIARY
or
INTELLIGENCE SUMMARY. 1st Northamptonshire Regt.

Army Form C. 2118.

Hour, Date, Place	Summary of Events and Information	Remarks and references to Appendices
Wed. 5th Left Batt. LOOS.	Relieved by 2/K.R.R.C. and became Left Reserve Batt. Relief completed 8.30 P.M. 2/Lt. B.G. MARSHALL killed about 6 A.M. by rifle grenade at Sap on HART'S CRATER. Dispositions as Left Reserve Batt. — 1 Coy. (Altars N. of Craters) — 1 Coy. cellars in LOOS near Rt. Batt. H.Q. — 1 Coy. in E. Way. — 1 Coy. & Batt. H.Q. in O.G.1.	S.P. Tollemache — Major
Thurs. 6th Left Res. Batt.	Just after midnight, Germans exploded a mine in front of SEAFORTH ALLEY not damaging our trenches. Left Front Batt. did not occupy Crater. Germans did. In consequence, dispositions slightly altered — viz — Coy. of Front Batt. from Enclosure move to N.E. of Crater, ready to support the left Coy. in front of New Crater. Coy. of Left Res. Batt. from E. WAY, moved up to Enclosure and placed under orders of O.C. Left Front Batt. for Tactical purposes. If this Coy. is sent forward, another Coy. of Res. Batt. to be moved up to Enclosure Avenue to hold Reserve Line. Work Done — 1 Coy. making Fire Bays in Enclosure Avenue — 1 Coy. providing carrying parties for 173rd Tun. Coy. and 26th Fd. Coy. — 1 Coy. wiring Support line from SCRUB LANE towards Crater. 1 Coy. wiring across top of LOOS Crater.	
Frid. 7th " "	Quiet day — Work for night 7/8th — Continuation of above Tasks.	
Sat. 8th " "	Quiet day — Relieve 2/K.R.R.C. in front line — Signallers, adv. Parties, Lewis Gunners and Carr. Parties at 3. P.M. Coys move 7.15 P.M. Relief completed 8.45 P.M. About 10 P.M. 2/Lt. C.N. Crawford was killed in front of HART'S CRATER by a fragment of shell	

3/ April 1916.

Army Form C. 2118.

WAR DIARY
INTELLIGENCE SUMMARY

1st Northamptonshire Regt

(Erase heading not required.)

Hour, Date, Place	Summary of Events and Information	Remarks and references to Appendices
9th Left Front Batt. LOOS	Dispositions — "C" Cy SCRUB LANE TO PICCADILLY. "B" Cy from latter point across LOOS CRASSIER TO BLACK WATCH ALLEY. "A" Cy from latter point to GORDON ALLEY where left joined right of 16th Div. "D" Cy in support in cellars N. of Crassier. 1 Coy 2/K.R.R.C. in cellars of Enclosure. Each Coy in front has 1 Platoon in Support line, with a cellar partly found from this Platoon.	S. P. Tollemache Major
10th " "	Enemy active with rifle grenades. Capt. MARTIN of the right Coy wounded in the head by a fragment of one. We retaliate with trench mortars. About 11 P.M. a patrol of left Coy under Lt Storey-Smith reconnoitred the small crater cannot by our camouflet. Germans were not occupying it, and no work had been done on it.	
11th " "	About 10:30 A.M. a small party of Bombers went up SEAFORTH S+P beyond our barrier, and got under the rear lip of Rifleman's Gate. From there they threw bombs into the crater. Then Pte Neville crawled up the lip and looked into the crater. He saw 6 dead Germans, but no live ones. No defensive works, but three holes supported by wooden frames. Possibly entrances to dug-outs. The party then returned to our barrier in the Sap. In the evening, Batt= relieved by 2/K.R.R.C. and returned to positions of Left Support Batt". 1 Coy Enclosure. 1 Coy cellars in LOOS. 1 Coy E.WAY. 1 Coy and Batt= H.Q. in O.C.1. Work. 3 Coys, 240 men, working on Enclosure trench, Resurrection, 1 Coy clearing E.WAY down to PICCADILLY	

4/ April 1916.

Army Form C. 2118.

WAR DIARY
or
INTELLIGENCE SUMMARY.   1st Northamptonshire Regt
(Erase heading not required.)

Instructions regarding War Diaries and Intelligence Summaries are contained in F.S. Regs., Part II. and the Staff Manual respectively. Title pages will be prepared in manuscript.

Hour, Date, Place	Summary of Events and Information	Remarks and references to Appendices
12th Support Bat: LOOS.	Quiet Day. Slight rain. Wind S.W. Work 300 men - (75 per Coy) completing Enclosure Avenue in Reserve Line	
13th "	Work as above. About 6.5.P.M. Germans shelled with 4.2.s, Batt: H.Q. in O.C.I. Fire very accurate, evidently observed fire. Trench blown in several places. Batt: Pioneers and H.Q. details worked very hard all night to repair Trench. (shelling ceased about 6.30.P.M)	
14th "	Quiet day. Relieved in evening by 1st Camerons. Relief complete 9.15.P.M. Work 2 carrying parties, each 1 Off = 50 men. - found by "A" and "B" Coy Draft of 10 other ranks arrived. Batt: moved to Billets in LES BREBIS. "A" area	J.P. To Vennecke Major
15th LES BREBIS.	Fine Sunny day. Some hostile shelling about 3.P.M. Café TREFUSIS, "A" Coy until QrMr Sergt A.D. + M.S and 2 men, wounded while fraying out the new Coy. Work 3 parties, each 2. Off:= 100 men (50 per Coy) for work under Trench Maintenance Coy.	
16th "	Quiet day. Bright Sun. Church Parade 11.A.M. (50 men per Coy) Work 2 carrying parties, each 1 Off: = 50 men (found by "C" and "D" Coys)	
17th "	Quiet day in billets. Concert in evening. Work. 2 parties, each 2. Off:= 1. Off:= and 50 men	
18th "	Work. Two parties each 2. Off:= 100.0 Other ranks (50 per Coy) for work under Trench Maintenance Coy.	
19th "	Quiet day in billets. rained most of the day.	

WAR DIARY
INTELLIGENCE SUMMARY

Army Form C. 2118.

1st Northamptonshire Regt.

April 1916.

Place	Date	Hour	Summary of Events and Information	Remarks and references to Appendices
LS BREBIS	20th	6.30 P.M. 8 P.M.	Coy parade at 10 minutes interval; order of march - B.C.A.D.; relieve 1st S.W. Borderers in right sub-section - Maroc Section.	S.D. Tottenham Major.
Right Sub Section MAROC	21st		Dispositions - "C" Coy from S.O. "S" of Boyau 1. (Left of 2nd Div.) to Sap.B (excl.) "D" Coy from Sap.B (incl.) To Boyau 10.A. and Sap.D (excl.) "A" Coy from Sap.D (incl.) to Boyau 13. and to LIVERPOOL STR (excl.) - where left of Batt" joined right of 2/K.R.R.C. One man killed on Patrol.	
	22nd		Very wet day - Patrols reconnoitred enemy's wire. Trench in bad condition; crumbling after the rain.	
	23rd		Relieved by 1st L.N. Lancs. Move into cellars in S. MAROC in support.	
			Work. 3 parties of 1 Offr. 2 N.C.O.s 70 men each, found by A.B. and D. C'y work on Support line from SEVENTH AVENUE southwards - revetting, clearing, lowering parapets and rebuilding parados. 1 Offr and 30 men "C" Coy, hire in Dug-out in reserve line, NEUF ALLEY and work from that line. 1 Offr and 30 men "C" Coy work on Reserve line under B'n Pioneer Offr. 1 N.C.O. & 14 men carrying for R.E.	
Support MAROC	24th		Weather fine and warm. Work, continuation of above; also Bomb Shelter constructed in NEUF ALLEY.	
	25th		" " " "	
	26th		Relieve 1st Loyal N. LANCS in front line. Dispositions.. "C" Coy from left of 2nd Div." at foot C'm Trench S of Boyau 1. to Sap.B incl. "A" Coy from Sap.B. excl. To Boyau 10.A. Sap.D (incl.) "D" Coy Boyau 10.B. incl. to Boyau 14 (excl.) "B" Coy from Boyau 14. incl. to LIVERPOOL STR each. Relief completed 10.50 P.M.	

Army Form C. 2118.

WAR DIARY
INTELLIGENCE SUMMARY.
(Erase heading not required.)

1st Northamptonshire Regt.

April 1916.

Place	Date	Hour	Summary of Events and Information	Remarks and references to Appendices
Right Sub Section MAROC	27th	2 A.M.	Officer's Patrol went out from left Coy's line, and found wire hitherto unobserved along the Sunken Road.	S.P. Tollemache Major
"	28th	A.M.	C.O. visited Bn H.Q. and afterwards Divl H.Q. in connection with proposed raid on enemy's front line.	
		4 P.M.	46th Battery R.F.A. cut some newly observed wire E. of sunken road. Observed from Fosse 5.	
		8.30 P.M.	Raiding parties assemble in front line opposite Bogai 14. Capt. Snell and Major Tollemache layout tape in the required direction, as far as the sunken road, which the raiding parties pass over and form up 50 yards in front of it.	
		8.40 P.M.	Parties move forward to beyond the sunken road — in 3 columns of single file — viz. Right Trench Party 1 N.C.O. 7 men under 2/Lt Phipps. Right Parapet Party 1 N.C.O. 7 men under 1st Lt Spry-Smith. Left Trench Party 1 N.C.O. 7 men under 1st Fricker. Capt. Snell, commanding the whole, headed the centre party consisting of 2 Bombers and 3 Bayonet men under a Corpl for blocking the C.T. Trench and followed by 2 orderlies of Stretcher bearers and 4 number for marking the gaps in the 2 line of enemy's wire.	
		8.50 P.M.	Artillery bombardment opened upon which raiding parties rushed forward to front outside enemy's inner wire.	
		9.0 P.M.	Artillery lifted to enemy's outpost line, maintaining a barrage on the front line on either flank of length of trench to be attacked.	
		9.12 P.M.	After taking 2 prisoners, bombing 3 dug outs, and shooting 5 Germans with revolver, fairly left the Trench and retired through a covering party of 20 men under Major Tollemache and Lieut Clayton, which had followed the raiding parties out as far as the sunken road. Only 3 wounded, who were all brought in. Both German prisoners were killed by shell fire near The German wire, escorts according to their being wounded. Whole party, including covering party was back in our trench by 9.25 P.M. Enemy scarcely retaliated at all.	

1/ April 1916.

Army Form C. 2118.

WAR DIARY
—or—
INTELLIGENCE SUMMARY. 1st Northamptonshire Regt
(Erase heading not required.)

J.P. Tollemach
Major

Place	Date	Hour	Summary of Events and Information	Remarks and references to Appendices
Maroc	28th	4.H.11	After quiet night, enemy released gas opp H.H.N.E. of L008, which by 5 A.M. had reached Maroc in section	
Right Front Batt		5 A.M.	Gas helmet worn for about an hour - Various strays were made with success attack 15th	
			Irish Div. on left of 1st Div. and were heavily repulsed. No unusual activity on our front.	
		9 P.M.	relieved by I.N. Lancs. moved to cellars S. M.4. R.O.c. - as right reserve batt -	
			Work: 2 offs 100 men French bording Muddle Alley. 1 off 50 men fare-stepping O.B. 1. Support Line. 1 off 30 men	
			living in Meat Alley and working on Reserve line. 1 off 30 men working on Boyau line round Fosse 5. 1NCO 10 men fort R.E.	
Right Support Batt	29th } 30th }		Quiet Day - Bright and sunny. Work same as above. 2 men on working party wounded.	
Maroc			" "	

2nd Brigade.
1st Division.

1st BATTALION

NORTHAMPTONSHIRE REGIMENT

M A Y 1916.

WAR DIARY OF INTELLIGENCE SUMMARY

Army Form C. 2118.

(Erase heading not required.) 1st Northamptonshire Regt.

May 1916

J.P. Tollemache Major

Place	Date	Hour	Summary of Events and Information	Remarks and references to Appendices
Right Reserve Bn. MAROC	1st		Quiet day. Work – 2 offs 100 men on MIDDLE ALLEY, Trench boarding and constructing T. heads	
		8.30 P.M.	1 Off + 30 men on Reserve Line from NEUF ALLEY to CHAONE ALLEY. 1 off + 50 men on O.B.1.	
			1 off + 30 men on Reserve Line from WALL AVENUE to O.B.3. 1 N.C.O. 14 men working under R.E.	
	2nd		2/Lieut C.L. SERGEANT joined from 3rd Batt, and posted to "C" Coy. 1 Platoon of "A" Coy + 2 Lewis Guns to LENS ROAD REDOUBT	
			Quiet day. Relieved in evening by 1/Cameron Highlanders 1st Bde. Relief complete 9.50 P.M. To billets in LES BREBIS.	
			Work. A off + 208 O.R. clearing CRASSIER TRENCH and WELCH TRENCH in 1st Bde area. Two parties each 1 off +	
			52 O.R. carrying for 173rd Fd Coy R.E. 1 Platoon "B" Coy. to Div. Bombing School FERFAY for 6 days.	
LES BREBIS "B" Area	3rd	1.30 A.M.	Return Alarm of Gas attack received from 16th Div. Cancelled 2 A.M.	
			Of a class of 7 men returned from a Bn. Bombing Course 3 (Pte) GROVER, FREEMAN and CLARKE) obtained "D" certificate	
		7.30 P.M.	Fatigue 2 N.C.O.s and 20 men. To report to 23rd F.A. Coy R.E. at Railway embkt. 7.30 P.M. each evening 3rd – 7th inclusive	
	4th	1.30 A.M.	Another alarm of Gas attack from 16th Div. "A.Int". Cancelled before 2 A.M. Quiet day. Fine and bright.	
		10.30 A.M.	"B" and "C" Coys marched out to woods 1 mile beyond PETIT SAINS, accompanied by cookers – back by 4 P.M.	
	5th		Quiet Day. The platoon of "A" Coy in LENS ROAD Redoubt relieved at 11 P.M. by a platoon from D. C"y	
		8.10 P.M.	Fatigues – 2 parties each 1 off + 52 o the ranks carrying explosives to mine gallery for 173rd C"y R.E.	
	6th	10.30 A.M.	Quiet Day. A and D Coys marched out to wood beyond PETIT SAINS with cookers returned 5 P.M.	
	7th	10 A.M.	Church Parade. 2 off + 50 men from C"y. Showery day. Platoon in LENS Rd Rt relieved 7 P.M.	
		2.30 P.M.	Draft of 85 o the ranks arrived from the Base. 2/Lieut C.E. WILSON joined from O.T.C. and posted to B. C"y	

2 May 1916

Army Form C. 2118.

WAR DIARY
INTELLIGENCE SUMMARY.
(Erase heading not required.) 1st Northamptonshire Regt

Instructions regarding War Diaries and Intelligence Summaries are contained in F.S. Regs., Part II. and the Staff Manual respectively. Title pages will be prepared in manuscript.

Place	Date	Hour	Summary of Events and Information	Remarks and references to Appendices
LES BREBIS	8th		3/Lt G.H. GADSDEN joined from Base.	
		9.15 p.m	Quiet day – Fresh S.W. wind. Sunny. In evening relieve 2nd B. Munster Fus" as Right Res Battn LOOS. C'y parade and move up at 10 min interval to N. MAROC billeted in cellars. Relief completed 10.40 P.M.	L.P. Tollemache Major
N. MAROC	9th		Wet day. Work on night 8th/9th after relief. 2 off = 104 O.R. Ranks wiring troops front line. Little work accomplished owing to want of corkscrew stakes. 2 off = 104 O.R. deepening KING STREET. Also fine carrying parties totalling 80 N.C.Os and men.	
"	10th		Fine day. Work as above. Little progress made with wiring, owing to hostile fire - night 9/10th 150x of Wire erected, from in front of HAYMARKET towards JERMYN STREET.	
"	11th		Night 10/11th	
"	12th	8.30 PM	C'y Parade 8.30 P.M. and move up to front line in relief of 2/K.R.R.C. Relief completed 10.40 P.M. Dispositions - "C" C'y - CARFAX ROAD - KING ST Extn. "A" C'y Sallu point C.5.b x W of LENS road. "B" C'y left front to SCRUB LANE. "D" C'y in outpost in SOUTH ST. Battn H.Q. by Post Office LOOS	
Rt Front Battn LOOS	13th		Much work on left C'y's line, which had been bombarded and blown in while occupied by 2/K.R.R.C. CORSE LANE defined and secured. FIR ST cleared and deepened. FIR ST/MOUNT SAP cleared and re-occupied.	
	14th		Quiet Day. Sniper plate fired upon with elephant gun. Relieved in evening by 2/K.R.R.C. Relief interrupted by alarm from left Battn = (2/O.P.: Sussex) where enemy after a bombardment entered trench and took away Lewis Gun. Returned to Rt Res Battn Billets N.M + ROC. Work 50 men carrying sandbags from mine tanks, 50 men clearing and deepening comn Trench "A" to "E" under HARRISON'S CRATER. 30 men wiring front line. 50 men carrying wire & stakes. Also 3 carrying parties totalling 80 N.C.O.s & Men.	
		10 P.M Midnight		

T2134. Wt. W708-776. 500000. 4/15. Sir J.C. & S.

Army Form C. 2118.

WAR DIARY
or
INTELLIGENCE SUMMARY.
(Erase heading not required.)

1st Northamptonshire Regt.

May 1916.

Instructions regarding War Diaries and Intelligence Summaries are contained in F.S. Regs., Part II. and the Staff Manual respectively. Title pages will be prepared in manuscript.

Place	Date	Hour	Summary of Events and Information	Remarks and references to Appendices
MAROC	15th		Wet Day. Quiet. Work. 1 off + 50 men arriving front line from JERMYN ST. Towers Triangle. 1 off + 50 men carrying	D.P. Follenade
		8.30 P.M	arriving material from VALLEY Xroads to JERMYN ST. and deep dugouts to Cpt C? K.R.R.C. 1 off + 40 men continuing	
			deepening of Com? trench A.T. & F. under HARRISON'S CRATER. 1 off + 30 men deepening & repairing P.T. heads in QUEEN ST.	Major
			Carrying parties totalling 11 O.N.C.O's + men. Total 5 off + 300 men.	
"	16th		Fine sunny day. Slight shelling in morning, directed at dummy battery close to Batt? H.Q. 2 men wounded. Work as above.	
"	17th		Work as above, except that carrying parties were reduced by 40 men. 4 off + 200 men on QUEEN ST.	
			2/Lieuts. G.V. NOAKS. M.T.BR. McWHA. G.B. THOMPSON + H.C. RAMSAY joined from Base.	
"	18th		Beautiful sunny day. Very Quiet. At 10 P.M. Batt? moved to LES BREBIS, billeting in D. Area.	
			Work 1 off + 54 O.R. report to Hants Forbes R.E. at Railway Crossing. 7.30 P.M. 1 off + 54 O.R. to 173rd C? R.E. at	
			Hole in The Wall. 8.30 P.M. 1 off + 54 O.R. same place 10 P.M.	
LES BREBIS.	19th	10 A.M.	Batt? parade. to march via PETIT SAINS to woods on LORRETTE HEIGHTS, 1 mile S. of HERSIN, arriving	
		12.30 P.M.	At 3 P.M. after dinners, Batt? fell in for Handling of Arms, followed by bomb throwing competition.	
		5 P.M	Teas; at 5.30 P.M. Bat? formed up and marched home, arriving 8 P.M.	
	20th		Quiet day - inspection of billets, rifles, clothing + equipment.	
	21st	7.30 P.M.	Work 1 off + 54 O.R. report to Hants Forbes C? at Station. 9.15 A.M. Church Parade. 2 off + 50 men for C?	
	22nd		Some rain. LES BREBIS shelled a good deal. D. C? go by Bus to HOUCHIN for bath. 2/Lt M.L. GIDDY joins from Base.	
		7.30 P.M.	Work 1 off + 54 O.R. to Hants Forbes C? 2 off + 108 O.R. to 173rd C? R.E. 8.30 P.M. and 10 P.M.	

4 May 1916

Army Form C. 2118.

WAR DIARY
or
INTELLIGENCE SUMMARY
(Erase heading not required.)

1st Northamptonshire Regt.

Instructions regarding War Diaries and Intelligence Summaries are contained in F.S. Regs., Part II. and the Staff Manual respectively. Title pages will be prepared in manuscript.

Place	Date	Hour	Summary of Events and Information	Remarks and references to Appendices
LES BREBIS	23rd	9 AM	Battn paraded with Drums, Lewis Guns, Limber, and Cookers — and marched via PETIT SAINS to Heights 1 mile S of HERSIN, on the LORETTE HEIGHTS. Have dinner. 3 P.M. Battn paraded, handling arms — followed by bomb throwing competition, and minor Tactics for LEWIS Guns. Tea 5 P.M. March back 6 P.M. — 8 P.M.	J. P. Tollemache Major
"	24th		Quiet day in billets. Coys whilst some were halls. Rain in afternoon. Concert in evening.	
"	25th	8 P.M.	(Some rain in morning.) Battn moved by Coys to MAROC and relieved 1st Glosters in Double Crassier Line. Battn H.Q. in HARROW ROAD, instead of O.G.1. where 3rd Bn had it. Relief completed 11.15 P.M.	
Left Battn MAROC	26th		Dispositions. During to certain action contemplated, the right Coy front of this Battn = sub-section was taken over by 2/1 (R.) Sussex Regt; leaving the left Battn = on a two Coy front — 1 Coy ("B") from Sap H (incl.) to Boyau 28. 1 Coy ("C") from latter point to HAYMARKET (excl.) A portion of the front line on either side of Boy. 28. where the 2 coys meet — i.e. from listening posts C. and D, is not held, as it is stated by 173rd Mining Coy R.E. to be undermined by the Germans. Each Coy has a bombing post on either side. Two Coys in Support, "D" Coy in O.G.1. working with right front Coy —, "A" Coy in SOUTH S1, between the LEWIS ROAD and HAYMARKET — working with left front Coy — carrying up rations, wiring material &c.	
"	27th		Quiet on this front — except for slight shelling of our trenches round The Triangle. It was observed that the German Trenches S. of Double Crassier were extra full of men. Some shelling about 11 P.M. S. of Double Crassier, & S.O.S. signal from Left Battn = Rgt Bn. No further details. A deserter came in to Rgt Bn. with much information.	

5/ May 1916.

Army Form C. 2118.

WAR DIARY
INTELLIGENCE SUMMARY.
(Erase heading not required.)

1st Northamptonshire Regt

Instructions regarding War Diaries and Intelligence Summaries are contained in F.S. Regs., Part II. and the Staff Manual respectively. Title pages will be prepared in manuscript.

Place	Date	Hour	Summary of Events and Information	Remarks and references to Appendices
Left Bn - MAROC	28th		C"y" in front line relieved - "B" C"y" by "D", "C" C"y" by "A". "B" moved to O.C.1. "C" to SOUTH ST	S.P. Tallemache Major.
"	29th	1 A.M.	Great activity in the trenches in preparation for intended offensive. Heavy Trench Mortars brought up and dumped in KING St. and Bogan 28. They and their heavy ammunition greatly interfering with freedom of communication of the front line. C"y" Crater parties etc. Reserve Machine Guns also brought up.	
"	30th	1 A.M.	"B" relieves "D" and "C" relieves "A" in front line. Continuation of above mentioned activity - all the world suddenly knew itself in the construction of dug-outs - an activity hitherto neglected. Germans fairly quiet, except for slight shelling. Our patrols active each night.	
"		8 P.M.	Orders received that the intended offensive is suspended. No reason given.	
"	31st		Day employed in clearing up trenches of accumulation of frightfulness collected for the offensive.	
"		10 P.M.	Relief of Battn by 2/K.R.R.C. H.Q. and 2 C"ys move into N. MAROC. 1 C"y to Bayon O.G.1. and 1 C"y in SOUTH St. between LENS ROAD and HAYMARKET.	
"			Work after relief. "A" C"y on QUEEN St. from HAYMARKET to JERMYN ST. D. C"y on O.G.1. from MAROC - LOOS road to SOUTH ST. The 2 C"ys from front line to N. MAROC, have a night off.	
"		*	add -	
"	29th	2 A.M.	Lieut. A.W. FRICKER killed, and 4 men wounded while wiring in front of KING St.	

2nd Brigade.

1st Division.

1st BATTALION

NORTHAMPSTONSHIRE REGIMENT

JUNE 1916.

Confidential

War Diary

Vol 23

1st Bn Northamptonshire Regt.

June 1916

WAR DIARY
INTELLIGENCE SUMMARY

(Erase heading not required.)

1st Northamptonshire Regt.

Army Form C. 2118.

June 1916.

Place	Date	Hour	Summary of Events and Information	Remarks and references to Appendices
N.MAROC	1st		Fine Sunny day. Disposition:- Battn = H.Q. - B. & C. Coy's in cellars in N. MAROC. D. Coy in O.G.I. N. of MAROC - LOOS road. A. Coy in SOUTH St. between LENS ROAD and *HAYMARKET. There are positions of Left Reserve Battn.	S. P. Tollemache Major
		9.30	German aeroplane came over MAROC - appeared to have engine trouble, and dropped in steep spirals to about 3000 ft., when it appeared to recover itself, and made. Neither our anti-aircraft guns nor our aeroplanes in the vicinity seemed to make any effort to attack the intruder.	
		9.30 P.M.	Work. Carrying parties totalling 50 working for 173rd Coy R.E. on N. & S. Craters. Other carrying parties totalling 120 bringing bombs & S.A.A. from MIDDLE ALLEY to Bomb Store MAROC. 1 Off. 20 men constructing a Traverse with loop-hole and a bombing post in MIDDLE ALLEY. A Coy making T heads and deepening SOUTH St. D. Coy deepening and strengthening O.G.I. from MAROC - LOOS road to SOUTH St. All the evening and into the night, very heavy artillery fire from the S. on The IVth Corps front. No news.	
	2nd		Fine bright day. Following officers joined from England. Capt. B.O. Smyth. 2/Lt. C.H. Ferguson (3rd Batt.) 2/Lt. A.G.H. Clarke. Peaceful day. No news of last evening's bombardment in direction of VIMY.	
	3rd	9.P.M.	Work. A. Coy continuing work on SOUTH St. as above - other coy's carrying and working as on 1st inst. Quiet Day. C.O. visits village line with Brig. r in morning. 2nd Coy and C.M. Cmdrs in afternoon. Work. A. Coy on T. heads in SOUTH St. B. Coy carrying parties and loopholed Traverse in MIDDLE ALLEY. C. Coy + 25 of D. on QUEEN St., cutting fire-step. D. Coy (less 25) carrying parties for minors and work on O.G.1	

WAR DIARY
or
INTELLIGENCE SUMMARY.

(Erase heading not required.) 1st Northamptonshire Reg.t

Army Form C. 2118.

June 1916

Place	Date	Hour	Summary of Events and Information	Remarks and references to Appendices
MAROC	4th		Quiet day. Due to relieve 2/KRRC Tonight. Separatory crater parties etc go in in afternoon. Crater party caught by a shell on taking over. An officer K.R.R.C killed. 2/Lt W.T.R.McWHt wounded. 2 men killed and 1 slightly wounded. C Coy move in relief at 8.45 P.M. Complete 10.45 P.M.	J.P. Tollemache Major
	5th		Dispositions D. Coy from N. Crassier to Staff HALLIES LANE. A Coy from later point to Bogan 28 "C" Coy from Bogan 28 to HAYMARKET excl. B Coy in Support. Reserve line 1 Platoon in DUG OUT ROW. Some shelling of centre Coys line near Triangle and support line CORDITE AVENUE	
	6th		FAIRLY QUIET DAY. 2nd Lt W.H. CHAMBERS – E.T.S SYFRET and MWG JACKSON join from Base.	
	7th		Enemy company again shelled 1 man killed 1 wounded. Believed at night by 2/KRRC. at 10 P.M. A small raid by 8 N.C.O.s and men was attempted against enemy work head on S. Crassier after getting successfully to close under enemy parapet. The attacking line and the party in reserve had 5 men wounded by bombs	
	8th		after spending 1 night in former quarters of left Bn Bn H. S. H.Q. and 2 Coy move at 4 P.M. into new H rest. B Coy in South St. C Coy in O.C.1. A. & D. to Area H near Artillery Row. Work Nights 7th/8 and 8th/9th 4 off.rs 10 N.C.O.s 140 men digging new trench from King 8th to front line opposite Russian Sap. 1 off.r 50 men under B.de Pioneer off.r - Carrying parties totalling 50 under 173rd C Coy R.E. Other carrying parties totalling 50, working for various Trench Mortar Batteries. Total 306. other ranks	
MAROC	9th		Quiet Day. New areas cleaned up and improved. Work same as above - Total 300 other ranks.	

Army Form C. 2118.

WAR DIARY or INTELLIGENCE SUMMARY.

(Erase heading not required.)

1st Northamptonshire Regt.

Place	Date	Hour	Summary of Events and Information	Remarks and references to Appendices
MAROC	June 1916. 10th		Very wet all morning. A few 5" shells on the billets about 2 p.m. No damage. Relieved by 10th GLOUCESTERS at 5 p.m. Coys marched to LES BREBIS, had tea, and proceeded to billets at PETIT-SAINS.	J. P. Tollemache Major
PETIT-SAINS	11th 12th		General clean up. 165 men on fatigue at MAROC in the morning.	
"	13th		Too wet for day in the country. Battalion marched to BRAQUEMONT at 5 p.m. for rehearsal of Memorial Service of Lord Kitchener to be held on 13th.	
"	14th		The Battalion, as strong as possible, marched to BRAQUEMONT at 10 A.M. Memorial Service at 11 A.M., lasted half an hour. Men excellently turned out and marched with large gathering present including our new May Genl.— Major General B. P. STRICKLAND C.M.G., D.S.O. Poured most of the morning. C.O. and Adjt. made a tour of the left group gun positions behind MAROC. 2/Lt H.G. MANNING joined Battalion.	
"	15th		Short parades in morning. 165 men on fatigue up to MAROC. Five men wounded (2 since died of wounds).	
"	16th		Battalion route march. Route:— PETIT-SAINS — BRAQUEMONT — BARLIN — PERSIN — PETIT-SAINS. Started out at 10 A.M. and returned at 1.30 p.m. Move fell out. At 11 P.M. hear Battalion will have to move up to MAROC to relieve 9th BERKS on 17th.	

WAR DIARY
or
INTELLIGENCE SUMMARY.
(Erase heading not required.)

Army Form C. 2118.

Place	Date	Hour	Summary of Events and Information	Remarks and references to Appendices
MAROC	17th		Moved up to MAROC at 12 Noon via BULLY-GRENAY and silenced 8th Berks in huts B. and came under Comd. of G.O.E. 1st Bde. Small fatigues of 60 carrying for T.M. batteries. Rest of Bn arrived, only 3 old hands about.	
"	18th		Quiet day. Came once more under orders of 2nd Bde in the evening. Fatigues of about 160 carrying for 173rd Coy R.E.	
"	19th		Busy making communication and Battalion was ordered all day. Work – Coys in their allotted tasks as per special programme ie wiring and digging. Unfortunately parties severely hit. "A" Bn. 2 killed, 9 wounded. "B" Six wounded. "C" 2/Lt SERTEANT badly wounded in leg also one man "D" One killed, two wounded. Chiefly Trench mortar & rifle grenades.	
"	20th		Carrying on making communication line. Coys on their special work at night. No casualties.	
"	21st		Construction of communication trenches carried on. Bomb accident caused about 6.30 pm to three S. Bearers whilst practice throwing + not its fully wound deal. Usual special work for Coys. Two casualties 2/Lt SERTEANT died of wounds at BETHUNE.	

WAR DIARY
INTELLIGENCE SUMMARY

1st Northamptonshire Regt.

Army Form C. 2118.

June 1916

Place	Date	Hour	Summary of Events and Information	Remarks and references to Appendices
N. MAROC	22nd		his fire lay and day warm. Plenty of wire methodically made. Ten brushes aeroplanes went over the line. Wire A. digging their new trench. B. wiring S. of CRASSIER; C. wiring the CRASSIER; "carrying for B"; "D" carrying for B and strengthening MAP just S. of CRASSIER.	J. P. Tollemache - Major
"	23rd		Some shrapnel in Maroc and rain continued during the night. Work carried on by bays as under. A. in new trench; B. wiring first line and kept the S. C. completed wire on CRASSIER, the alarm at 4.30 a.m. for mine and quiet day. A MG Coy & 20th MIDDLESEX attached to us for M[achine] Gun work. C Coy completing new trench and S. by wiring it.	
"	24th		The 2 Cos. 20th Middlesex arriving at 4 P.M. are at divided into four parties, each of which is mixed with a half Coy of Northamptonshire. The whole forming 4 mixed Cos called A. B. C. D. The men are mixed within the platoon in the proportion of about 1/3 Middlesex to 2/3 Northamptons. Many of the Platoons are commanded by North'ton Middlesex off's who also have the 2nd in Co'd of the mixed Co's	
"	25th		The mixed Bat'n moves into right front Batt'n sub-section MAROC in relief of 1/KRRC. Advanced parties and signallers move at 1 P.M. Companies in succession from the left, with Platoons at 10 min. interval. First Co - "B" at 1.30 P.M. Last Co - "A" at 5.30 P.M. Relief complete 7.30 P.M. C. & D. Co's in support in cellars in S. Maroc.	

WAR DIARY or INTELLIGENCE SUMMARY

Army Form C. 2118.

1st Northamptonshire Regt.

June 1916.

Place	Date	Hour	Summary of Events and Information	Remarks and references to Appendices
S. MARIE	25th	cont.d	Disinfectors A. Cy CALONNE ALLEY (excl.) to NEUVE ALLEY and Sap. C.1. (excl.) B. Cy CALONNE ALLEY (excl.) to NEUVE ALLEY and Sap. D.1. (incl.) "B.1." Cy from latter front (incl.) to Boyau 15 (excl.) "B" Coy from latter point to B.H.K. (incl.). Preparations were made to light smoke candles and throw "P." (smoke) bombs along entire front during night 25/26th. This was postponed but M.G. fire and artillery strafe took place.	J.P. Tollemache Major
"	26th		Lt (Temp Capt) H.S.J. ATTWATER C ony & A. Cy killed by Trench Mortar bomb. Lieut A.G. CLARKE slightly wounded. Orders rec.d to discharge smoke candles and P. bombs from right to Sap. C1 at 3.P.M. but order cancelled owing to weather, which was wet.	
"	27th		Very wet day. Right Cys a trench & good deal blown in by Trench Mortars. A stokes Mortar Off.r & 2 men buried Support line of Right Centre Cy also blown in. To a lesser degree than right Cy. B. Cy 20th Middlesex defeat short bursts of artillery fire.	
"	28th	1.10.A.M.	Smoke candles and P. (smoke) bombs discharged along whole Battn Front, accompanied by M.G. fire and short bursts of artillery fire. Some retaliation. Wet morning. Fine in afternoon.	
		8.A.M.	B. Cy, mingled with B. Cy 21st Middlesex, form B and B.1. Cys and take over the right half of the line	
		10.P.M.	A Cy " " " " " " " " " " left " " "	
"	29th		Preparations to make Germans expect attack or raid on this front in order to assist intended operations against Triangle N. of the Double Grassier. German Trenches shelled - gaps cut in our wire - and bridges built over our trenches in view of enemy.	
"	30th	9.10 P.M. (Quiet Day)	Attack on Triangle by K.R.R.C. and on N. face of Grassier by Rl Sussex. Unsuccessful owing to concealed M.G. on N. face of Grassier. Some German prisoners taken. Trench entered in two places, where we blew mines, but tunnel under Grassier was not reached.	

L 2nd Bde.
   1st Div.

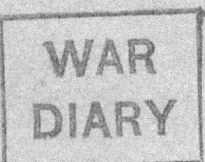

1st BATTALION

NORTHAMPTON REGIMENT.

JULY 1916.

1/2

1st/4 Bn. Northamptonshire Regt.

- July 1916 -

July 1916.

WAR DIARY
of
INTELLIGENCE SUMMARY.
(Erase heading not required.) 1st Northamptonshire Regt.

Army Form C. 2118.

Vol 22

D.P. To Menache Major

Place	Date	Hour	Summary of Events and Information	Remarks and references to Appendices
MARCC. Right Battn	1st		Results of operation on our left at The Triangle become more clear. Trench gained but had to be abandoned owing largely to fire of two M.G.s concealed in N. side of Crassier. Attack along N. Crassier itself operated by M.G. and over.	
	2nd		Quiet day in our own line. Trenches little damaged by retaliation of last night. 2 C.oy. 20th Middlesex arrive to relieve the 2 C.oy. 31st Middlesex. The 20th M.x C.oy. go in support of the right centre sub left centre. "C" C.oy. goes in on right. D.C.oy. on left. A & B C.oys to turnel cellars in support.	
	3rd		Remainder of 20th Middlesex arrive and take over. Battn marches to LES BREBIS - has dinner, and marches via Noeux les Mines to RUITZ, accompanied by Transport, arriving 10 P.M. Draft of 28. O.R. arrived	
	4th	6.P.M.	Battn marched at 6.P.M. to M+RLES LES MINES, arriving 8.30.P.M.	
MARLES LES M.	5th		Remained in billets, sorting kits etc, ready to move. Many cases of Stores left under charge of Mairie	
	6th	12 Noon	Marched to LILLERS arriving 2.P.M. Divisn. Entrained 3-30 P.M. Train left 4-15 P.M. arriving GUYDAS 12 m.n.	
	7th	1.A.M.	Marched via NHOURS to FLESSELLES, arriving 5-15 A.M. Very wet day - Remained in billets	
	*6th		2/Lt. KNIGHT and MORKAM joined at LILLERS Station, from Base.	
FLESSELLES	8th		Remained in billets until 8.P.M. when Battn marched to Via VILLERS-BOCAGE and MONTIGNY to FRECHENCOURT. Delayed at road junction in BEHENCOURT by passage of 3rd B.de 11-45 - 19-50. reached billets 1-30 A.M. (9th)	
FRECHENCOURT	9th	4.30.P.M.	Marched at 4.30.P.M. to BRESLES arriving 7.P.M. via ALBERT to BERNANCOURT BECOURT arriving 11.30 P.M.	
BRESLES	10th		Quiet day in billets. Men got a lift in a Tech. march 8.45. to BECOURT. Transport proceeded to DERNANCOURT.	

Army Form C. 2118.

WAR DIARY
INTELLIGENCE SUMMARY.
(Erase heading not required.) 1st Northamptonshire Reg.

Instructions regarding War Diaries and Intelligence Summaries are contained in F.S. Regs, Part II. and the Staff Manual respectively. Title pages will be prepared in manuscript.

July 1916.

Place	Date	Hour	Summary of Events and Information	Remarks and references to Appendices
Bécourt Wood	11th		Remained in bivouac. Off[rs] reconn[d] battle ground. 1st B[n] in position, with 2 batt[ns] from N.W. corner of MAMETZ Wood to BAILIFF Wood. Then other 2 Batt[ns] being in old German lines between FRICOURT and LA BOISSELLE. 3rd B[n] in ALBERT.	J.P. Tollemache Major
"	12th		Remained in bivouac. * Working party of 400, under 2nd in C[md], marched to LOZENGE Wood, and thence carried over	
		8 P.M. To 2 A.M.	Tahrs, etc thro' CONTALMAISON to the front line. Considerable shelling in the village. Some casualties. Party carried back some 70 wounded, mostly German, from cellars of CONTALMAISON Chateau. a work which would seem to have been the duty of the 2nd Field Ambulance, extracted which was retained at Fricourt for the purpose.	
"	13th		Remained in bivouac. at 8.30.P.M. party of 1 off[r] 25 men sent up to assist in wiring front line.	
"	14th	6 A.M.	Moved forward to O.B. front and support line, just E. of BECOURT Wood. 7 P.M. returned to Bivouac in Wood.	
"	15th	12.15 A.M.	Moved to positions N. of LOZENGE Wood, on either side of Sunken road from FRICOURT to CONTALMAISON- taking the place of the 10th Glosters. who moved up to front line.	
"	16th	8.30 P.M.	Moved up by C[oys] at 10 min intervals, and took of CONTALMAISON Village line from 1st Glosters on right and from 2nd Munsters on left - from N.W. corner of MAMETZ Wood, thro' the Cutting, to N.W. corner of Village. C[oys] from right to left - D. B. C. A. relief completed by 10-30 P.M. 3rd B[n] moved out to attack German 2nd Line 3rd B[n] having taken German 2nd line, our C[oys] carry up tools, wire, water &c to both Glosters and Munsters also work at digging out Black Watch Alley. at 8.P.M. 68th B[n] on our left made an unsuccessful attempt on the German trench in front of POZIERES.	
"	17th			

July 1916.

Army Form C. 2118.

WAR DIARY
INTELLIGENCE SUMMARY
(Erase heading not required.) 1st Northamptonshire Regt.

Instructions regarding War Diaries and Intelligence Summaries are contained in F.S. Regs., Part II. and the Staff Manual respectively. Title pages will be prepared in manuscript.

July 1916.

Place	Date	Hour	Summary of Events and Information	Remarks and references to Appendices
N.E. of CONTALMAISON	18th	9:30 P.M.	2/Lt R.V.H. Knight and 12 other ranks killed by shell fire in the village line + about 25 wounded. Relieved 1st Gloucesters and 2nd Munsters in O.G. 1 and 2. relief complete by 11 P.M.	D.P. Tollemache Major
O.G.1 & 2.	19th		In above line, right on C=== Trench left in X.5.d. S. of junction of POZIERES Trench with O.G.1. and of MUNSTER Alley with O.G.2. H.Q. at X.12.a. (incl) left in X.12.a.34. just S. of the C=== Trench. In evening recon. orders to attack the two Trench junctions. Prepare to do so by surprise without preliminary bombardment, but assisted by 4 Stokes mortars, to form a barrage beyond the points attacked, viz. O.G.1 + 2, and points 50"s of POZIERES and MUNSTER Trenches with object of establishing blocks in all four trench junctions.	
	20th	2:30 P.M.	Trench Mortars opened, and the 4 assaulting parties moved out simultaneously, followed by consolidating parties. Each assaulting party consisted of 1 off= 10. O.R. "2nd MUNSTER ALLEY 2/Lt CHAMBERS. O.G.2 - 2/Lt BARTHORP. O.G.1 - 2/Lt GADDESDON. POZIERES Trench Lt JACQUES. Immediately parties started, enemy opened machine gun fire from several directions. Right party reached MUNSTER Alley. The other parties could not make their objectives. Lt BARTHORP. was killed or wounded as he reached the Trench junction in O.G.2. 4 of his party only remained wounded. These were driven back by hostile bombing, and Lt CHAMBERS party they withdrew. 2/Lt GADDESDON and all his party attacking O.G.1. were wounded. Of the left party attacking POZIERES Trench, Lt JACQUES alone reached the German parapet, dropped in a shell hole, and got back with difficulty. Bombing parties under Capt CLAYTON continued bombing up O.G.1, but we did not succeed in extending our flank on either front or support Trench. Casualties 3 off= 2/Lt=F.C. COCKERILL and G.H. GADDESDON wounded. 40 other ranks. Lt BARTHORP, wounded and missing (believed killed) M.R.	4500 S.B

T2134. Wt. W708—776. 500000. 4/15. Sir J.C. & S. 2/Lt=

Army Form C. 2118.

WAR DIARY
or
INTELLIGENCE SUMMARY.

(Erase heading not required.) 1st Northamptonshire Regt.

Instructions regarding War Diaries and Intelligence Summaries are contained in F.S. Regs., Part II. and the Staff Manual respectively. Title pages will be prepared in manuscript.

July 1916.

Remarks: D.P. To Vernacher Major   4416

Place	Date	Hour	Summary of Events and Information
O.G.1 & 2	21st		Left our front Coy's line in O.G.1. Taken over by 9th Australian Battz; up to BLACK WATCH Alley. Parties from A and D. Coy's dig an advanced line in conjunction with N Lancs - afterwards called LANCASHIRE Trench. B. Coy's put out a line of picquets 200 yds in front of German Switch line. To remain out all day.
"	22nd		In same position, with picquets formed by B. Coy on left flank, in front of SUSSEX Trench. Preparations made for an attack on MUNSTER Alley by B. Sussex Regt. and on Switch Line by K.R.R. B. Coy Northants Regt. To advance if K.R.R. established themselves in German line and form a line of picquets in front of them. C. Coy. To stand ready to move forward and consolidate. 1st Bn to attach Switch line on right of K.R.R.
"	23rd	12.30 A.M.	Above attack commenced. All units late at forming up positions. Great congestion in Gloster Alley. K.R.R. advanced and portions reached German line. B. Coy 1st Northants also advanced close behind K.R.R. and got into German Trench with them, bombing to both flanks – about 300 x of Trench held. Capt. CHISHOLM Cmdg B. Coy 1st N.H. took command of the combined parties, and consolidated the Trench gained. The German Trench to right and left had not been taken, and Germans were bombing from both flanks, therefore, as his supply of bombs was exhausted, Capt. CHISHOLM withdrew his party back to LANCASHIRE Trench. K.R.R. were then withdrawn to reorganise. B. Coy returned to D.G.2 and C. Coy occupied LANCASHIRE Trench - which had been considerably shelled and worked at digging it out. D. Coy with (Melson) occupied the post (CLARK'S POST) at end of GLOSTER Alley, which had been held during the night by a mixed detachment of 1st N.H. and were on other H.Q. by 2nd Coys.

T2134. W1. W708-773. 500000. 4/15. Sir J. C. & S.

Army Form C. 2118.

WAR DIARY
INTELLIGENCE SUMMARY

(Erase heading not required.) 1st Northshire Regt.

July 1916.

Place	Date	Hour	Summary of Events and Information	Remarks and references to Appendices
	23rd		O.C. 2. heavily shelled, 2nd E.D.BADCOCK killed. 2/Lt E.S.GROBINSON wounded. 2/Lt M.G.RUMSAY wounded.	D.P. Tollemache. Major.
ALBERT	24th	7.P.M.	Relieved at 7.P.M. by S.W.Bordeners - marched by Coy to ALBERT. Since 12th inst. when Bn. was in BECOURT 8. Offrs. and 260 other ranks, including many platoon seg ts. have been killed and wounded. Big draft badly wanted.	
"	25th		Remained in billets in ALBERT. Draft of 1 seg t. 18. Rank and File arrived.	
"	26th		Marched by Coy. at 20 mins interval, commencing 9.A.M. via main AMIENS road. Halted for dinner and marched as a Battn. to billets at FRANVILLERS, arriving 2.30 P.M.	
FRANVILLERS	27th		Remained in billets, Coys went out bathing in the SOMME near BONNAY.	
"	28th		TALAVERA Day - regimental sports in commemoration of exploits of 48th Reg t. on that day.	
"	29th		Remained in billets - Coys went again to the SOMME and bathed.	
"	30th		Batt n Church Parade - 11 A.M. Orders rec d 2 P.M. To march in evening to HENENCOURT WOOD Batt n Parade 6.15. P.M. Draft of 20 arrive. Reach bivouac 8. P.M.	
HENENCOURT	31st	11.A.M	Brig r inspects Batt n in mass. In evening Brig r + C.O. all t ground for training.	

4426
EB

COVER
FOR
BRANCH MEMORANDA.

Unregistered.

Referred to	Date	Referred to	Date
6ᵗᵒ Armata		Bollettinos	
180		From 180. P.a. By Barber	

" 2nd Brigade.
1st Division

1st BATTALION

NORTHAMPTONSHIRE REGIMENT

AUGUST 1 9 1 6

Army Form C. 2118.

Vol I

WAR DIARY
INTELLIGENCE SUMMARY.
(Erase heading not required.) 1st Northamptonshire Regt.

August 1916.

Place	Date	Hour	Summary of Events and Information	Remarks and references to Appendices
HENENCOURT Wood.	1st	8.30 A.M.	Battn. Parade. March out and practise attacks and deployment against hostile trench line.	O.P. To Mernache
"	2nd	9.30 A.M.	Preliminary heats to select Bn. representatives for Divl. Sports. Trg of War Team; G.S. Waggon and Limbered Waggon.	
"	"	9 A.M.	Coy. parade for Coy. Training - Practise deploying and movement in open order. 2/Lt F.H.R. TYLER joined.	
"	3rd	"	Coy Parades in morning. 9 P.M. Battn parade for practice of Night Attack.	
"	4th	"	" 2.30 P.M. Divl. Sports - Army and Corps Commanders present.	Major
"	5th	"	2nd Bn. won 1/4 mile and Relay race. 2nd & 3rd in Offrs jumping and in G.S. Limber. Draft 1/31 O.R. arrive.	
"	"	"	Coy. Parades in morning. 5 P.M. Battn. Parade for practice of night attack. Draft of 39 O.R. arrive.	
"	6th	2 A.M.	C.O, Adjt and 4 Coy Cmdrs. conft at Bde. night operations. 12 Noon - Church Parade.	
"	"	"	2/Lt M.C. JACKSON rejoined from Base (5 m inst). 2/Lt E.W.R. JACQUES and 2/Lt F.W. Twigg to Lewis Gun Course (3 m inst)	
"	7th	9 A.M.	Coy Parades. 5 P.M. Battn. Parade. Practise attack for night operations - returned 9.30 P.M.	
"	8th	9 A.M.	" Draft of 29 O.R. who had previously been sent to 10th Lincolns, restored to the Battn.	
"	9th	12.30 A.M.	Battn. parades for night operations in conjunction with the L.N. Lancs. Bde. Divl. Comdr present. Return 5.30 A.M.	
"	"		2/Lt. WILSON returns from 6 weeks Officers course at BOULOGNE also C.S.M. ROUGHTON	
"	10th		Wet morning. parades cancelled Coy parades 10.7.4 to 12.30 P.M.	
"	11th		Coy Parades - practise musketry and bayonet fighting. 2/Lt W. TAPPIN and 100 other ranks arrive from base.	
"	12th		Coy Parades - Orders recd. That Bde. will move in evening of 13th.	

WAR DIARY or INTELLIGENCE SUMMARY

Army Form C. 2118.

(Erase heading not required.) 1st Northamptonshire Regt.

August 1916.

Place	Date	Hour	Summary of Events and Information	Remarks and references to Appendices
Intermediate Line	Aug 13		The Battalion having completed its work made all necessary arrangements went forward & took its allotted place by letters to Coy. Comd. at times. Relief by the 21st and Berkshires took place.	
Lavence Wood	Aug 14		Assumption of the night, Major Hon. D.P. TOLLEMACHE 2nd Coy. 6th, who went up to reconnoitre line was slightly wounded by shell. The morning was spent in repairs and work on the W. & S. Batteries which had been smashed and the C.T. batteries - not really important -	
			Bayonets & R.E. Stores delivered the B. Batteries to [illegible]. We are and take the morning as the made [illegible] carry [illegible] any unnecessarily. There ordered to [illegible]. having only 2 men. Then the Bk said you like by [illegible] supply the ammn to [illegible] was considered.	HEAVY GALE
Support trench	Aug 15		The day was spent making [illegible] trench. At 5 P.M. the Battalion received orders that [illegible] [illegible] was to A.P. to be relieved from the 2nd Royal Sussex. There was a [illegible] of the Staff - by order [illegible] Coy. [illegible] "C" Company then pushed out Coy. NC.O.s one under 2nd Lt. McBaw & one under 2nd Lt. Hurn. They noted & found no one attempt was made to take the Enemy front trench but was taken 2nd Lt. Bessant was wounded 2nd Lt. Chambers & 2nd Lt. Myers wounded. Casualties — 1 killed 2 wounded.	
Support trench	Aug 16		At 9.30 A.M. 2nd Lt. Myers was wounded. Having spent the night in a shell hole. The remainder of the night was without incident of success. Parties of [illegible]	

WAR DIARY or INTELLIGENCE SUMMARY.

1st Northamptonshire Regt.

Army Form C. 2118.

3/ August 1916.

Place	Date	Hour	Summary of Events and Information	Remarks and references to Appendices
Fontaine les Croiselles	Aug 3rd (contd)		It was too still to render approach work absolutely impossible for our own in taking the attack. There is no doubt were ambushed. Orders issued and at 10.25 PM C & D Companies attacked and entered their position, with B Royal Sussex operating on their right, & consolidated the trench between S3 C.8 and S3 d 6.9. The same night the 2nd Royal Sussex evacuated trenches & were taken by three nights. A counter attack which was successfully stopped by Capt Scard and C Company and resulted in all the enemies efforts to break down the position of trench being nil & no attack was pressed home. Capt Scard D.S.O. & 2/Lt Seagram and 2/Lt Myr killed. 2/Lt Barber, 2/Lt Ferguson & 2/Lt Chips wounded. 2/Lt Chambers was found dead & reported O.R.s casualties 4 killed & 28 wounded. 27 missing. Sept 02. The Bn was spent investigating the new line and the relief of Bn was taken by A Company under Capt Clayton. 2/Lt Hulme, 2/Lt Laker was killed & 2/Lt Crookes W.&M.& 2/Lt Pendleton	
Fontaine	Aug 4th		At 2.45 PM we brought up some stokes mortars and rifle grenades as well as combed down the trench relinquished by B Sussex sectors. 1st Royal North Lancashires made a frontal attack and succeeded in capturing upon them portion of the trench to the Rt. But with very little difficulty. This position was occupied much simplified by A Company making a flank bombing attack simultaneously.	

WAR DIARY
INTELLIGENCE SUMMARY
1st Northamptonshire Regt

Army Form C. 2118.

Place	Date	Hour	Summary of Events and Information	Remarks and references to Appendices
High Ground South of High Wood	August (contd)		The news was brought up that 2nd Ldrs & 2nd Suff. had lost all their ground. **G.V.** Our Casualties: Killed 11, Wounded 32, Missing 1. Total 44. **E.T.S.** "A" Company on patrol out on outpost Company sent at 2 P.M. and moved into a new within a line of posts on the Ridge. 2 Companies of the Royal Sussex and one of the total were sent up to consolidate the line. **J.C.** In the work about the Sussex ground on the Right from the direction of High Wood amongst the paths and would doubtless confuse us a while, forced Capt. Claytor was killed and 2nd Lt. Lee wounded. Our Casualties Killed 2 Wounded 12 Total 14.	
	Aug 5th	About 7 O.M	The Enemy advanced in four columns the outpost Coy to retreat withdraw from its position on the Ridge. The position was soundly attacked by B & A Companies and the fight lasted all morning. During this time **2nd** Reinforcement was killed **W.** & 2/Lt Napier and 2/ Rayner Sykes were wounded. After a little unopposed watching preparation B & A Companies and 2 Companies of Sussex went into again at 2.30 P.M. and after a very severe fight established a post about 30 yards in rear of the newly taken trench from which an excellent view could be obtained of the valley Lignicultire and also all Enemy movements were seen. Hamelin Line not now	A.E.C.... Col.

5/ August 1916

Army Form C. 2118.

WAR DIARY
or
INTELLIGENCE SUMMARY. 1st Northamptonshire Reg.t
(Erase heading not required.)

Place	Date	Hour	Summary of Events and Information	Remarks and references to Appendices

Aug 2nd
Contd

Consolidated and carried on to the 2nd Welsh on right. The relief was in progress throughout the night and the Regiment moved back in Bivouac & went at about

4 P.M. 2nd

The thanks and congratulations of all the Higher Commanders were duly received by the Regiment for a particularly brilliant & glorious part in the attack. All its objectives were gained and in spite of very heavy losses the spirit and tenacity of the Regiment was maintained throughout. Casualties — 9 Other Ranks killed, 9 wounded, 91 missing, 25 Other R.

Bivouac Wood Aug 3rd

Everybody slept until midday. At 6 P.M. the Contable Rifles marched as advance for Inspection by Lt Col Bethell who addressed the Batt. in warm and in which he showed during the serious the loss in the lines. A full return of casualties were collected
and the ranks by Col 7 days were as follows — 18 Officers, 356 Other ranks —
of the Other ranks 51 were killed, 265 wounded, 40 missing.
Not all day. At 7 P.M. Lt. ? P.O.C. 2nd Rh. Roy Sco Fusrs. invited ashore to the

Burnt Woods Aug 4th

beloved officer. Capt. L G Bowstedler D.S.O. Capt A C Child M.C. and 4/pt Bellingham D.C.M.
and congratulated "B" Coy and the Stokes Mortar who, thanks to parade, on
the magnificent work of the Regiment

6/ August. 1916.

Army Form C. 2118.

WAR DIARY
or
INTELLIGENCE SUMMARY.
(Erase heading not required.)

Hour, Date, Place	Summary of Events and Information	Remarks and references to Appendices
Becourt Wood 22nd Aug.	This evening there was another official message from Brigade circulated for information that to the effect that early this morning Captured Guns were to be called Northampton Trench and Clarks Trench respectively to commemorate the captures by the Regiment and Capt Clark the gallant Commander of B Coy.	
Becourt Wood 23rd Aug.	Another day of not anything exciting happening except one of the men went to Albert and obtained a bath and clean change of clothing. Reconstitution of the Battalion has taken with a close change of clothing. The Commanding Officer made arrangements for instructors to instruct Casualties amongst N.C.O.'s. A draft of 8 N.C.O.'s arrived from England to be redistributed to N.C.O.'s of long experience of active service with the Bold in France.	
Becourt Wood 25th Aug.	Morning occupied by programmes of training. Bombing was by The question of ration_ communication practice very considered and Games to Athletic Report received of the 6.30 pm services from reports of Welshes Battalion at B.39 C.M. 93 c.2 the Brigade telegraph himself at 7 pm. Shew continuing 17 pm. Sd/Lt 12 pts a Sgt in the unit and 3/7 Champion Sd 6.30 CM 93 c.2 Lippy him all with death, 2 another casualty.	

(73989) W4141—463. 400,000. 9/14. H.&J.Ltd. Forms/C. 2118/10.

August 1916.

Army Form C. 2118.

WAR DIARY
or
INTELLIGENCE SUMMARY.
(Erase heading not required.) 1ˢᵗ Northamptonshire Regᵗ

Hour, Date, Place	Summary of Events and Information	Remarks and references to Appendices
BECOURT WOOD. Aug 26ᵗʰ	Day spent preparing the scheme for the trench attack, all being cut and up tonight. Commanding Officer 6.30 P.M. Battalion paraded for C.O's inspection.	
BECOURT WOOD Aug 27ᵗʰ	Orders to move up by Companies at 10 minutes intervals starting at 4 P.M. in relief to 1st CAMERONS in LOZENGE WOOD. Relief complete by 5.15.	
LOZENGE WOOD Aug 28ᵗʰ	A day of hard work. 100 men of C Company dug 200 yards of a new communication trench leading from MAMETZ WOOD to MILLS ST. In the afternoon every available man was used to carry to the trench mortar Bombs and S.A.A. to front line. Lieut. HIGH W.O.D. (Lyt RJKACEY Surrey), 2ⁿᵈ 3ᶠᵉˢˢ MARTIN & 6ᶜᴅᴜᴳᴵsᴀ and 106 the men joined the battalion	
LOZENGE WOOD Aug 29ᵗʰ	A repitition of yesterdays 100 men of "D" Coy on the communication trench all day the remainder of the Battalion on other fatigues carrying trench Mortar Bombs to the front line and dropping in the Divisional signal cable in the neighbourhood of FRICOURT.	

Army Form C. 2118.

WAR DIARY
or
INTELLIGENCE SUMMARY.
(Erase heading not required.) 1st Bedfordshire Regiment

Place	Date	Hour	Summary of Events and Information	Remarks and references to Appendices
LAZENWOOD	30/8/16		The battalion dug in some convenient line 100 men of A Coy digging under very bad conditions in the communication trench. Company Commanders warned at about 9.30 P.M. that the Batt would relieve the 1/4 Gloucesters L.H. on the front line in High Wood in early morning. Other Coys attend to 4 P.M. 31st for relief of 1/4 Gloucesters. Standing by and getting ready for the relief which was started at 4.30 P.M.	D.P. Tollemache Major
LOZENGE WOOD HIGH WOOD	31st 8/16		Relief of 1/4 Gloucesters completed by 8.10 P.M. "D" and "B" Companies holding A trench in High Wood. D on the Right. A draft of 27 other ranks joined the Battalion. Major Hon. D.P. TOLLEMACHE reports from 143rd Field Ambulance and occupies adv. H.Q. in BLACK WATCH Trench HIGH WOOD.	

Appendix 1.

Army Form C. 2118.

WAR DIARY
or
INTELLIGENCE SUMMARY. 1st Northamptonshire Regt
(Erase heading not required.)

August 1916

Hour, Date, Place	Summary of Events and Information	Remarks and references to Appendices
Bécourt Wood 22nd Aug	A message was sent round from Brigade in the evening stating as follows:- "G.O.C. 1st Northampton On coming out of action I desire to thank Lieut Col W.R. Cuthill the Officers, N.C.Os, and men of the 1st Battalion Northamptonshire Regt for their splendid and gallant conduct during the recent operations. No praise can be too high for the manner in which they stuck to their work. The bravery and resolution all ranks showed in the push to drive in our lines the whole spirit of Officers and the initiative displayed was magnificent throughout and I am proud to have had Officers, N.C.Os, and men in the Brigade under my command. Signed A.B. Hubback Brigadier General Commanding 2nd Infantry Brigade.	Special Order of the Day by G.O.C. 2nd Bde 22/8/16. ACCuthill Lt Col

2nd Brigade.
1st Division.

1st BATTALION NORTHAMPTONSHIRE REGIMENT

SETEMBER 1916.

WR 24

1st Bn Northamptonshire Regt

WAR DIARY.

September 1916

Army Form C. 2118.

WAR DIARY
INTELLIGENCE SUMMARY.
(Erase heading not required.)

1st Northamptonshire Regt

Instructions regarding War Diaries and Intelligence Summaries are contained in F. S. Regs., Part II. and the Staff Manual respectively. Title pages will be prepared in manuscript.

September 1916.

Place	Date	Hour	Summary of Events and Information	Remarks and references to Appendices
HIGH WOOD	1st		Battⁿ holds a 2 Cᵒʸ front. D.Cᵒʸ on right, joining 4/R⁵ Sussex at E. edge of Wood. B.Cᵒʸ on left, with a Cᵒʸ of 60th holding remainder of line to W. edge of Wood. 2 Lewis guns with each front line Cᵒʸ. C.Cᵒʸ and 2 Lewis guns in BLACK WATCH Trench, sent to relv⁵ Battⁿ H.Q. which was occupied by 2 i/c Cᵒʸ, 2 Lewis guns & Sig. Off⁻; Battⁿ H.Q and A.Cᵒʸ at N. end of BAZENTIN le Grand. - Draft of 30 O.R. arrive, also 2/Lieuts. K.H. McCLURE. G.E.E. SMITHETT. R.W. GATES. D.K. COOPER. A.S. RAYNER. W.H. BEARD.	L.P. Tollemache Major
"	2nd		Weath⁻ Cleaning and improving QUEENS, GLASGOW, ANDERSON, BLACK WATCH and ELGIN Trenches.	
"		1 a.m.	About 1.a.m. a line of Germans advanced a short distance along front of B.Cᵒʸ and threw bombs which fell 10 yds in front of our parapet. Fire was opened and caused them to retire.	
		3 AM	Both Cᵒʸˢ sent out strong patrols about 3.A.M. and found no Germans in front of their line. During the night a sniping front was established in old German dug-out 5 yds in front of D.Cᵒʸˢ line. From this front Snipers claim to have killed about 10 Germans during the day	
		2 P.M.	Smoke barrage on German line N of the wood. Heavies bombarded German line in the wood.	
		4.45 P.M.	Message rec⁻ᵈ That Germans were massing in WOOD LANE.	
		5.30 P.M.	Black Watch arrive to relieve. Relief complete 6.20 P.M.. Batt⁻ moves to billets in ALBERT.	

T2134. Wt. W708—776. 500000. 4/15. Sir J. C. & S.

WAR DIARY
INTELLIGENCE SUMMARY

Army Form C. 2118.

2/ September 1916.

1st Northamptonshire.

Place	Date	Hour	Summary of Events and Information	Remarks
ALBERT	3rd		Quiet day in billets. C.O's inspection of kits, rifles etc. Inspection of billets by 2nd in C.	P. To Memache - Major
"	4th		Baths in morning. C.oy. in drill order inspected by C.O. in afternoon.	
"	5th		2nd in C.oy. attended enquiry at 1st Bn. H.Q. on CATERPILLAR VALLEY as to Heavy Artillery shooting short in HIGH WOOD. At 9 p.m. 2 washing parties of 250 and 200, went up in motor lorries to work near BAZENTIN. Remainder of Batt.n moved up to during afternoon to QUADRANGLE TRENCHES	
QUADRANGLE	6th	11 A.M	On 2nd B.n moving up from Reserve to support. Working parties rejoin up there. Conference at Bn. H.Q. Plan of attack on 9th and on HIGH WOOD considered, contingent on success of 3rd Bn. on 8th - sent in W. portion of Wood. In afternoon 2nd in C.mdt and B.C.mdt go up to HIGH Wood to see what work can be put in hand in preparation for above. Draft of 30. O.R. arrive. Capt. SPREY-SMITH rejoins from Lewis Gun Course.	
"	7th		Quiet day. C.oy. practise bombing, attack from Trenches etc in view of new draft and impending operations.	
"	8th	6.P.M	Batt.n erecting. To move up to HIGH WOOD. 2nd in C.mdt move up to 2nd Bn. H.Q. to keep touch with 3rd B.n attack. 3rd. B.n attacked Western portion of HIGH WOOD - partially successful at first, especially on the left, where 1st Cheshires penetrated into the wood to 2nd line of German Trenches - but lost considerably and withdrew owing to lack of support.	
"	9th		Batt.n under orders to move up to HIGH WOOD - but considerable delay during to 3rd B.n requiring trenches for organising a fresh attack, refilling dumps etc. Our own store had also to be re-established - N. Lanes found carrying party of 200 for the purpose - who entered ELGIN Trench at 12. Noon	

WAR DIARY or INTELLIGENCE SUMMARY

Army Form C. 2118.

1st Northamptonshire Regt.

September 1916.

Place	Date	Hour	Summary of Events and Information	Remarks and references to Appendices
HIGH WOOD	9th	12.30 P.M.	C⁰ʸ began to move up ELGIN Trench. "D.C⁰ʸ" leading and taking over left of "B" Coy front, making right of 2nd Munsters at Sap 4. "B.C⁰ʸ" following. "D" took over the right of the line in the wood. Front line C⁰ʸˢ only got into position about 3 P.M. while "C" The Support C⁰ʸ was utterly blocked in the trenches and was unable to get into position until after 6 P.M. when the attack was over. "A" C⁰ʸ in reserve, managed to force its way thro' the crowd into BLACK WATCH Trench during the evening.	D.P. Tollemache Major
"		4.45 P.M.	B. and D.C⁰ʸˢ attacked from the right edge of the Wood to Sap 4. A crater being blown on the right, on the site of the crater blown for the 1st B⁰ⁿ attack on 3rd inst. first taken by Black Watch + Turks &c. No artillery preparation written. The wood + but a short Stokes mortar bombardment, which was ineffective. For the instant our men went over the parapet. The Germans opened a very heavy rifle and M.G. fire. Our attack was unable to reach their objective except on the right, where the crater (The débris of which injured several of our men) was occupied by 2/Lt CLARKE and his platoon. This platoon was supported by another under 2/Lt COOPER and Lewis Gun. The Germans counter-attacked strongly with bombs, but the Lewis gun out of action, and drove out our men. 2/Lts A.H.G. CLARKE and D.R. COOPER were missing (the former known to be wounded). The majority of the men of these 2 platoons were killed wounded or missing. The 3rd platoon of B C⁰ʸ on the left of the above were also hard hit. 2/Lt H.G. MANNING being badly wounded. D.C⁰ʸ on the left of B. met with no better success, but more men got back. 2/Lt W.G. JACKSON killed. Total casualties 4 off. 135 other ranks.	

4/ September - 1916.

WAR DIARY
or
INTELLIGENCE SUMMARY.
(Erase heading not required.) 1st/5th Manchester Reg.

Army Form C. 2118.

Place	Date	Hour	Summary of Events and Information	Remarks and references to Appendices
HIGH WOOD	10th	6.AM	C" Coy Takes over front line at C" in support. B & D Coys sent down to Batt H.qrs. from this line and come under orders of O.C. 1st Northumbrian Dvn of 17. D. R Fus, and also following officers (from Batt) Lieut. S. CAREY Reg) 3/7 R.D. MARTIN, F.G. WILSON (5th Bn) & C. RENTON (Tank) G. LINDLEY Regt B.R.L. SMITH (Tank) A.E. WARD (Tank) & E. COLE Reg	V.P. Toulouse Hgo
"	11th		3rd Bn hands over line in W. hollow of wood to 2nd Bn - 2 Coy 1st N. Lans. taken over this Batt - relieved by 21st LONDON. 47th Dvn - 2 Lans. Coy by 24th LONDON. Relief complete 11-30 AM. Marched by Coys to N. end of BEGOURT Wood and bivouaced - arriving about 2.30 PM	
BAZIEUX WOOD	12th		Marched at 5 AM (Starting point Railway bridge W. of ALBERT 6-30 AM) to BAIZIEUX Wood.	
"	13th	10 AM	C.O. & 2nd in C" attend at Div. A.Q. at 10-30 AM. Batt marched to billets at BRESLE arriving 11-30 AM.	
BRESLE	14th		Batt: cleaning up kits and billets. Programme drawn up for 3 weeks Training.	
"	15th		Coys commence course of physical drill, drill w/o arms, bomb throwing, musketry instruction, bayonet fighting etc.	
"	"	P.M.	Footmens of big battle - Taking of HIGH WOOD - FLERS, MARTINPUICH, COURCELETTE MORVAL etc.	
"	16th		Quiet time in billets - Coys Training proceeding. Small reinforcement of 10. O.R. arrive	
"	17th		Church Parade 11 A.M. Coys went to have baths at BAIZIEUX	
"	18th		1st Bde scrous up - 2nd Bde under orders to move - Coy training suspended - Batt at BAIZIEUX for about 300 men - remainder have to go unwashed. Wet and muddy day.	

5/ September 1916.

Army Form C. 2118.

WAR DIARY
or
INTELLIGENCE SUMMARY.

(Erase heading not required.) 1st Northamptonshire Regt.

Instructions regarding War Diaries and Intelligence Summaries are contained in F. S. Regs., Part II. and the Staff Manual respectively. Title pages will be prepared in manuscript.

Place	Date	Hour	Summary of Events and Information	Remarks and references to Appendices
BRESLE	19th	1 P.M.	Battn paraded 1 P.M. – Starting Point HENENCOURT – 2 P.M. Marched via MILLENCOURT & ALBERT, & BECOURT, and LOZENGE WOOD to MAMMETZ WOOD, arriving 7 P.M. Ground wet; dug-out shelters waterlogged. Troops made bivouacs with waterproof sheets.	D.P. Tollemache Major
MAMETZ Wd	20th		Showery morning. At 1 P.M. orders received to vacate present bivouacs by 4 P.M. and move back to ALBERT to billet. C'y move at intervals, commencing 3 P.M. order to B.C.O.D. Transport very much blocked both getting up & and coming down from BOTTOM Wood. Roads deep in mud and very congested. Lorries etc. & blocking road. Transport arrives 1.30 P.M.	
ALBERT	21st		Quiet day cleaning up arms etc and billets. Baths for C & D Coys in morning, for A & B in afternoon.	
			2/Lt F.V. INGE and Pte HEATHER and 60 O.R. join from Base.	
	22nd		C.O. inspects Coys in Drill Order. At 3 P.M. Battn paraded for presentation of medal ribbons by Brig. Genl Temp Capt J. CLARK receives the Military Cross. Sergt HURST the D.C.M. Eight others the Military Medal.	
	23rd		Quiet day in billets.	
	24th		Lt T. THORNELY, and 2/Lt G.L. TOTTON. join from Base.	
	25th	4 P.M.	C Coy commence to move up (D.C.B+) to support reserve Trenches, CHESTER St & MILL ST – arriving 9.30 to 10 P.M. Battn H.Q. in CHESTER St. L.N Lanes and 2/60th in front line – Btn Service in support.	
Pte Posthm	26th		All available men digging out DROP STARFISH and CORK Alleys. A Coy digging new C'on Trench.	
S of HIGH Wood			N.B. 2/Lt A. St C. COLDWELL joined from Base 25th inst.	

6. September, 1916.

Army Form C. 2118.

WAR DIARY
of
INTELLIGENCE SUMMARY. 1st Northamptonshire Regt
(Erase heading not required.)

Instructions regarding War Diaries and Intelligence Summaries are contained in F. S. Regs., Part II. and the Staff Manual respectively. Title pages will be prepared in manuscript.

Place	Date	Hour	Summary of Events and Information	Remarks and references to Appendices
S. of High Wood	27th		B and C Coys move up to FLERS Line and are placed at disposal of O.C. 2/K.R.R. "C" Coy attacked across the open between O.C. 1 + 2. with a view to taking a further portion of O.G.1. while the 2/K.R.R. assisted by bombers of our C. Coy made a bombing attack up O.G. 1 + 2. There was no effective artillery preparation; the German Trenches were strongly defended; The attack was unsuccessful. 2/Lt E. COLE killed. 2/Lt R. W. GATES wounded, about 30 O.R. killed and wounded.	
"	28th		Major TOLLEMACHE moved up to 2/K.R.R. H.Q. to take charge of the 2 Coys at disposal of O.C. 2/K.R.R. "D" Coy placed at disposal of O.C. 2/R.t Sussex Regt "A" Coy employed carrying up bombs etc.	
"	28th		Efforts were made to gain ground up of O.G.1. by bombing; some ground was gained but the Trench junction connecting O.G.1. with the new Trench taken by the 1/L.N. Lancs was not reached. About 5 P.M. a Zeppelin was sighted E. of our position. Between 6.30 P.M. and 8.30 P.M. Batt.s concentrated at BAZENTIN and was relieved by 18th LONDON in reserve position. Moved to billets in ALBERT.	
ALBERT	29th	2 P.M.	Batt.s parades and marches to billets at MILLENCOURT. 2/Lt T. C. BLANDFORD joined from Base.	
"	30th		Quiet day in billets nothing to report	

2nd Brigade.

1st Division.

1st BATTALION

NORTHAMPTONSHIRE REGIMENT

OCTOBER 1916.

1st Northamptonshire Regt. Vol 25

WAR DIARY

October 1916

Army Form C. 2118.

WAR DIARY
OF
INTELLIGENCE SUMMARY.
(Erase heading not required.) 1st Worcestershire Regt.

October 1916

Instructions regarding War Diaries and Intelligence Summaries are contained in F.S. Regs., Part II. and the Staff Manual respectively. Title pages will be prepared in manuscript.

Place	Date	Hour	Summary of Events and Information	Remarks and references to Appendices
MILLENCOURT	1st		Preparing for move to back area. Spare baggage and Lewis Gun carts sent to FRECHENCOURT.	
"	2nd		" " Transport marched by road, starting 6 A.M.	
"	3rd	5.45 AM	Batt marched to main ALBERT — AMIENS road, when all 3 Btns were to entrain.	
		10. A.M.	Entrained in French buses and proceeded via AMIENS and DISEMENT to ACHEUX where Batt	
			went into billets - then in billets by 6 P.M. Transport arrived 8.30 P.M.	
ACHEUX	4th		Inspection of billets by C.O. Coys start preliminary Training.	
"	5th		Coys continue preliminary training.	Training Programme
"	6th		Training commenced as per programme see Appendix I	
"	7th		" " " "	
"	8th		All Coys have baths in billets.	
"	9th		Coys training as per programme.	
"	10th		" " " " — A Coy commenced musketry on the range.	
"	11th		" " " "	
"	12th		" " " " Draft of 24 Other Ranks arrived	
"	13th		" " " "	
"	14th		" " " " Draft of 18 Other Ranks arrived	

2/

October 1916

Army Form C. 2118.

WAR DIARY
-or-
INTELLIGENCE SUMMARY.
(Erase heading not required.)

1st Yorkshire Regt.

Instructions regarding War Diaries and Intelligence Summaries are contained in F.S. Regs., Part II. and the Staff Manual respectively. Title pages will be prepared in manuscript.

Place	Date	Hour	Summary of Events and Information	Remarks and references to Appendices
ACHEUX	15th	11 A.M.	A & B. Cos Church parade. C & D Cos have baths – Football in afternoon –	
"	16th	3 P.M.	Memorial service for all Ranks killed in the Somme battle. Lt Col. H.K. BETHELL leave ?? Battn on appointment to C= the 7th Inf Bde. Major Hon D.O.T. DALEMAICHE takes over command of Battn and is appointed Temp. Lt. Col.	
"	17th		Coy Training continued. A Coy night firing on range. 1st Rainbayes & 135+12597 to join Battn	
"	18th		" " " B Coy " " " "	
"	19th	8 A.M.	Battn parades for B= Route march via CHEPY – MIAULY – TOEUFFLES – Home 1 P.M. J. O. Tan Roots joins B =	
"	20th		C Coy Training in morning. at 2.30 P.M. The Div= Com= inspects the Battn in Mess, and addressing the Battn Complimented it on its appearance, and on its record in the field. B. & D. Coys Night firing on range. at 8th H.Q.	
"	21st		Training continued – Football match v. B= Indiana in afternoon. Conference of C.Os.	
"	22nd		Baths for all Coys. Quiet day in billets. C.O. inspects billets of A & B. Cos.	
"	23rd		C Coy Continue Training – C.O. attends demonstration by French Mortars & O.P. towards the Battn.	
"	24th		Parade under Coy arrangements owing to rain.	
"	25th	9am	A & D Coys parade for "Practice of the attack formation" B & C Coys unoccupied in the morning. A & D Coys in the afternoon. Rifles returned for repair by Armourer. 7.P.M. moon bombarded.	

T2134. Wt. W708-776. 500000. J/15. Sir J. C. & S.

October 1916.

Army Form C. 2118.

WAR DIARY
or
INTELLIGENCE SUMMARY.
(Erase heading not required.) 1st Northamptonshire Regt.

Place	Date	Hour	Summary of Events and Information	Remarks and references to Appendices
LEHEUX	25		No 5208 R.Q.M.S J. Buck Awarded Meritorious Service Medal.	
	26		No parades during the day, owing to the bath having been inaccessible.	
	27	10.30	Divisional Route March. Batten under half strength on account of inoculation. Route Aclieux – Toutencourt – main Doullens – Mailly road – Chipilly – Home home. 1 P.M.	
	28	8.45am	Battn parades for the attack. H.Q. Working coys, 2 Pioneer coys, 1 Dismantling coy. Football in the afternoon.	
	29		No church parade owing to the weather. First Line Transport proceeds to OISEMONT.	
	30		Companies practising new organisation of bombing squads. Parados erected in the afternoon.	
	31	5am	Battn parades for move to BRESLE. Entrained at 7.45am Arrived BRESLE 3.45 P.M.	

2/Lt Coldwell 2/Lt
31-10-16

2nd Brigade.

1st Division.

===========

1st BATTALION

NORTHAMPTONSHIRE REGIMENT

NOVEMBER 1916.

WAR DIARY

INTELLIGENCE SUMMARY.

Army Form C. 2118.

1st Northamptonshire Regt.

Vol 26

Place	Date	Hour	Summary of Events and Information	Remarks and references to Appendices
ARBRE	1916 Nov 1		Parade under Coy arrangements. Lieut R.T.P. Humpleby left for Talbetion to take up the appointment of adjutant to the Divnl school of instruction. Parade under Coy arrangements. Lieut J.C.O. Marriott left the Battn to take up Staff Captaincy of 74th Brigade. Capt A. Macnaught appointed A/Adjt.	
	2		Parades as usual. 2nd Lt. B.C. Douglas appointed Transport Officer.	
	3		Brigade field day. A & B Coys arrived. Football in the afternoon.	
ALBERT	4	9.45am	Battn paraded to march to Albert, arrived 1.15pm. Billets fair & sft.	
	5	11.30am	Holy Communion service.	
	6		Parades under Coy arrangements. Nil parade in afternoon. 2nd Lt. H.G.S. Martin however assumed a.) Coy, and Capt. L.H.M. Moeller Lieut K.H. McClure transferred from D Coy, to 2nd in command of C Coy. Lieut A. Thornley to be 2nd in command of "D" Coy. 2nd Lt. W.N. Prowd attached to 179th Trench Mortar Coy.	
	7		Lieut A. Thornley to STAPLES for Lewis gun course. Parade as usual. 2nd Lt. Robert Chalice Feasey joined Battn today from Cadet School. Posted to D Coy. Parades as usual. Recce East of ALBERT between BECOURT and BAZENTIN Road.	A.J.C. Cottrell 2nd

Army Form C. 2118.

WAR DIARY
or
INTELLIGENCE SUMMARY.
(Erase heading not required.)

1st Northamptonshire Regt.

Instructions regarding War Diaries and Intelligence Summaries are contained in F. S. Regs., Part II. and the Staff Manual respectively. Title pages will be prepared in manuscript.

Place	Date	Hour	Summary of Events and Information	Remarks and references to Appendices
ALBERT	8		Parades as usual	
	9	"	" " "	
	10.	"	" " " Lieut H.H. McLure assumed command of B Coy, vice Capt J.C. Chisholm. The Major-Genl approves of Capt J.F.M. Pioneer, and Capt L.J.S. Martin wearing the badges of rank, for which they have been recommended.	
	11		Church Parade in Cinema at 11.45 a.m. 1 Officer and 40 men per Coy.	
	12		Parades as usual, but Coys parade in Canvas leggings.	
	13.		Canvas leggings to be worn at further orders is given.	
	14		Parades as usual.	
	15		2 Officers and 2 Sgts per Coy to 2 R. COURT CIRCUS with Coys to view Trenches and dug outs made by the 1st Divn Pioneer Coys.	
	16.		The remainder of the Officers and 2 other N.C.Os per Coy with proceed to R. COURT CIRCUS to view trenches and dug out.	
	17		Cleaning up of billets	
	18	10.30am	Battn parade to go into huts in HIGH WOOD, arrive at 1.30 P.M.	
	19		Clean up the camp. Coys go and get wood to make fires. all otherwise 2ft.	

Army Form C. 2118.

WAR DIARY
of
INTELLIGENCE SUMMARY. 1st Northamptonshire Regt.

(Erase heading not required.)

Instructions regarding War Diaries and Intelligence Summaries are contained in F.S. Regs., Part II. and the Staff Manual respectively. Title pages will be prepared in manuscript.

Place	Date	Hour	Summary of Events and Information	Remarks and references to Appendices
HIGH WOOD	20		C.O. goes up to look at the line.	
	21		Coy Commdrs " "	
EAUCOURT L'ABBAYE	22		Batta goes into the line N.E. of EAUCOURT L'ABBAYE. A and C Coys go into the front line, B & D in support. Digging party starts to dig a trench to connect front line Coys, 200 yards apart. Relief complete 11 p.m. 2nd Wards (D Coy) 2 Taylor (C Coy) and digging party.	
	23		Front line Coys improve their own trenches. Digging party continue to make the trench. Worked on the previous night. 2nd Ld Hickie (D Coy) 2nd Welburn (B Coy) in the digging pty.	
	24		Trench completed between front line Coys. 2nd Isaacs (D Coy) 2nd Blandford (A Coy) in the digging party.	
	25		B & D Coys relieve A & C Coys on the front line, who went into the ra-lets at EAUCOURT L'ABBAYE. Rain during the day which made trenches in a dreadful state. Carns B became fed. Began to come down to the dressing station. Improvements to front line coys to put sods with white ore, on them where no steps. While in front line.	
	26		Day spent in improving the lines, which was in every depth of 18" of mud.	
	27		Batta relieved by 1st Bn Glos Caster Regt. Relieve took 12 hours. Total casualties O/R's 8 killed 15 wounded.	

O.C. Howell 2 Lt.

Army Form C. 2118.

1st Northamptonshire Regt.

WAR DIARY
or
INTELLIGENCE SUMMARY.
(Erase heading not required.)

Instructions regarding War Diaries and Intelligence Summaries are contained in F. S. Regs., Part II. and the Staff Manual respectively. Title pages will be prepared in manuscript.

Place	Date	Hour	Summary of Events and Information	Remarks and references to Appendices
MAMETZ WOOD	28	7.30 a.m.	Battn arrives at the camp in Mametz Wood. A few more stragglers turning up during the day.	
	29		Most of the available men of the Battn go on fatigue. Capts. Martin, Ayles, & Henson went with 2nd Lieuts: & 2nd Nilson.	
	30		go to ALBERT for 3 days rest. Fatigues all day. All companies provide as many men as possible	

A.P. Hawke 20?

2nd Brigade.

1st Division.

1st BATTALION

NORTHAMPTONSHIRE REGIMENT

DECEMBER 1916.

Army Form C. 2118.

WAR DIARY
of 1st/4th Hampshire Regt
INTELLIGENCE SUMMARY.
December 1916

(Erase heading not required.)

Instructions regarding War Diaries and Intelligence Summaries are contained in F.S. Regs., Part II. and the Staff Manual respectively. Title pages will be prepared in manuscript.

Vol 27

Place	Date	Hour	Summary of Events and Information	Remarks and references to Appendices
MANSETT WOOD	Dec 1st		210 men provided for fatigue	
	2nd		161 men provided for fatigue. 16 men passed to TRESHENCOURT on trotting course	
	3rd		Capt & 3 NCOs 2nd Lt J.E.E. Sackett & 8 men passed on leave. Given transport to M.G.C.	
			8 men transferred to 179th Tunnelling Coy R.E.	
	4th		A guard of 1 off, 1 NCO & 3 men furnished to guard R.E. stores at LONGUEVAL. 2 offrs off to A/Sgt.	
			9/Hpts off to A/Cpls. 2/Hpts app to L/C 3/Pte app to to serve M.M.	
	5th		1 Sgt 21 O.R. joined the Batn. Lieut P.S.R. Humphery & 1 Captain from Divl School	
	6th		200 men provided for fatigue	
	7th		Clean up camp in the morning. Batn parade 10.45am. Dumm: 20 at HQ went on local works	
			Relieved 1/6th in the front line at TRONES CROSSING (M.19.6.6.) A.C. & B. Coys in line, R & D reserve.	
			1 support. D. Coy d.p. fatigue & working parties. New support line at night. D/here coy return	
			Casualties 2 slightly wounded	
	8th		Fatigues as for 7th. Casualties nil	
	9th		A & C coys relieved by B & D. A coy in d.p. fatigue at night in new support line. C coy	
			joined fatigues. Casualties (killed wounded) 2 O.R. M. Dowell, N. Murfield, W. Pocock	
	10th		Casualties 3 killed, 3 wounded (1y T.M. and 2 coy fatigue as for 7th. A.S.O. Wilcox 2 wdd.)	

Army Form C. 2118.

WAR DIARY
of
INTELLIGENCE SUMMARY. Northamptonshire Regt.
(Erase heading not required.)

Instructions regarding War Diaries and Intelligence Summaries are contained in F. S. Regs., Part II. and the Staff Manual respectively. Title pages will be prepared in manuscript.

Place	Date	Hour	Summary of Events and Information	Remarks and references to Appendices
High Wood & Camp	11		Relieved by 2/Royal W. Kents. Relief complete 7pm. (Batt⁰ in High Wood & Camp by 9.30 pm.) Accommodation scarce.	
	12		Baths, fatigues by Coy's furnished (100 & 70 apr'y). No fatigues. Draft of 160 strong from 2/4th Bath (2nd Lieut Fairclough) Northants Regt joined the Batt⁰. Major Fitch (Manchester Regt) joined Bath.	
	13		Draft officers as follows: A24, C28, C52, D58. One offr & 7 NCO's & 15 ORs per Coy (Bn deriv? ?s day. 2nd Lieut Strudford, Sgt Turner, proceed to South Army school of instruction. Ø monthly ?return?	
	14		2 offrs 16 H COs 230 men furnished for fatigues. RSM Greaves places proposals. Troops slightly arrived. Capt L H Mackenzie officially reported to England.	
TIERS LINE	15		Camp cleared up for May. Remainder the ??? which did not arrive 7th. Bath parade at 2pm to relieve 60th in TIERS LINE. Relief completed 5.30 pm. Four reporters wounded. Fatigues altogether 2 offrs 125 ?? cour???? fatigues.	
	16		Found troops overland route to ford???. Coys clear up trenches. Fatigues 3 offrs 120 men (same as previous days)	
	17		Coys busy sheltering ?? clean dug-outs to provide accommodation officers & ??. Fatigues 1 offr & ?? men during the next ??? D. Casualties 2 wounded.	
HP Colwell	2nd Lt			

Army Form C. 2118.

WAR DIARY
of Northamptonshire Regt
INTELLIGENCE SUMMARY.
(Erase heading not required.)

Instructions regarding War Diaries and Intelligence Summaries are contained in F. S. Regs., Part II. and the Staff Manual respectively. Title pages will be prepared in manuscript.

Place	Date	Hour	Summary of Events and Information	Remarks and references to Appendices
	18		Small fatigue parties of men in morning making bombs etc. Fatigues not previously noted 2 offrs 20 men. Draft of 109 OR joined the Battn.	
BAZENTIN	19		Coys made as much accumulation as possible to men being during the day. Relieved by 1 N.L. Relief complete 6.15 p.m. Whole Battn in BRIQUETERIE HUTS by rear MAMETZ WOOD by 8 p.m.	
	20th		Party of 200 men under Lt Thornley & 2/Lt Guthrie go to the CORBY DNOP (Talus), hangers (cadj). Two Officers 11 NCOs & 146 OR on fatigue during the day. 1 Sgt 9 OR joined the Battn. Lt Col Ramsay joined the Battn. U Coy 1 and Lt Rayne & 7 NCOS + men went on leave. 200 men on fatigue. 2 casualties (killed 1 wounded) 19 slightly went to FK.	
	21st			
	22nd		3 6 OR 5 offrs on fatigue during the day.	
TRENCHES	23rd		Battn relieve the 60th in the front line. Relief complete 6.10 p.m. New support line improved at night. 3 wounded.	
	24th		Consd. with damage done to one front by our own artillery. Some work on previous night. Casualties 1 wounded.	
OBL (Mash	25th		Profound quiet day. Got no appearance. Capt Walker, 2/Lt Wilson, Roberts & McFall on look out patrol, went to 50 yards.	150

WAR DIARY of 1st Northumberland Fus[iliers] Regt
INTELLIGENCE SUMMARY

Army Form C. 2118.

Place	Date	Hour	Summary of Events and Information	Remarks and references to Appendices
	26		Pats 13 & 16 withdrew in accoun't of our own artillery barrage. Bayonet tuned. Short shooting (a frequent occurrence).	
BAZENTIN HUTS	27		Relieved by 2 Names. Three Companies relieved by 6 P.M. Relief of 4 Coy 3 hours late owing to incoming unit mistaking direction. Whole Relief in Bazentin Huts by 11 PM. Total casualties 7 wounded 1 died of wounds.	
	28		Baths. From 12 PM till 4 PM. Game of cleaning up Tents &c. 8 ORs forwarded divisional School. 30 OR proceeded to B Coy.	
	29		3 Offrs & NCOs 200 OR on fatigue during the day.	
ALBERT	30		BOYs 130 OR on fatigue during the day. Batt proceeded to ALBERT, via TRAMWAY. Draft of 10 ORs Joined the Bn. Capt Aybott, 2nd Lts Wilson Markie proceed on Leave. 1 Offr 334 OR on fatigue during the day. 2nd Lts Craster & Sergeant No 240 OR Divisional patrol.	

A.J.C. Ellwood
Capt & Adjt

1ST DIVISION
2ND INFY BDE

1ST BATTALION
NORTHAMPTONSHIRE REGT
JAN - DEC 1917

WAR DIARY.

1st. NORTHAMPTONSHIRE REGIMENT.

2nd. INFANTRY BRIGADE.

1st. DIVISION.

JANUARY.1917.

1st Northamptonshire Regiment

WAR DIARY.

January 1917

WAR DIARY or INTELLIGENCE SUMMARY

Army Form C. 2118.

1st Battn Northamptonshire Regt

(Erase heading not required.)

Place	Date	Hour	Summary of Events and Information	Remarks and references to Appendices
MILLENCOURT	Jan 1		Battn moves to Millencourt from ALBERT. Parade 2 PM under Lt Col Lawrence 3rd DSO	
	2		General cleaning up of billets etc.	
	3		Elementary training starts. Companies parade under their own arrangements	
	4		Very wet day, which considerably interrupted parades. 51 soldiers & 4 officers from Hosp & 25 toys joined	
	5		Parades as usual in the morning. Lecture by the Bde Major to all officers in afternoon.	
	6		Companies parade under Sgt-majors. All officers on the whole day Riding Exam Schl etc. Capt M.D. Macnaghten, & Capt F.P.C. Bydell awarded the Military Cross. C.S.M. Pandy awarded the D.C.M. London Gazette 2-1-17.	
	7		Battn parades for church at 10 am. Lt Semby, 2 Lieut La Sundby & 1 Lieut in charge of 2 Rangers & 110 OR proceed to Mons front wat out, FRESHEN COURT. Attended by general & adjutant Lt Thornally & 24 Catholics proceed to England on 10 days leave. Battn parades and is taken inspected by G.O.C. 2nd NDS, Strength 15 officers, 720 O.R.	
	8		No 15581 L/c R. Staples (M.B.Y) proceeds to England upon a commission with a view to obtaining a commission	
	9		Training continued	

158.

W.F.C. Moore 2/Lt

Army Form C. 2118.

WAR DIARY

INTELLIGENCE SUMMARY. 1ST NORTHAMPTONS WAR 2637

(Erase heading not required.)

Place	Date	Hour	Summary of Events and Information	Remarks and references to Appendices
ALBERT	10		Move to ALBERT. Battn paraded at 10am with 1st & 2nd line transport and arrived in ALBERT 11.30am. 2 offrs 7 225 OR. Capt MILLEN OC Rt at 6.30 am and proceeded to ALBERT for fatigues joining Battn in billets on completion. 2 WNKS R and 10 OR proceeded to 4th Army musketry camp for musketry training.	75&c
	11		Training continued. 2 Offr 125 OR on fatigue 2022 SF MILLS proceeded to R.F.C. on probation. 2 Offrs 225 OR on fatigue. Rowing continued	
	12			
	13		Draft of 2 Capts 93 OR arrived. Training cont. Church parade at 12 noon. 2 Offrs 126 OR on fatigue	
	14		Training continued. 2nd Lt Renton, A J an 93 OR proceeded on leave. Bombing accident occurred during the morning owing to faulty No 5 ammn. 2nd Lt Price, G.L Capts Sgt Cotter 30 R all wounded.	
	15		Training continued. Officer chief side (outpost) a draft of 150 R arrived.	
	16			
	17		" Training continued. Draft of 103 OR arrived.	

A.P. Moore 2nd Lt.

Army Form C. 2118.

WAR DIARY
or
INTELLIGENCE SUMMARY.
(Erase heading not required.)

1st North[ampton]shire[?] B[att]n[?]

Instructions regarding War Diaries and Intelligence Summaries are contained in F. S. Regs., Part II. and the Staff Manual respectively. Title pages will be prepared in manuscript.

Place	Date	Hour	Summary of Events and Information	Remarks and references to Appendices
ALBERT	18		Training continued usual fatigues. C.Q.M.S. Fitzhugh attended a course on the 7th batt'n Reg. at Northamptonshire Regt. Sgt. Powell attended a course in the 5th T.R. Battn[?] Capt. A.F. Macrae[?] at Prov[?]. on tour. Commanding officer attended off'rs court	
	19		2nd/Lt N M Nesbit struck off strength from June 17th/17. No 20339 Pte Clarke S reported for duty from apprehended Dun ALBERT	
			Usual training & fatigues 2nd/Lt[?] C Smith struck off the strength 17th June 1917	
	20		No 20339 Pte L Clarke tried by F.G.C.M. & remanded for F.G.C.M.	
	21		Training cont. Commanding off'r inspected baths. No 27549 Sgt Huse posted to R.I. industries	
			2nd/Lt M H joined batt'n from England. 2/Lt B.R. Ritchie[?] to base. Died of wounds	
	22		Training programme continued. 2/Lt N. L. Warr & E.W. Lindsay proceed on leave	
NARLOY	23		March to NARLOY. Paraded 8:15am arrived 12:30 pm	
BRESLE	24		Batt march to BRESLE. Paul[?] of R.a.m.c. arrived 1:30pm. Watch twenty thirty cth[?]	25c
	25		Relieved off the A.B.E. at A.M. [?] 2nd/R.Sussex and received[?] opera from [?]	
	26		Coys Parade independently. Football [?] the battn[?]	

A.F. Col[?]

Army Form C. 2118.

WAR DIARY
of
INTELLIGENCE SUMMARY. 15th Yorks & Lancs (Leeds Pals) Bn

(Erase heading not required.)

Instructions regarding War Diaries and Intelligence Summaries are contained in F. S. Regs., Part II. and the Staff Manual respectively. Title pages will be prepared in manuscript.

Place	Date	Hour	Summary of Events and Information	Remarks and references to Appendices
BRES	27		Brigade route march 9 men fell out	756c
	28		Voluntary services. Brigade church parade cancelled	815
	29		Training continued, deployment attack formations etc	
	30		" "	
	31		Manoeuvre parade, as the Brigade did Brigade route march. 8 men fell out	

R.J. Titherton

WAR DIARY.

1st. NORTHAMPTONSHIRE REGIMENT.

2nd. INFANTRY BRIGADE.

1st. DIVISION.

FEBRUARY. 1917.

WAR DIARY

INTELLIGENCE SUMMARY

Army Form C. 2118.

1st Batt. Cameronians Scottish Rifles

February 1917

Place	Date	Hour	Summary of Events and Information	Remarks and references to Appendices
BRESLE	Feb 1st 2nd		Paraded as usual. Football in the afternoon. Cleaning up of billets etc, after breakfast	
MERICOURT SUR-SOMME	3		Move to MERICOURT. Parade at 9.30 am. Arrive at 3.40 pm. 1 man fined to come with Bn.	
	4		C.O. and 3 Company Comdrs go to visit the line. East washing during the day	
CHUIGNOLLES	5		Battn move to CHUIGNOLLES. Parade 11.45 am, Arrive 3.30 pm. Half Coy on lorries, rest on march. Gen HIRSCHAUER (Comdg 18th French Corps) watches the Brigade march past.	
	6		Advance parties of 1 officer and 14 NCOs per Coy go up to the line, and sleep the night with the French, to take over stores etc.	
FRONT LINE	7		Battn moves up to trenches and relieves 108th French Regt. Parade 8 pm, very suddenly the French motor lorries the troops. Cold, wet & very muddy.	
	8		10 pm. Very quiet during the night. Enemy & our artillery both have to be done.	
BARLEUX	9		Quiet day	
	10		Brig-Genl. goes round the line with C.O.	
	11		C.O. & Cameron took round 2nd in Command. Dug 2nd and 3rd Recs. go round & visit the F.O. Major-Genl. Bn. Innt. Commander. Dug 2nd and 3rd Recs. very comfortable	
BOULOGNE	12 13		Moved into reserve, relieved by 10th Brigade on dug outs. Battn strength 962. 163 men.	
HUIGNES	14		Capt Macnaught returns from leave. 2nd pioneers & NCOs 200 men. C.O. & Cameron took round 2nd in Command. Relieved by 1st Cameronians.	
	15		10 pm. 2 N.C.O.s 50 men on fatigue during the morning. 2nd in Command CHURCHES in by 7.30 pm.	
	16		Roll Call 6.15 +.3.30pm. Move in & relieve CHURCHES in by 7.30 pm. Same in the afternoon. Cleaning up of billets. 2 Coys parade in morning, 2 Coys later.	
	17		Training Dismissed gas helmets inspected all found serviceable. Everyone issued with box respirators, new pattern.	

A.V. Collins Lt Col
2nd/7

Army Form C.

WAR DIARY
of 1/1 Northamptonshire Regt
INTELLIGENCE SUMMARY. Feb 1917

(Erase heading not required.)

Place	Date	Hour	Summary of Events and Information	Remarks and references to Appendices
ELVERDINGHE	Feb/18		Battalion march to B. melting	758c
	19		training. Parades for Musketry, Musketry and Physical	EB
	20		Mgr. Jund inspect men during morning. In the evening day.	
	21		Foot counting at Fortrain. Paraded 2 boys in morning, 2 in afternoon	
	22		First full parade. Checking of wind at noon	
FRONT LINE	23		Relieve 1st Gloucesters in the front line. Relief completed at 5p.m. My coy is taken over	
HUNLUN			before dusk	
	24		Quiet day. Front line boys shew and rifle fire.	
	25		Two (B) Lewis guns to fire the German working parties. German went up about	
			1.00pm. found a coming shells, a few to be in theirown. Patrols 1/2 of 7 to R.E. R2 D.2.5 Enemy	
	26		Relieved by 63rd Rifles. Completed by 8pm. to theirs 8.4/9 Manticoen by four grounds, probably	
	27		Battalion in all boys during the night. Casuals that [...]	
	28		Capt. F.S.M. Pearson joins [...] March, Sunday. Preaching until 80 O.R. P.P.L.S. B.eggamesarf, for the purpose of receiving a bath.	

W.C. Coldstream
2nd Lt.

WAR DIARY.

(WITH APPENDIX).

1st. NORTHAMPTONSHIRE REGIMENT.

2nd. INFANTRY BRIGADE.

1st. DIVISION.

MARCH. 1917.

"ORIGINAL"

Army Form C. 2118.

WAR DIARY
of 1st Northamptonshire Regt.

INTELLIGENCE SUMMARY.
(Erase heading not required.)

Instructions regarding War Diaries and Intelligence Summaries are contained in F.S. Regs., Part II. and the Staff Manual respectively. Title pages will be prepared in manuscript.

Vol 20

Place	Date	Hour	Summary of Events and Information	Remarks and references to Appendices
In Billets BEQUINCOURT Front line RANCOURT	March 1st		Proposed raid. Capt Pierson (2nd in C) and 2nd in House as adjutant – Reader – Heather – Renton go to BEQUINCOURT to train for it.	
	2nd		Relieve 6 D'on Front line. Quiet relief complete by 8 PM. 2nd Lieut Stevens surrenders "A" Coy.	
	3rd		Quiet. Companies clean much bomb trenches.	
	4th		Capt Pierson's party worked up trenches over Hap in range fire. Two prisoners captured in the early morning, one aged 26 owing information by the adjutant who owing to this little knowledge of the German language, was unable to finish that by after reply. Quite angry and sent to … at completed for line to be cannot put upright.	
	5th		Raid carried out at 3:30 am. Germans showed to be away. Left Coy bombers on the left centre into the German line. Rifle and many snipers by their dug outs and entered their tempting one entered. 2 officers to take prisoner, killed German chief trench CANNOT CHANGEMAN.	
	6th		Meal on advance with German line 2 posted to retreat. Wiered 30 on retreat after three. No gases of trees enthusiastic. Our party in the German line was less surprised. Maps were afterwards found, some way from of the dugouts see map. Dog tired, gave way afterwards found and have. Guns found after stick trouble. It had been turned by the German aid. Have completed by 10:30 am containing to L 9 howser, pouring tent, more G.	
BEQUINCOURT	7th		Relieved by 60th Rifles. Battn in dug outs.	
	8th		BEQUINCOURT. Battn in dug outs. Conceal by Cant 95th men at CH. V E G NOLLES 2nd FET CROMWELL Johnson.	
	9th		Clean up. No prisoners. Conceal by Cant 95th men at CH. V E G NOLLES 2nd FET CROMWELL Johnson.	
	10th		Heavy firing where we found to a … mounting of …	
	11th		Brig General faces the Bathing party	
CHUIGNOLLES	12th		Bathn moved to CHUIGNOLLES, whole Battn in the 8 PM. 2 Wks BERTIN + Guns Journed.	
	13th		Parade from 9 – 12:30, 2.3.30	
	15th		7.15 am – 8, 9. 12.30, 2.3.30	
	16th		,, ,, ,, Practice march along 88 formation	
	17th		Batt. G find pickets 2 Corps during the attack. Leaves by brigade on new ,,	

ASR Cottwell 2 Lt

Army Form C. 2118.

WAR DIARY

of 1st Northants Machine Gun Regt.

INTELLIGENCE SUMMARY.

(Erase heading not required.)

Instructions regarding War Diaries and Intelligence Summaries are contained in F. S. Regs., Part II and the Staff Manual respectively. Title pages will be prepared in manuscript.

Place	Date	Hour	Summary of Events and Information	Remarks and references to Appendices
CHUGNON	18		Foot washing by Coys. Report of raid into the Zone.	
BRIE	19		Relieved the MUNSTERS in Reckergment in front of BRIE. Very quiet, no sound of a gun. Cavalry and cyclists going through all day.	
	20		Now cavalry and cyclist go towards MONS-EN-CHAUSSÉE (patrol) Patrols of BOCHE manages to enter ESTREES-EN-CHAUSSÉE (no only village for miles around totally unshelled) and burn two houses. Found it to be full of large numbers of civilians (mostly women & children). No sign of military eqpt. Seen a few people sent to BOVINCOURT & NESMANO. Found 18 boy and 1 offr + 100 ors G in an old 25a prisoners & young children. No sign of military eqpt. seen	
	21		Relieved by 51st Division. Regt relieved by 45 Brownich Fusiliers. Took over Camp on westward of 25b R.I.C., no troops arrived. Whether the whole Bgde ought to move in an open field in the rear as made by the A.S.C. no tents arrived.	
	22		Go to billets camp on westward slope G.J./R. Bde Hdqrs. under R.A.F.s Camp pitched. Reg fatigues on BRIE Bdge till 12 midnight very heavy fatigues down till 12 midnight	
	23			
	24			
	25			
	26			
	27			
	28		Fatigues Carried. Sun. Ch. 4 P.M. 30 Sgt. Forzal & Cpl. Newman awarded D.C.M. Sgt. transferred with Key Nobs.	
	29		+ 800 or Bdgs. 150 or 20s to MUNGR-BRAYONNE. forced	
	30		Nissen huts for advanced army Hdqrs. Hem's	
	31		Same as yesterday	

ASP Coldborn Bt

War Diary

1st Division No. G.277/14/17.   2nd Brigade No. G.38/47.

G.O.C.
2nd BRIGADE.
----

1.   I much appreciate the fine offensive spirit shown by all ranks of the 1st Northants and 1st L.N. Lancs in the raids they carried out.

        Their efforts were deserving of better results, and had it not been that the enemy were in a great state of preparedness I am convinced that the success in both cases would have been great.

2.   In spite of being met by a Barrage, and knowing that the enemy was quite prepared, the way the raiding parties advanced and endeavoured to achieve their object is much to be admired. It shows that the right spirit is there, and I look forward to the day when the opportunity will come of action under more favourable circumstances, the result of which can never be in doubt.

3.   The arrangements for these raids, in every detail, could not have been better, and every credit is due to those responsible.

4.   Kindly have the above conveyed to all ranks.

                                (sd). E.P. STRICKLAND,
                                          Major General,
8th March, 1917.   Commanding 1st Division.

- 2 -

O.C. Loyal N. Lancs.   O.C. 2nd T.M. Battery.
O.C. Northamptons.   H.Q. Left Sub-Group.
O.C. No. 2 M.G. Coy.   O.C. X/1 T.M. Battery.

        Forwarded for information.

                                Captain, Brigade Major,
9th March, 1917.   2nd Infantry Brigade.

WAR DIARY.

1st. NORTHAMPTONSHIRE REGIMENT.

2nd. INFANTRY BRIGADE.

1st. DIVISION.

APRIL. 1917.

Army Form C. 2118.

WAR DIARY
of 1/5 Northumberland Regt

INTELLIGENCE SUMMARY.

(Erase heading not required.)

Instructions regarding War Diaries and Intelligence Summaries are contained in F. S. Regs., Part II and the Staff Manual respectively. Title pages will be prepared in manuscript.

Place	Date	Hour	Summary of Events and Information	Remarks and references to Appendices
BRIE	APRIL 1st 2nd 3rd		All Coys at work on the roads. Total strength of Batt. 30 offrs 1011 OR. Signallers out on a bright scheme. High command exercises with R.F.C. & S.R. Stunts by visual. Two motor lorries 19 pm. Battl. out in morning 9am. Exalt form special rifle reconnt. The army Commander inspected two Coys appreciation of the country ahead of us were shown in the interesting battle plan of the Brigade shown up by the formation in their descent. The Yorkshiremen officer made a small party Capt. S.S.D. Simon arrived on this military order. "For an enemy and hostility a simple one which carried out a raid on the night of 6-4-17 when the right column of attacked first penetrated into company by a barrage of grenades and hand mortar it was not first partially crumps to recognise the situation and set after the enemy to open strongly into."	
	4th		2 & 3 Coys under orders of 34th Field Coy RE to S.E. mine. C & J am roads. Coy Parade in afternoon.	
	5th		Some work as usual. 11.30am. Inoculation 12.15 pm Returned to L/SM.GS. Parade 1/30 pm Reflection	
	6th		Same work as usual. All in by 5pm.	
ENGUINGHEM	7		Church Parade 2 offrs and 25 O.R. per Coy	
	8		7am - 7.45am Bayonet fighting & physical training. 9-12.30 pm. Platoon drill etc	
	9		Manoeuvre 2- 3.30 am Training of specialists. Very wet weather.	
	10		Whole Battalion falls in Rifle parade in morning.	
	11		Training 9.30 for 9.7th.	
	12		Coy practice attack 1st D. platoons then as a Coy. 9-11.30am. Coy drill and Lewis gun drill 11.30 - 12 noon. 9-3.9 reconnoitred and appointed 2nd in command

Army Form C. 2118.

WAR DIARY
or 1st Yorkshire Lancashire Regt
INTELLIGENCE SUMMARY.
(Erase heading not required.)

Place	Date	Hour	Summary of Events and Information	Remarks and references to Appendices
Dernancourt	13		A.B.& D Coys. Coy and Platoon drill. Handling of arms 7-10.30am. Manoeuvres by Platoons for "Bosun" in harn.	
	14		C. Coy. Practice of attack over broken ground. 9.15 noon. A.C. & D. Coy manoeuvres, advance under fire, attacking strong points. 2.15 noon. B Coy. Attack practice.	
	15		2.30pm. 50 OR per Coy. Church parade. 2nd Lt N. Elliot joined the Battalion.	
MORCOURT	16		Batt. moves to MORCOURT. Parade of 45 NCOs RCs in Coy 1.30pm. Training of Specialists from 2-3pm.	
	17		9am - 12 noon. Coy manoeuvres. 12 noon-12.30pm. NCOs under Capt Wake 7-8pm. Training of Specialists	
	18		As for yesterday. B Coy "Attack on Strong Point" under C.O. Casualties owing to enemy...	
	19		" " " 2/Lt CALDWELL proceeds on leave.	
	20		" " "	
	21		Scheme. Battalion in the Attack. A Coy Right assaulting Coy, C by 2nd assaulting Coy. B " in support D " in support	
	22		Attack on a front of 400 yards.	
	23		Battalion tactics. 2 Coys in the morning, 2 in afternoon. Training.	
	24		Brigade field day. Wounded no reporting team.	
	25		2 NCOs & 10 non. & 3rd D'ford proceed to England on leave. Training.	W.C. Russell

A.5834 Wt.W4973/M687 750,000 8/16 D.D.& L.Ltd. Forms/C.2118/13.

Army Form C. 2118.

WAR DIARY
of 1st Northampton Shire Rgt
INTELLIGENCE SUMMARY.
(Erase heading not required.)

Place	Date	Hour	Summary of Events and Information	Remarks and references to Appendices
Moncore-Bt	26		Training. Bisset Bombing and Riflemens competitions. To coy comp took an average of 82.4 for Bn. & found a total of 8.12 for Riflemens competitions arranged.	
	27		Training. Draft 8.1.9 OR joined the Bath. A coy was dismissed per comp when the Bn. left.	
	28		Training. Brigade sports in the afternoon.	
	29		5 pm. Ceremonial parade. Capt. J. S. G. Roberts assumed acting Major. 2 Offrs + 60 OR for Ceremonial parade. a draft 3 6 OR (all signallers) joined Bath. 2 N.H. M.W. Taylor joined Bath.	
	30		Training. The other night patrol april 29th has been sent to Savoy? hill. On approaching it was discovered to be no enemy. No information has been carried out by Rolemer that Bath. at Mackinson hill with the been carried out commanding Officer. One no not to attack a full ent have been found 2 to 3 m. Orders were issued to the following period. Boulais, and fresh attacks has been made to the following periods and was prepared today and tomorrow.	

D.F.C. Moore
2 Nt L

WAR DIARY.

1st. NORTHAMPTONSHIRE REGIMENT.

2nd. INFANTRY BRIGADE.

1st. DIVISION.

MAY. 1917.

Army Form C. 2118.

Vol 32

WAR DIARY
of 1st Northamptonshire Regt.

INTELLIGENCE SUMMARY.

(Erase heading not required.)

MAY. 1917.

Instructions regarding War Diaries and Intelligence Summaries are contained in F. S. Regs., Part II and the Staff Manual respectively. Title pages will be prepared in manuscript.

Place	Date	Hour	Summary of Events and Information	Remarks and references to Appendices
MORLANCOURT SUR SOMME	May 1st		Refitting in the morning. Battn. got back to billets at 12.30 p.m. Church parade.	
	2nd		Battn. takes 2 coys parade in the morning and 2 in the afternoon. An officer and 2 N.C.O's per coy. go to MERICOURT to the 23rd Field Coy RE to learn transport of & bridges & unlimbering.	
	3rd		Advanced guard scheme in the morning. Available training in the afternoon.	
	4th		Scheme in the morning. (9D) Coys outpost scheme. a.m. Advanced guard p.m.	
	5th		Training	
	6th		2 officers and 60 O.R. per coy attend church parade.	
	7th		Battn. takes its officers and men's guards to section shooting on the range.	
			Very hot weather. Excellent bathing parts in the village.	
	8th		General advance and outpost scheme.	
	9th		Outpost scheme.	
	10th		Advanced and flank guards scheme. Boys acted as enemy to A.O.T. attack.	
	11th		Proceeds on leave to England. Scheme. Attacking (through a wood).	
	12th		A & D Coys practice trench to trench attacks. B Coy enemy garrison. C Coy attack & strong point under the supervision of Commanding officer Regt. Reports in the afternoon.	
	13th		2 officers and 60 O.R. per Coy attend church parade.	
	14th		Training afternoon. Specialists training. A Coy does night operations.	
	15th		Outpost scheme in the morning. Cookers & water cart went out and rations drawn out. Bath taken in the river in the afternoon. Football, volleyball etc. C Coy did evening training.	
	16th		Battn. acted as enemy to 1st 103rd Brigade. C Coy did advance guard jobs.	

A.5834 Wt. W4973/M687 750,000 8/16 D. D. & L. Ltd. Forms/C.2118/13.

WAR DIARY
INTELLIGENCE SUMMARY

1st Royal Hampshire Regt.

Army Form C. 2118

Vol 3

Place	Date	Hour	Summary of Events and Information	Remarks and references to Appendices
MORCOURT	17		Battn Baths. L.G. action musketry. Rifle grenade practice to live grenade firing. Bombing sections firing No 23 live grenade. A Coy numerical red rifle. Rifle section practice Rapid loading and fire control	
	18.		Draft of 11 O.R joined Battn with Bath. First parade on the ranges. Very hot replicas. Rifle obtained. was good.	
	19.		Battn moved to Villers-Bretonneux. Struck at 2pm, arrived at 6pm in billets	
VILLERS-BRETONNEUX	20.		2 officers and 60 O.R. per Coy attend Church parade.	
	21.		Route March. Drill Parade.	
	22.		" "	
	23.		" Officers reconnoissance in afternoon under the officers	
	24.		2 N.C.O R M°Cready & Guyatt sent to England. 12 O.R joined. Per Route March in morning. Baths Taken. Officers ditto. Inter-Coy relieve under 2nd i/c G.S.Q Robinson. Battalion sports in the afternoon.	
	25.		Divisional sports in the afternoon.	
	26.		Route March in morning.	
	27.		Coy Parades in the morning. Bath parade in afternoon. Entrained for BOUZENCOURT at 1.15am	
	28.		Coy parades, musketry taken. Conducting Etc. Afternoon Bath parade in afternoon. By Coy.	
	29.		2 Lt. T.C. Jennings joined Battalion. Route March. Shell bath. C.O.'s Conference talk in afternoon. By Coy. Prize for rifle practice on the range. afternoon 5.p.m. Physical and Bayonet training	
	30.			
	31.		Route march in the morning, 10 hours per Coy. awst Reunion under in afternoon officers	

A.S.F. Ashley

WAR DIARY.

1st. NORTHAMPTONSHIRE REGIMENT.

2nd. INFANTRY BRIGADE.

1st. DIVISION.

JUNE. 1917.

Army Form C. 2118.

WAR DIARY
of 1st Northamptonshire Regt.

INTELLIGENCE SUMMARY.
(Erase heading not required.)

Place	Date	Hour	Summary of Events and Information	Remarks and references to Appendices
Nr CASSEL	16		All Officers' Coys & pers. informed by hearing Colonel Ham 11.AM. & 12.	
	17		2 offr & 60 OR to coy, arrived Cassel passed	
	18		A Coy by first, packed transport, marched to S.S. Woolwich & morning	
			2 Lieut D. Cantlie, R.A.O. Caton, R.L. Sawin & 1 S.A. Thamasgan join 7th & arrive at Bailleul 1.45	
			Batn arrived at 4.30 AM. & 3 pm batn. in camp (10 offrs 200 OR) whole coys paraded 4.15 pm arrived P. Front Day	
INGHOOFDE	20		Batn paraded at 4.30 AM orders received to return Braine (made 3 R.D. same) arrived as in Egypt AM.	
			May Lt Wort. M. ordered Army med hosp	
COUDEKERQUE	21		Batn formed up & Stan marched to COUDEKERQUE arrived & in the pm.	
	22		Morning and drilling & Inspection Rifles ever fell out. officers and sundry lines p.m.	
			Batn paraded, Warm march to ?½ & 3.30 arm marching to bus on WISE Rd BOOS DE. Poona in the pm.	
	23		3. company NOTRE DAME, 1 mile E. of COXYDE Bains 3	
Nr COXYDE BAINS	24		2 offrs & 60 OR came Bains DE.	
	25		Coy in each woods mornings/ several absences 2 coy billets on wiskers	
	26			
	27			
	28			
	29		Coys manoeuvres	
	30		B Coy on rapid attack on wood, cross country at noon. D Coy & B Coy on BRAINE in the afternoon.	
			May Mostly Clearing off of injured. C coy & D Coy	
	31		2 2/Lts Lt A.C. to Church Parade	

WAR DIARY.

(WITH APPENDICES).

1st. NORTHAMPTONSHIRE REGIMENT.

2nd. INFANTRY BRIGADE.

1st. DIVISION.

JULY. 1917.

WAR DIARY
of 1st Northamptonshire Regt
INTELLIGENCE SUMMARY

Army Form C. 2118.

Vol 34

Place	Date	Hour	Summary of Events and Information	Remarks and references to Appendices

Army Form C. 2118.

WAR DIARY
of 1st Northumberland Regt.
INTELLIGENCE SUMMARY.

(Erase heading not required.)

Place	Date	Hour	Summary of Events and Information	Remarks and references to Appendices
	16th Sept.		The enemy appears to have made three main attacks, as far as intelligence shows, on our Brigade front. The left of the 48th Div. The right of the 6th Div. attacked by bombers along Bon-Avis trench, in particular on B.7 & B.8 about 6.15 right across our Front at 6.30 to 7 o'clock on their left at about 8.15 from the same direction as our first attack, all supported by creeping barrage. The enemy succeeded in creeping barrage. The enemy succeeded in getting up new concentrations of MGs, apparently placed under cover. Our night reports of our Coys were that Reserve Coy (C) was going up to reinforce C.B.7 & B.8 on bomb attack, that another party with some apparently accurate MGs must have been dealt with to maintain the salient, that the salient, the 5-long through that a request be sent by aeroplane for fresh ammunition & reinforcements. That B. The now holds by the line from the Ruins Quarries, MG. ...unable to hospital see on the wooded at B.15.B.9, trench ... passed on their side to the right where B & C held on. Any communication trench infantry retired in ours & appeared as B.15.B.1 to aeroplane, at 8.30am a party (appeared as officers) 15 prepared to bomb down in an line in of MG stopping them by our fire very accurate. Whole right flank back 4.0 of the near right half (500 men approx) were cut up by Infantry on our backs, and surrounded. The Regt.(32nd Jaeger) which was the German opposite was discovered that the Germans were on them rolling two way behind from L.L. direction, and the advance offered for the right about half & front about 500 men (unbroken by the 2nd Cos. sinces the fight was so bad is the Brigade Reserve. As to go to relieve and wait for further orders. The Bn. returned to the assembly trenches in the wood, about 500 men. Our front line was presented on the 21st Goblin Regt by MG fire & our front line was presented on the 21st Goblin.	

WAR DIARY
or
INTELLIGENCE SUMMARY.
(Erase heading not required.)

Army Form C. 2118.

Place	Date	Hour	Summary of Events and Information	Remarks and references to Appendices
	18th cont.		Officers Commanding: Lt.Col. Hon. D.P. Tottenham Capt. L. L. Aylett Lieut. J.R. Hunter " J.B. Thompson " J.H.A. Mann " P.A. Heather 2nd Lt. R.P. Needham " T. Rodan " A.R. Jennings " F.C. Blanchard " R.C. Baxter " E.M. Jones " C.E. Binnai " D.C. Chisholm " F.E. Rith " R.C. Booty " W.H. Coyne " T.W. Symons " J.H. Smith " R.R. Macaulay Capt. F. Hayes (RAMC att.)	{mentioned}

Army Form C. 2118.

WAR DIARY
or
INTELLIGENCE SUMMARY.

(Erase heading not required.)

Instructions regarding War Diaries and Intelligence Summaries are contained in F. S. Regs., Part II. and the Staff Manual respectively. Title pages will be prepared in manuscript.

Place	Date	Hour	Summary of Events and Information	Remarks and references to Appendices
RINON CAMP	July 11		The Arabs who were the rest of the Camp ourselves carried to Egypt & returned in the evening.	
			Inspected & cleaned the morning Kit & arms. Y.M.C.A. Lecture in the evening.	
Entrenching	12		Brigade occupied of the hillside. D.Coy & P.O.B. A.Coy relief.	
POST-B Reene			Defences. Bathing in the afternoon.	
	13.			
	14.		Kit inspection and cleaning of equipment.	
(AN)VEADE	15.		Batln moved at 6.45 am. to ZHYVEADE arr: in the 2 pm.	
			Batln moved at 6.45 am. to ARMBOUTS CAPPEL left ZHYVEADE at 11/12.15 pm. Dist 13¼/22.50 arrived	
ARMBOUTS	16		to ARMBOUTS CAPPEL 6:30 am. Dist 11. & 12.15 pm.	
CAPPEL			Batln moved on. Fell no other were carried.	
	17		Church parade C.6. Trust at 9 am on Crosby wind 2nd 287 other ranks.	
	18.		Orders received. Co. 3 men at 5pm. Batln all in trenches by 5pm from 7 & 287 other ranks.	
ST POL	19		Moved to meet M.B. ST POL, at 5pm. Batln all in trenches by 8pm from new orders.	
	20.		Parade from 9-9.30, 11-11.30 and 5-6. Training & new drafts begun.	
	21		" 9, 12.30, 2, 3.30 pm., 2-4, 5-6 pm. L.Coy. away to shooting range on rifles.	
			" 9, 12.30, 2, 3.30 pm. Old single fourth under went to rifle range.	
	22		Afternoon and Bathing. Brigade Church Parade & 9.30am. 2 Officers and 150 other ranks return 2 Lieut/&th	
			Brigade Church Parade & 9.30am. 2 Officers and 150 other ranks return. 2 Lieut A.W. Walsh reported for duty.	
	23		Parades: 11 Ridge R. Moore of 2nd Lieut J.S. Aspinal reported for duty.	
			Parades: 7.15 am - 7. 12 - 1 - 3.30 - 5-6. Capt J.C.D. Moore on appointment.	
	24		7 miles route march by Divr. Brigade Colable dress. Pic. Saw fair fall in	
			measured Field Day. A draft of 1 Officer 128 other ranks 2nd Lieut Balfour joined the Battalion from K.O. Laucaster Regt.	
	25.		Sp Coys am Left arithy in the Battalion from K.O. Laucaster Regt.	

A.S.P. Ellcott
2nd Lt

WAR DIARY
INTELLIGENCE SUMMARY
(Erase heading not required.)

Army Form C. 2118.

Place	Date	Hour	Summary of Events and Information	Remarks and references to Appendices
	26			
	27			
	28			
	29			
	30			
	31			

Copy.

No.4.

H.Q. 1st Div. (For information).
O.C. Royal Sussex.
O.C. Loyal N.Lancs.
O.C. Northants.
O.C. K.RR.C.
O.C. F.G.Coy.
O.C. T.M.Battery.

2ND INFANTRY BRIGADE INTELLIGENCE SUMMARY.
Covering period 24 hours to 6 a.m. 9th July 1917.

Reference Map - Sheet 13.S.W. 1/20,000.

1. **OPERATIONS.**

   Patrols. The following patrols were sent out from our Right Battalion front.-
   (i). A patrol of 2 Officers, 2 N.C.Os and 6 O.R. left our trenches at M.16.c.65.65 at 10.45 p.m. They passed through our wire and advanced on the enemy wire projecting Eastwards beyond the salient in his trenches at M.16.c.9.9. 2/Lieut. A.R.McANALLY was in command of this patrol.

   The party crossed "No Man's Land" until they reached the enemy's wire 100 yards East of the apex.

   2/Lieut.McANALLY and Sgt.RIVETT cut a gap through this wire about 6 feet wide. The party was then disposed, and lay in wait of any Germans that might appear.

   They laid about ¾ of an hour and formed a covering party for No.2 patrol which passed through the gap, carried out their reconnaissance and returned to our trenches.

   2/Lieut.McANALLY then replaced his men and waited.

   About 10 minutes later a German Officer strolled along BEHIND the wire with his hands in his pocket.

   Our officer waited until the German Officer reached the gap and then sprang up and advanced on him covering him with his revolver and challenged him, whereupon the German started and cried "Gott in Himmel".

   2/Lieut.McANALLY then noticed a party of 20 or more German soldiers following their officers about 5 or 6 yards behind him.

   Seeing that it was useless to confront this party on their own side of the wire, he shot the officer apparently killing him. The remainder of our party then opened fire on the German party and threw two bombs amongst them.

   A number of them fell, and several of them were heard groaning as if badly wounded. The exact casualties can only be surmised.

   The remainder of the German party then started bombing our men, who withdrew under their Officer's order.

   Machine guns were opened on our party returning, about half way across "No Man's Land" (Machine Gun thought to be firing from the apex) which however regained our trench with no casualties at about 1.0 a.m.

   (ii) Patrol No.2. 10.30 p.m. a patrol consisting of Lieut.THOMSON, 1 Sgt and 6 O.R. left our trenches at M.16.c.5.8. and proceeded along left track towards enemy line

   The ditch running at right angles to this track in centre of "No Man's Land" was crossed by means of 6 feet planks.

   The enemy wire was reconnoitred and found to consist of two rows of Chevaux de Frise and loose wire thrown about.

   The ground between the ditch and enemy wire is very marshy with a good many either ponds or shell holes filled with water. The ground however is passable, but a crossing would be rather slow. Patrol could only approach within 15 yards of enemy wire owing to the presence of 6 Germans who were between their own wire and trench.

Very Lights were being fired by this party.

Enemy wire is about 15 yards in front of their trench.

Point of trench particularly observed is about 15 yards West of apex.

The enemy's defences at this point consist of breastworks in apparently good condition.

Patrol then withdrew at 11.30 p.m. and proceeded towards the enemy line on the right of the track, passed through the wire about 50 yards East of the apex.

Patrol then moved half left to examine wire running parallel with the trench.

This was found to be rather thick, and in the wire was an advanced post occupied by the enemy; one of the garrison of this post was heard to cough.

A bag of German bombs was found in "No Man's Land" fixed to the ground about 15 yards in front of this wire.

Patrol returned at 12.25 a.m.

(iii). Nos.3 & 4 Patrols. These patrols went out from M.15.b.3.3 where there was a gap in our own wire.

Captain GARWY and 2/Lieut. BORROW were in charge. They made their way to a mound; in front were one patrol covered by the other; reconnoitred some broken ground round a heap of stones and found it unoccupied. Both patrols then turned up the bank and went to the German wire.

The wire here is very thin, but there is not a clear gap.

The existing wire consists of knife rests and concertina.

The patrols returned at 2.30 a.m.

Work. A certain amount of work was going on in the German lines.

The night was dark and damp. Very little hostile activity.

(iv) A patrol left our lines at M.15.b.2.4. and proceeded to M.15.b.45.50. Here there was a gap cut in the German wire, also a gap opposite to it in our wire. The enemy wire consists of 3 or 4 rows of knife rests, making an entanglement 30 to 40 yards thick; this however can be got through with a little care as few of these frames are wired together.

Patrol returned at 12.50 a.m.

(b). Artillery. Our artillery carried out a rapid bombardment of enemy trenches in M.9.d., M.10.c. and M.15.b. with 18 pdrs. and 4.5" hows. at 2.0 p.m. with good effect.

4.15 p.m. to 4.45 p.m. another bombardment of enemy trenches in M.15.a.& b., M.16 a.& b. and M.10.c. The shooting appeared to be good.

   Note. Patrol (iv) was the patrol sent out by Right Bn. on night of 7th/8th and referred to in yesterdays Summary.

2. ENEMY'S DEFENCES AND ORGANISATION.

(Trench Mortars.) Trench Mortar emplacements are suspected at M.9.c.80.65, M.9.c.80.20. and M.15.b.9.7.

3. ENEMY ACTIVITY.

(a) Infantry. Day normal. During night of 7th/8th inst from 1.a.m. to 2.30 a.m. hostile machine guns swept BARE SUPPORT and BAT ALLEY. The night of the 8th/9th inst was very quiet. An enemy sniper was active at 8.10 p.m. firing from M.9.c.55.30.

(b). Aerial. Nothing to report.

(c). Artillery. Hostile artillery was very active again throughout the day. 8", 5.9", 4.2" and 77 mm were used and at one point 9.2" were reported.

Left Battalion Front. The Battalion area was shelled consistently. The support line and right company appeared to receive the most attention.

Right Battalion Front. BARE ALLEY, Battn.H.Q., the Reserve line and and O.P. at M.21.b.9.3. were most heavily shelled. The Reserve line was shelled with very heavy shells reported to have probably been 9.2".

Back Areas. The Bridges and Pier head were shelled with Naval guns and shrapnel from 3.30 p.m. to 4.30 p.m. Several direct hits were made on the bridges.

The Right Support Battalion H.Q. and vicinity were continuously shelled chiefly with 5.9" and 4.9" though some 8" were used. Several hits (direct) were made on NIEUPORT & NIEUPORT BAINS ROAD. Shelling is reported to have come from Easterly and North-Easterly direction.

NIEUPORT BAINS was heavily shelled with 8",5.9" and 4.2". The O.P. at M.14.d.0.6. received six direct hits with 5.9" and was much damaged.

Hostile artillery activity recommenced at about 5.30 am. today

(d). Trench Mortars. Trench Mortars were active on BARE ALLEY, Support line and O.P. of the Right Battalion and also Nos.7 and 9 M.G.Battle emplacements.

The front line in M.15.a. and support line of Left Battalion were intermittently shelled with heavy trench mortars. The O.P. at M.15.a.20.95. received a direct hit but was not damaged.

4. INFORMATION. (a) Movement.

7.45 a.m. 4 men were seen at M.15.a.95.90. one of them pointed towards our lines.

11.30 a.m. 3 men were observed M.16.a.7.0. They were all wearing white bands round caps.

11.40 a.m. 5 men were observed moving about behind screens at M.10.c.5.1.

1.5 p.m. One man was observed to run down Dune at M.11.a.3.3.

1.50 p.m. Two men were observed looking over the parapet at M.15.a.85.75. One was wearing a steel helmet and the other a grey cap with blue band. The latter carried field glasses.

1.55 p.m. periscope observed in trench at M.15.b.2.8. This point has been repaired with sandbags.

3.25 p.m. One man was seen at M.15.a.7.9.

2.15 p.m. Two men were seen at M.9.c.80.65 where a T.M. dugout is suspected.

Two men were also seen at M.9.c.60.40.

6.15 p.m. One man was seen at M.15.a.75.95.

8.15 p.m. One man was seen running along trench at M.9.c.8.2.. He was fired on by our snipers but not hit.

5. MISCELLANEOUS.

While our artillery were shelling M.18.d. at about 5.p.m. a thick dense cloud of smoke was seen and a few explosions were heard. A dump was probably hit or some buildings set on fire.

Between 3.50 a.m. and 4.15 a.m.(9th inst) three enemy shells fell in his own front line. On each occasion an orange coloured rocket was fired which burst into several stars. The shells fell about M.9.c.75.80.

The enemy's wire in front of his support line at M.9.c.9.2 has been blown in for 10 feet.

Subterranean noises as if iron girders were vibrating were heard in our front line whilst our guns were vibrating at about 5.30 pm. The noises were heard at M.15.a.75.75. and M.15.a.60.50.

Enemy transport were plainly heard in the direction of M.15.b.70.85. on paved road.

(Signed). H.V.BARNES.

2/Lieut,
2nd Brigade Intelligence Officer.

9th July 1917.

2nd Brigade No. G. 3/1/1.

REPORT ON THE OPERATIONS OF JULY 10TH, 1917.

Reference Map - Secret Map attached.

1. PERIOD PREVIOUS TO THE ATTACK.

For some day previous to the attack the enemy had subjected our line to intermittent bombardments, shelling the whole area East of the River YSER, particularly local Headquarters and communication trenches.

On the West of the River he shelled NIEUPORT BAINS heavily at times, and hit or knocked out the majority of O.Ps. The trenches on the Western bank were also shelled; the three bridges at the mouth of the River were rather heavily shelled on the 9th - some damage being done.

There was a considerable amount of hostile Counter-Battery fire, and back areas were shelled.

The hostile infantry activity was below normal, very little movement being seen, and the nights were particularly quiet, both as regards artillery and infantry. There was the normal amount of hostile machine gun fire at night.

Hostile aircraft was active during the days of 5th, 6th and 7th, flying considerably over our lines, but on the 8th and 9th it was less in evidence.

2. HOSTILE ARTILLERY PROGRAMME UNTIL 7.10 p.m. on the 10th inst.

5.30 a.m.	Enemy heavy artillery started a casual shelling of the reserve line, the bridges, and NIEUPORT BAINS.
6.45 a.m.	Shelling much increased, heavy barrage on front line for an hour.
7.45 a.m.	Barrage lifted to Support and Reserve lines.
8.45 a.m.	Barrage lifted to S.W. side of the YSER.
9.45 a.m. to 9.50 a.m.	Lull.
9.50 a.m.	Barrage on Support lines.
10.50 a.m.	Barrage lifted on to S.W. side of the YSER.
11.50 a.m.	Barrage dropped to front line.
11.50 a.m. to 11.55 a.m.	Lull.
11.55 a.m.	Barrage on S.W. side of the YSER.
12.55 p.m.	Barrage dropped to support line.
1.55 p.m.	Barrage dropped to front line.
1.55 p.m. to 2.10 p.m.	Lull.
2.10 p.m. to 7 o'clock.	The front and support lines and S.W. bank of the YSER and the bridge heads were continuously barraged.

There was a distinct lull of about 10 minutes at 6.10 p.m.

From 1.15 p.m. a continuous barrage was maintained on the bridges and Western bridge-head. Shells at least 8" calibre were falling at rate of 4 a minute.
Another distinct barrage was put across the houses at the Eastern end of NIEUPORT BAINS.

The times given above are only approximate and while a barrage is reported in one place it means that the shelling was heaviest here.

The Battalion Headquarters were apparently maintained under a continuous barrage except during the lulls.

The bridges were destroyed at the following times :-

By 8.30 a.m.	MORTLAKE BRIDGE was cut in two.
By 12.55 p.m.	KEW BRIDGE WAS DESTROYED.
By 4.45 p.m.	RICHMOND BRIDGE WAS SMASHED.

The tunnels and covered trenches on the Eastern side of the YSER were blown in before 4 p.m. and there was no covered means of approach to the bridge heads.

Throughout the day all back areas, Headquarters, Battery positions and ways of approach to the front area were kept under a steady fire, and the frequency with which all lines and means of communication were cut by this bombardment added extraordinarily to the difficulties of control of the situation.

3. COMMUNICATION AND REPORTS.

The situation was reported by continual messages from Observation Posts of the Support Battalion, and retaliation was asked for by the Brigade on numerous occasions. Touch was maintained with the Divisional Artillery throughout, but it was found best to control the fire from artillery O.Ps.

Reports of the situation were received from Battalions East of the YSER by pigeon; all telephone and wireless communication was out by 10.15 a.m.

Message timed.	Extracts from messages.
11. 7 a.m.	O.C. 2nd K.R.R.C. reported that Right Coy.H.Q. was blown in, Battalion H.Q. was being heavily shelled, he was reinforcing right with one platoon. (Pigeon message).
5.15 p.m.	O.C. 2nd K.R.R.C. estimated casualties at 35% (Pigeon message).
6.30 p.m.	O.C. 1st L.N.Lancs.Regt. reported C.R.E. had gone forward to investigate repairs necessary to No.1.Bridge and that he was trying to send two orderlies over the River in tubs.
7.10 p.m.	O.C. 2nd K.R.R.C. reported that he had two companies with no officers; that Battalion H.Q. had been moved into tunnel in BEACH ALLEY; that he was endeavouring to reinforce; enemy planes were flying low. (Pigeon message).
7.10 p.m.	White rockets bursting into two white lights- Bombardment heavy. (@ Note. This was taken to be the S.O.S. signal and acted on as such, but the green lights appeared as perfect white).
7.19 p.m.	Movement can be seen about German Reserve line
7.25 p.m.	Golden rain rockets opposite both Battalions.
7.44 p.m.	A lot of movement over our lines. Right Battalion. Groups of men.
7.45 p.m.	Enemy attacking.
7.52 p.m.	Enemy have overrun Right Battalion, probably also left.
7.50 p.m.	Telephone message was O.C. 1st L.N.Lancs.Regt. that he was holding West of canal as his front line.
7.55 p.m.	O.C. 1st L.N.Lancs.Regt. reported by telephone that a few of the 2nd K.R.R.C. had swam across the River and report they are absolutely overrun.
Untimed.	Enemy have reached BARE SUPPORT and SISTON LANE roughly. Dugouts burning, prisoners going back. Enemy apparently waiting.
Telephone message.	Small party of 2nd K.R.R.C. putting up a fight close to Battalion Headquarters.
8.15 p.m.	Enemy advancing in extended order to water at M.15.c.
8.20 p.m.	Enemy working round our left at M.14.b.5.5.
8.50 p.m.	Small group of our men behind river barricade about Eastern end of No.1.Bridge.
8.45 p.m.	Dugout near Right Battalion H.Q. burning.
8.57 p.m.	Golden rain rockets opposite Left Battalion.
9. 4 p.m.	Large enemy party at M.14.b.5.5. also Machine Gun. Probably local H.Q. Many messengers.

9.10 p.m.   Enemy at N.14.b.5.5. Advancing slightly and reinforcing
             firing line.
9.15 p.m.   Enemy crossed BACK WALK on our extreme left making for
             BEACH AVENUE. Think trying to surround Battalion H.Q.
9.30 p.m.   Field guns appear to have been brought into position
             behind the sand dunes.
11.10 p.m.   About 40 "BOSH" are holding Eastern end of No.1.Bridge.
             Enemy holding Right Bank of Canal between No.2 & 3 Bridges.
1.35 a.m.   Captains BUTLER & SMITH and Lieut. GRACIE and
             Artillery Liaison Officer have swum back. They report
             enemy digging hard by BIRD RESERVE. They think this
             will be his main line of resistance. Could artillery
             get on please. Enemy also active round KITCHENS.

        The extracts given above are only on points of particular
interest.

4. INFANTRY.

        The hostile infantry attacked in three waves, each wave
consisting of a line of groups of men. Each group estimated at
between 6 & 8 men strong. They are reported by survivors from
the Right Battalion to have debouched from their lines at the
junction of the Battalion front, i.e., about N.15.b.20.25. and
to have split into two, one half going to their left and
working down BASE TRENCH and the other half to their right
towards Right Battalion Headquarters at N.15.d.25.65. The
enemy is believed to have reached the Battalion Headquarters in
about an hour. The enemy infantry carried out their assault
under a creeping barrage.

        Against the Left Battalion the enemy is believed to have
attacked in groups over the top and to have had a particularly
large working party along the coast.

        As will be seen in the messages given in para. 3 the first
rear observers saw of the enemy was groups of men on the whole
front simultaneously. These groups were in three waves and
after the first creeping barrage of the assault there was a
distinct lull in the hostile artillery fire, though a slow
barrage was maintained on the bridges and NIEUPORT BAINS.

        Parties of the enemy carried small flammenwerfer which
were used for firing dugouts. Smoke bombs are reported to
have been used, and also "stick handle" bombs. They wore
grey uniforms with steel helmets and either wore white or
yellow armlets according as to whether they were bombers or
flammenwerfer carriers.

        The enemy is believed to have used light machine guns
as he swept the whole length of the N.E. bank of the YSER
from the dunes whilst another machine gun near the left
Battalion Headquarters took a large party of "C" Coy. 1st
Northamptonshire Regt. in the rear. The machine gun reported
by observer at N.14.b.5.5. had a heavy mounting resembling our
Vickers Gun tripod; the mounting being carried separately by
one man.

        Officers who succeeded in getting back estimated our
casualties in killed and wounded at the moment of attack
as being from 70% to 80% of the effectives. The majority
of the dugouts were blown in and their occupants either
killed, wounded or imprisoned. The trenches were in most
places nearly levelled and the communication trenches
hopelessly blocked. That there was considerable resistance
offered was evident from the fact that many of the enemy
groups extended, stopped or proceeded cautiously from time to
time, but actually fighting was impossible to observe from O.Os.
owing to smoke.

        Survivors of "C" Company of the 1st Northamptonshire Regt.
state that their company resisted until practically all of them
were knocked out, and the remnant almost surrounded. A few of
these managed to escape across the river. There are no
survivors from the other companies. The enemy penetrated into
NOSE TRENCH and NOSE SUPPORT on the right. The Battalion
Scout Sergeant escaped by making his way round to the Battalion

Headquarters of the Border Regt. (left Battn, 32nd Div), informed them of the situation and told them that the enemy were working their way round behind them. The Officer Commanding this Battalion at once formed a defensive flank and strong points thereby stopping a further advance on the enemy's part.

At about 8.30 a.m. a party, apparently officers, were seen near Right Battalion H.Q. fighting at close quarters till the last.

On the Left Front the enemy appeared to be seriously held up about SISTOW LANE as there was another short artillery preparation (directed by very lights from aeroplanes) and another distinct attack where the Reserve Company of the 2nd K.R.R.Corps appeared to make their stand.

Survivors who passed close by here report seeing many dead Germans and a considerable number of our men killed in the open. They report that at the Regimental Aid Post of the 2nd K.R.R.Corps the enemy bombed stretcher bearers and wounded.

The signal for lifting the hostile barrage appeared to be golden rain rockets.

The Machine Gun Officer who collected a party of 30 men at the river barricade, threw his gun into the river before crossing to prevent it falling into the hands of the enemy.

A party of about 16 men of the 2nd K.R.R.Corps who were unable to get out of their dugout on the 10th had two smoke bombs thrown in amongst them by the enemy who molested them no further. On the 11th they got out of their dugout and succeeded in getting making their way back across the river.

5. CASUALTIES. The following numbers of all ranks were East of the River, not including Machine Gun Company, Trench Mortar Batteries and Tunnelling Company.

	East of YSER.		Rejoined.		Casualties.	
	Off.	O.R.	Off.	O.R.	Off.	O.R.
1st Northamptonshire Regt.	20	508	0	9	20	499
2nd K.R.R.Corps.	20	501	3	46	17	455
TOTAL.	40	1009	3	55	37	954

6. AIRCRAFT. Hostile aircraft flew over our lines during the lulls in the bombardment, and when the enemy infantry attacked they flew very low over the whole area firing machine guns. The bridges over the YSER were barraged by them with machine gun fire. They directed artillery fire by very lights and they are reported to have opened fire (machine gun) on slightest movement East of the River during the preliminary bombardment.

7. OUR ARTILLERY. The Divisional Artillery was firing continuously throughout the day.

Counter Preparation was ordered at 10.45 a.m. and was continued more or less throughout the day, though later some of the Heavy Artillery was employed on neutralising fire, but without causing much diminution of enemy's fire.

There can be little doubt that the enemy has adapted the same tactics as have been so successfully employed by us in attack lately, but with the extra advantage that we were provided with dugouts which were not shell proof, with trenches never very good and much damaged, and that our aeroplane arrangements were so incomplete that the enemy were at entire liberty in the air, and we obtained no information of any value from our own Air Service.

For the same reason the Counter-Battery work appeared far less effective than is generally the case.

(sd). G.C.KEMP,
Brigadier General
Commanding 2nd Infantry Brigade

14th July, 1917.

WAR DIARY.

(WITH APPENDICES).

1st,. NORTHAMPTONSHIRE REGIMENT.

2nd. INFANTRY BRIGADE.

1st. DIVISION.

AUGUST.1917.

Army Form C. 2118.

WAR DIARY
of 1st Warwickshire Regt.
INTELLIGENCE SUMMARY.

(Erase heading not required.)

Instructions regarding War Diaries and Intelligence Summaries are contained in F.S. Regs., Part II. and the Staff Manual respectively. Title pages will be prepared in manuscript.

Place	Date	Hour	Summary of Events and Information	Remarks and references to Appendices
Le Clifton Camp	August 1st		Boys parade independently, skirmishing and attacking formation. Boys attack strong point in the afternoon.	
	2nd		Lecture to all officers C.S.M's and Platoon Sgts in the afternoon.	
	3rd		Inspection of Battalion by Co. (Major Rackham) followed by special march.	
	4th		Boy attack strong point lead to C.B.S.F. Boys rifle exam firing, all inspectors and reinforcements finishing	
	5th		All Coys fire on field firing range, then on firing by training. Phase 5 to 7 joint battalion.	
	6th		Brigade church parade. Deputy Chaplain General conducted the service.	
		morning	Manoeuvre formations practised afternoon rifle and private section attacking	
	7th		General action - lewis gun firing. Bombing, sections retiring. 2nd & 5.7.F musketry practices.	
	8th		Specials training & church parades, morning firing 2nd & A.S.S. Bayonet exam Battalion	
	9th		All testing and grenade practice, firing 2nd & 5.S. Bayonet exam Battalion	
			sent were out on tactics. Manoeuvres practised in the afternoon.	
	10th		Training on lewis gun by training. Manoeuvres practised in the afternoon. B.O.B inspection	
			Rifle exam cont'd of C.S. Coys. Afternoon rifle parade action on the guns.	
	11th		2.30 - 2 Batt's afternoon general training in the afternoon	
	12th		5.30 to T.B. Pakington's pond	
	13th		Coy training 9-12 am general training in the afternoon	
			Voluntary service at 8.30 am.	
	14th		Manoeuvre practice 8.30-12 am. Afternoon specialist training except D. Coy and	
			Coy firing at rifle range at 6 Coy. Att'd in the afternoon.	
	15th		Coy training in the morning. Battalion half holiday. Except C.S. C & Coys Brigade horns	
			Route march in the morning. Afternoon rest.	
	16th		Tournament in the afternoon. Drill and manoeuvres practised in the afternoon.	
	17th		Specialist training in the morning. All coys field firing on the range in the afternoon	
	18th		Special training 12noon - 6 am on the 18th to 18th at 7 p.m.	
			No parade.	

Army Form C. 2118.

WAR DIARY
of 1st Northamptonshire Regt
INTELLIGENCE SUMMARY.
(Erase heading not required.)

Instructions regarding War Diaries and Intelligence Summaries are contained in F. S. Regs., Part II. and the Staff Manual respectively. Title pages will be prepared in manuscript.

Place	Date	Hour	Summary of Events and Information	Remarks and references to Appendices
	19		Brigade Church parade.	
	20		Company training in the morning. Ceremonial drill 2 pm to 4.30 pm.	
	21		2nd & 3rd Brigade race meeting in Jarna commenced. Friends from Thomas & 2 noon.	
			C/Col J. Caird of the 50th of the 50th to the 50th to the 50th.	
	22	8.20.12	Preparations for the attack. Lay all morning. Dotailed parades in the afternoon.	
	23		Morning Coy training and the usual training in the afternoon. Div & Bde parades.	
	24		Morning Coy training and the usual the division. Afternoon Coy training.	
	25		Returned to ceremonial parade. Made Coy training. The Army commander.	
	26		Divisional ceremonial parade. Divisional parades at 9 o'clock.	
	27	2pm & 6.50 pm	As per Corps Divisional parades. Morning Coy training. Coy training in afternoon.	
	28		Special return by Brig & Coms 9 am. New arrangements for use of trench. Dept of 6 R joined the Battn.	
	29		Route march. Cancelled owing to very wet weather 5 to 6 very wet.	
	30		No parades except Recreational training from 12-30 pm. Draft of 18 O.R. joined Battn.	
	31		Route march. Start 8.20. Arrived back 12.45 pm. Draft 1 Offr 10, NCOs 15, Privates 75.	
			Special attack scheme. Cooperation with No. 19 Inf Brigade.	

Capt Col.

1ST BATTALION, THE NORTHAMPTONSHIRE REGIMENT.

1917 Appendix.

August   **LE CLIPON.**

1st   Coys. parade independently, skirmishing and artillery formation. "B" Coy. attack strong point under C.O. Lecture for all Officers, C.S.M's and platoon Sgts. in the afternoon.

2nd   Inspection of battalion by Col. (Major Rackhouse) followed by route march.

3rd   "B" Coy. attack strong point under C.O. A. B & C Coys. rifle section firing. All bombers and Lewis Gunners fire & throw bombs.

4th   All Coys. fire on field firing range. When not firing Coy. training. Draft of 8 O.R. joined battalion.

5th   Brigade church parade. Deputy Chaplain General conducted the service.

6th   Morning. Manoeuvre formation practised. Afternoon, rifle and grenade sections rifle firing. Lewis Gun sections Lewis Gun firing. Bombing section, wiring. 2nd Lt. J.F.E. Monckton joined the Bn.

7th   Specialist training during the morning. Tactical scheme in the afternoon.

8th   All bombing and grenade sections bombing under 2nd Lt. Martin, Lewis Gun sections on range, training when sections not bombing or firing. 2nd Lt. A.S.S. Bayley joined battalion.

9th   Rifle sections & L.G's fire. Coy. training. Manoeuvres practised in the afternoon.

10th   8.30 - 12. outposts. Afternoon rifle grenade sections threw live grenades. G.O.C's inspection.

1917   Appendix.

August

10th (contd)   2nd Lt. J.B. Pilkington joined.

11th   Coy. training 9 - 12 noon. Special training in the afternoon.

12th   Voluntary service at 8.30 a.m.

13th   Manoeuvre practice 8.30 - 12 noon. Afternoon specialist training, draft of 5 O.R. joined. Capt. Pickering assumed command of A Coy.

14th   Coy. training in the morning. Battalion in the attack in the afternoon.

15th   Route march in the morning. Afternoon half holiday, draft of 5 O.R. joined. Brigade boxing Tournament in the afternoon.

16th   Specialist training in the morning. Drill and maneouvre practice in the afternoon.

17th   Specialist training in the morning. All Coys. field firing on the range in the afternoon. Night operations 12 pm - 6 am on the 18th, Draft of 7 O.R.

18th   No parade.

19th   Brigade church parade.

20th   Coy. training in the morning. Ceremonial drill 2 pm to 4.30 p.m.

21st   2nd & 3rd Brigade have rehearsal for Divnl Ceremonial parade from 8.40 am - 12 noon. Capt. J. Clark M.C. struck off the strength on being posted to the 204th Employment Coy.

22nd   8.30 - 12. Battalion on the attack. A. Coy. act as enemy. Specialist training in the afternoon.

1917 Appendix.

August

23rd   Wet day. Coy. training and specialist Training in the afternoon. Draft of 5 O.R. joined.

24th   Rehearsal for ceremonial parade by the division, Afternoon coy. training.

25th   Divisional ceremonial parade. March past before the Army Commander.

26th   2 offrs & 60 O.R. per coy. church parade at 9.45 a.m.

27th   Special scheme by coys. from 9 - 11 a.m. 11 a.m. specialist training; coy. training in afternoon.

28th   Route march, cancelled owing to very bad weather. Draft of 6 O.R. joined Battn.

29th   No parade except recreational training from 5 - 6. Very wet.

30th   Route march. Start 8.30 a.m. arrived back 12.45 p.m. Draft of 6 O.R. joined battn.

31st   Special attack scheme. Co-operation with motor M.G., M.G. Coy. T. Mortars & R.E.

                                  A.St. G. COLDWELL.

Fourth Army No. G.S. 843.

1st Division.

     I want to let the Division know how pleased I was with their appearance on parade this morning. The turn out of all ranks was particularly good, the handling of the arms was very smart and the march past struck me as quite excellent especially in three battalions which marched with a swing and a precision I have seldom seen equalled.

4.

It is very evident that there is a high standard of discipline maintained in all units and I congratulate the Division as a whole on their fine spirit and soldier-like appearance on parade. Whatever duty they may be called upon to perform I know that they will do it right well and that none could do it better.

(Signed) H. RAWLINSON,
General.
Commanding Fourth Army.

H.Q. Fourth Army.
25th August, 1917.

1st Division No. 7722.

ALL UNITS.

The Divisional Commander desires that the message of the Army Commander should be conveyed to all ranks of the 1st Division.
A copy should be posted in all Canteens and Recreation Rooms.
He wishes to congratulate all ranks on their very smart turn-out, and on the Parade generally. Considering that little or no practice has been carried out, the results were particularly good.
In this, as in all other respects, the 1st Division has more than upheld its reputation.

(Signed) H. SPENDER CLAY,

Lieutenant Colonel.
AA & QMG. 1st Division.

August 25th, 1917.

Copies.

Fourth Army No. G.S.843.

1st Division.

I want to let the 1st Division know how pleased I was with their appearance on parade this morning. The turn out of all ranks was particularly good, the handling of the arms was very smart and the march past struck me as quite excellent, especially in three battalions which marched with a swing and a precision I have seldom seen equalled.

It is very evident that there is a high standard of discipline maintained in all units and I congratulate the Division as a whole on their fine spirit and soldier-like appearance on parade. Whatever duty they may be called upon to perform I know that they will do it right well and that none could do it better.

(Signed) H. RAWLINSON,
General,
Commanding Fourth Army.

H.Q., Fourth Army,
25th August 1917.

1st Division No. 7722.

ALL UNITS.

The Divisional Commander desires that the message of the Army Commander should be conveyed to all ranks of the 1st Division.

A copy should be posted in all Canteens and Recreation Rooms.

He wishes to congratulate all ranks on their very smart turn-out, and on the Parade generally. Considering that little or no practice has been carried out, the results were particularly good.

In this, as in all other respects, the 1st Division has more than upheld its reputation.

(Signed) H. SPENDER CLAY.

Lieutenant Colonel.

AA & QM.G. 1st Division.

August 25th 1917.

Army Form C. 2118.

WAR DIARY
or
INTELLIGENCE SUMMARY.
(Erase heading not required.)

WAR DIARY
or
INTELLIGENCE SUMMARY.

Army Form C. 2118.

(Erase heading not required.)

Instructions regarding War Diaries and Intelligence Summaries are contained in F.S. Regs., Part II. and the Staff Manual respectively. Title pages will be prepared in manuscript.

Place	Date	Hour	Summary of Events and Information	Remarks and references to Appendices
	19		Regimental guard paraded.	
	20		Training in the morning. Regimental tactics & P.O. Ex's 3 & 4.	
	21		2nd Brigade launched attack on Jaffa. Advanced Brigade form Reserve 8am — 2.30pm.	
	22		9.30 No.3 Coy & M.G.s attack the village of Deir. Supported by the 2nd Inf. Bn. Coy.	
	23		Bn. training and Musical Ride. Parade to see the afternoon training of the Division	
	24		Rehearsal for Ceremonial parade to be held ??????	
	25		Divisional Ceremonial parade. March past the Commander-in-Chief	
	26	9am to 10.30	Bn. on tactical scheme	
	27	6am to 9am	Bn. on tactical scheme	
			Route march. Arrived in camp at 3pm	
	28		No parade. Usual reveille Reveille from 5.6. noc acts	
	29		Route march. Started 8.30am, arrived back 12.45pm	
	30		????????????	
	31		????????????	

1ST BATTALION. THE NORTHAMPTONSHIRE REGIMENT.

1917   Appendix.

August   **LE CLIPON.**

1st — Coys. parade independently. skirmishing and artillery formation. "B" Coy. attack strong point under C.O. Lecture for all Officers, C.S.M's and platoon Sgts. in the afternoon.

2nd — Inspection of battalion by Col. (Major Backhouse) followed by route march.

3rd — "B" Coy. attack strong point under C.O. A. B & C Coys. rifle section firing. All bombers and Lewis Gunners fire & throw bombs.

4th — All Coys. fire on field firing range. When not firing Coy. training. Draft of 8 O.R. joined battalion.

5th — Brigade church parade. Deputy Chaplain General conducted the service.

6th — Morning. Manoeuvres formation practised. Afternoon, rifle and grenade sections rifle firing. Lewis Gun sections Lewis Gun firing. Bombing section, wiring. 2nd Lt. J.P.E. Monckton joined the Bn.

7th — Specialist training during the morning. Tactical scheme in the afternoon.

8th — All bombing and grenade sections bombing under 2nd Lt. Martin. Lewis Gun sections on range. training when sections not bombing or firing. 2nd Lt. A.C.S. Bagley joined battalion.

9th — Rifle sections & L.G's fire. Coy. training. Manoeuvres practised in the afternoon.

10th — 8.30 - 12. outposts. Afternoon rifle grenade sections threw live grenades. G.O.C's inspection.

1917   Appendix.

August

10th (contd)   2nd Lt. J.B. Pilkington joined.

11th   Coy. training 9 - 12 noon.
                Special training in the
                afternoon.

12th   Voluntary service at 8.30 a.m.

13th   Manoeuvre practice 8.30 - 12
                noon. Afternoon specialist
                training, draft of 5 O.R. joined.
                Capt. Pickering assumed command
                of A Coy.

14th   Coy. training in the morning.
                Battalion in the attack in the
                afternoon.

15th   Route march in the morning.
                Afternoon half holiday, draft
                of 5 O.R. joined. Brigade
                boxing Tournament in the
                afternoon.

16th   Specialist training in the
                morning. Drill and manoeuvre
                practice in the afternoon.

17th   Specialist training in the
                morning. All Coys. field
                firing on the range in the
                afternoon. Night operations
                12 pm - 6 am on the 18th, Draft
                of 7 O.R.

18th   No parade.

19th   Brigade church parade.

20th   Coy. training in the morning.
                Ceremonial drill 2 pm to 4.30
                p.m.

21st   2nd & 3rd Brigade have rehearsal
                for Divnl Ceremonial parade
                from 8.40 am - 12 noon.
                Capt. J. Clark M.O. struck off
                the strength on being posted to
                the 204th Employment Coy.

22nd   8.30 - 12. Battalion on the
                attack. A. Coy. act as enemy.
                Specialist training in the
                afternoon.

2.

Appendix.

1917

August

23rd — Wet day. Coy. training and specialist training in the afternoon. Draft of 5 O.R. joined.

24th — Rehearsal for ceremonial parade by the division. Afternoon coy. training.

25th — Divisional ceremonial parade. March past before the Army Commander.

26th — 2 offrs & 60 O.R. per coy. church parade at 9.45 a.m.

27th — Special scheme by coys. from 9 – 11 a.m. 11 a.m. specialist training; coy. training in afternoon.

28th — Route march, cancelled owing to very bad weather. Draft of 6 O.R. joined Battn.

29th — No parade except recreational training from 5 – 6. Very wet.

30th — Route march. Start 8.30 a.m. arrived back 12.45 p.m. Draft of 6 O.R. joined battn.

31st — Special attack scheme. Co-operation with motor M.G., M.G. Coy. T. Mortars & R.E.

A. St. G. COLDWELL.

Fourth Army No. G.S. 843.

1st Division.

I want to let the Division know how pleased I was with their appearance on parade this morning. The turn out of all ranks was particularly good, the handling of the arms was very smart and the march past struck me as quite excellent especially in three battalions which marched with a swing and a precision I have seldom seen equalled.

4.

It is very evident that there is a high standard of discipline maintained in all units and I congratulate the Division as a whole on their fine spirit and soldier-like appearance on parade. Whatever duty they may be called upon to perform I know that they will do it right well and that none could do it better.

(Signed) H. RAWLINSON.
General.
Commanding Fourth Army.

H.Q. Fourth Army.
25th August, 1917.

1st Division No. 7748.

ALL UNITS.

The Divisional Commander desires that the message of the Army Commander should be conveyed to all ranks of the 1st Division.

A copy should be posted in all Canteens and Recreation Rooms.

He wishes to congratulate all ranks on their very smart turn-out, and on the Parade generally. Considering that little or no practice has been carried out, the results were particularly good.

In this, as in all other respects, the 1st Division has more than upheld its reputation.

(Signed) H. SPENCER CLAY.
Lieutenant Colonel.
AA & QMG. 1st Division.

August 25th, 1917.

1ST BATTALION. THE NORTHAMPTONSHIRE REGIMENT.

1917   Appendix.

August   **LE CLIPON.**

1st   Coys. parade independently, skirmishing and artillery formation. "B" Coy. attack strong point under C.O. Lecture for all Officers. C.S.M's and platoon Sgts. in the afternoon.

2nd   Inspection of battalion by Col. (Major Ackhouse) followed by route march.

3rd   "B" Coy. attack strong point under C.O. A. B & C Coys. rifle section firing. All bombers and Lewis Gunners fire & throw bombs.

4th   All Coys. fire on field firing range. When not firing Coy. training. Draft of 8 O.R. joined battalion.

5th   Brigade church parade. Deputy Chaplain General conducted the service.

6th   Morning. Manoeuvre formation practised. Afternoon, rifle and grenade sections rifle firing. Lewis Gun sections Lewis Gun firing. Bombing section, wiring. 2nd Lt. J.F.R. Monckton joined the Bn.

7th   Specialist training during the morning. Tactical scheme in the afternoon.

8th   All bombing and grenade sections bombing under 2nd Lt. Martin. Lewis Gun sections on range, training when sections not bombing or firing. 2nd Lt. A.S.S. Bagley joined battalion.

9th   Rifle sections & L.G's fire. Coy. training. Manoeuvres practised in the afternoon.

10th   8.30 - 12. outposts. Afternoon rifle grenade sections threw live grenades. G.O.C's inspection.

1917   Appendix.

August

10th (contd)   2nd Lt. J.B. Pilkington joined.

11th   Coy. training 9 - 12 noon.
        Special training in the
        afternoon.

12th   Voluntary service at 8.30 a.m.

13th   Manoeuvre practice 8.30 - 12
        noon. Afternoon specialist
        training, draft of 5 O.R. joined.
        Capt. Pickering assumed command
        of A Coy.

14th   Coy. training in the morning.
        Battalion in the attack in the
        afternoon.

15th   Route march in the morning.
        Afternoon half holiday. draft
        of 5 O.R. joined. Brigade
        boxing Tournament in the
        afternoon.

16th   Specialist training in the
        morning. Drill and manoeuvre
        practice in the afternoon.

17th   Specialist training in the
        morning. All Coys. field
        firing on the range in the
        afternoon. Night operations
        12 pm - 6 am on the 18th. Draft
        of 7 O.R.

18th   No parade.

19th   Brigade church parade.

20th   Coy. training in the morning.
        Ceremonial drill 2 pm to 4.30
        p.m.

21st   2nd & 3rd Brigade have rehearsal
        for Rival Ceremonial parade
        from 8.40 am - 12 noon.
        Capt. J. Clark M.O. struck off
        the strength on being posted to
        the 204th Employment Coy.

22nd   8.30 - 12. Battalion on the
        attack. A. Coy. act as enemy.
        Specialist training in the
        afternoon.

1917   Appendix.

August

23rd   Wet day. Coy. training and
            specialist Training in the
            afternoon. Draft of 5 O.R.
            joined.

24th   Rehearsal for ceremonial
            parade by the division.
            Afternoon coy. training.

25th   Divisional ceremonial parade.
            March past before the Army
            Commander.

26th   2 offrs & 60 O.R. per coy.
            church parade at 9.45 a.m.

27th   Special scheme by coys. from
            9 - 11 a.m. 11 a.m. specialist
            training; coy. training in
            afternoon.

28th   Route march, cancelled owing
            to very bad weather. Draft
            of 5 O.R. joined Battn.

29th   No parade except recreational
            training from 5 - 6. Very
            wet.

30th   Route march. Start 9.30 a.m.
            arrived back 12.45 p.m.
            Draft of 6 O.R. joined battn.

31st   Special attack scheme.
            Co-operation with motor M.G.,
            M.G. Coy. T. Mortars & A.E.

                                            A.St. G. COLDWELL.

                                            Fourth Army No. G.S. 843.

1st Division.

        I want to let the Division know how pleased
I was with their appearance on parade this morning.
The turn out of all ranks was particularly good, the
handling of the arms was very smart and the march past
struck me as quite excellent especially in three
battalions which marched with a swing and a precision
I have seldom seen equalled.

4.

It is very evident that there is a high standard of discipline maintained in all units and I congratulate the Division as a whole on their fine spirit and soldier-like appearance on parade. Whatever duty they may be called upon to perform I know that they will do it right well and that none could do it better.

(Signed) H. RAWLINSON,
General.
Commanding Fourth Army.

H.Q. Fourth Army.
25th August, 1917.

1st Division No. 7732.

ALL UNITS.

The Divisional Commander desires that the message of the Army Commander should be conveyed to all ranks of the 1st Division.

A copy should be posted in all Canteens and Recreation Rooms.

He wishes to congratulate all ranks on their very smart turn-out, and on the Parade generally. Considering that little or no practice has been carried out, the results were particularly good.

In this, as in all other respects, the 1st Division has more than upheld its reputation.

(Signed) H. SPENDER CLAY.

Lieutenant Colonel.
AA & QMG. 1st Division.

August 25th, 1917.

1ST BATTALION, THE NORTHAMPTONSHIRE REGIMENT.

1917　　　　　　　　　　　　　　　　　　　　　　　　Appendix.

August　　　LE CLIPON.

1st　　　Coys. parade independently, skirmishing and artillery formation. "B" Coy. attack strong point under C.O. Lecture for all Officers, C.S.M's and platoon Sgts. in the afternoon.

2nd　　　Inspection of battalion by Col. (Major Rackhouse) followed by route march.

3rd　　　"B" Coy. attack strong point under C.O. A. B & C Coys. rifle section firing. All bombers and Lewis Gunners fire & throw bombs.

4th　　　All Coys. fire on field firing range. When not firing Coy. training. Draft of 8 O.R. joined battalion.

5th　　　Brigade church parade. Deputy Chaplain General conducted the service.

6th　　　Morning. Manoeuvre formation practised. Afternoon, rifle and grenade sections rifle firing. Lewis Gun sections Lewis Gun firing. Bombing section, wiring. 2nd Lt. J.F.E. Monckton joined the Bn.

7th　　　Specialist training during the morning. Tactical scheme in the afternoon.

8th　　　All bombing and grenade sections bombing under 2nd Lt. Martin, Lewis Gun sections on range, training when sections not bombing or firing. 2nd Lt. A.S.S. Bayley joined battalion.

9th　　　Rifle sections & L.G's fire. Coy. training. Manoeuvres practised in the afternoon.

10th　　　8.30 - 12. outposts. Afternoon rifle grenade sections threw live grenades. G.O.C's inspection.

1917 Appendix.

August

10th (contd) — 2nd Lt. J.B. Pilkington joined.

11th — Coy. training 9 - 12 noon. Special training in the afternoon.

12th — Voluntary service at 8.30 a.m.

13th — Manoeuvre practice 8.30 - 12 noon. Afternoon specialist training, draft of 5 O.R. joined. Capt. Pickering assumed command of A Coy.

14th — Coy. training in the morning. Battalion in the attack in the afternoon.

15th — Route march in the morning. Afternoon half holiday, draft of 5 O.R. joined. Brigade boxing Tournament in the afternoon.

16th — Specialist training in the morning. Drill and manoeuvre practice in the afternoon.

17th — Specialist training in the morning. All Coys. field firing on the range in the afternoon. Night operations 12 pm - 6 am on the 18th, Draft of 7 O.R.

18th — No parade.

19th — Brigade church parade.

20th — Coy. training in the morning. Ceremonial drill 2 pm to 4.30 p.m.

21st — 2nd & 3rd Brigade have rehearsal for Divnl Ceremonial parade from 8.40 am - 12 noon. Capt. J. Clark M.C. struck off the strength on being posted to the 204th Employment Coy.

22nd — 8.30 - 12. Battalion on the attack. A. Coy. act as enemy. Specialist training in the afternoon.

1917   Appendix.

August

23rd   Wet day. Coy. training and
        specialist Training in the
        afternoon. Draft of 5 O.R.
        joined.

24th   Rehearsal for ceremonial
        parade by the division,
        Afternoon coy. training.

25th   Divisional ceremonial parade.
        March past before the Army
        Commander.

26th   2 offrs & 60 O.R. per coy.
        church parade at 9.45 a.m.

27th   Special scheme by coys. from
        9 - 11 a.m. 11 a.m. specialist
        training; coy. training in
        afternoon.

28th   Route march, cancelled owing
        to very bad weather. Draft
        of 6 O.R. joined Battn.

29th   No parade except recreational
        training from 5 - 6. Very
        wet.

30th   Route march. Start 8.30 a.m.
        arrived back 12.45 p.m.
        Draft of 6 O.R. joined battn.

31st   Special attack scheme.
        Co-operation with motor M.G.,
        M.G. Coy. T. Mortars & R.E.

                                    A.St. G. COLDWELL.

                                    Fourth Army No. G.S. 843.

1st Division.

I want to let the Division know how pleased
I was with their appearance on parade this morning.
The turn out of all ranks was particularly good, the
handling of the arms was very smart and the march past
struck me as quite excellent especially in three
battalions which marched with a swing and a precision
I have seldom seen equalled.

It is very evident that there is a high standard of discipline maintained in all units and I congratulate the Division as a whole on their fine spirit and soldier-like appearance on parade. Whatever duty they may be called upon to perform I know that they will do it right well and that none could do it better.

(Signed) H. RAWLINSON,
General.
Commanding Fourth Army.

H.Q. Fourth Army.
25th August, 1917.

1st Division No. 7722.

ALL UNITS.

The Divisional Commander desires that the message of the Army Commander should be conveyed to all ranks of the 1st Division.

A copy should be posted in all Canteens and Recreation Rooms.

He wishes to congratulate all ranks on their very smart turn-out, and on the Parade generally. Considering that little or no practice has been carried out, the results were particularly good.

In this, as in all other respects, the 1st Division has more than upheld its reputation.

(Signed) H. SPENDER CLAY,

Lieutenant Colonel.
AA & QMG. 1st Division.

August 25th, 1917.

WAR DIARY.

1st. NORTHAMPTONSHIRE REGIMENT.

2nd. INFANTRY BRIGADE.

1st. DIVISION.

SEPTEMBER. 1917.

Army Form C. 2118.

WAR DIARY
or
INTELLIGENCE SUMMARY.

of 1/7th O. & B. Staffordshire Regt.

(Erase heading not required.)

Instructions regarding War Diaries and Intelligence Summaries are contained in F. S. Regs., Part II. and the Staff Manual respectively. Title pages will be prepared in manuscript.

Place	Date	Hour	Summary of Events and Information	Remarks and references to Appendices
Helipon	20.		Marched as usual. Relieved training in afternoon. B coy night operations D/463.	
	21.		R. & V. quick train.	
	22.		Attack scheme. Open to dose, movement of R.B.C's. Trip over the general. Parts smart-drilled.	
	23.		Officer staff ride.	
	24.		Lager 600ft per coy, Cheval frise & brush. Race meeting in the afternoon (2 and 3 coy).	
			Officer scheme. Draft of 5/24 o.r. joined Battn. Special training in the morning. Officers	
			training in the afternoon.	
	25.		Attack practice.	
	26.		Public. Let. on outposts. 5th Bn. Kitcham. 1/2 a.m. to 12 p.m. myself proceeded with Lieut.	
			Painter, Squires, Brown Jones.	
	27.		Brigade practice attack scheme. 2nd Lieut's and Jones jones Bathalion	
	28.		10 officers join our staff ride. Remainder to Pion camp. Placed turning morning & training	
			Officer staff ride for 1/24 officer did not go on 28th. Recruits in camp.	
	29.		Weeds Machine (Lewis) section was inspected by 8th Yorkshires. Dep. 0/40 or joined on 2 0 3	
			Inspection the Major Mitchel.	
	30.		Deff. 60 or church parade.	

A. P. C. Moore
Lt. Col.

Army Form C. 2118

WAR DIARY
of 1st Northamptonshire Regt
INTELLIGENCE SUMMARY.
(Erase heading not required.)

Instructions regarding War Diaries and Intelligence Summaries are contained in F. S. Regs. Part II. and the Staff Manual respectively. Title pages will be prepared in manuscript.

Place	Date	Hour	Summary of Events and Information	Remarks and references to Appendices
Aldershot Camp	Sept 1		Staff war for all officers, C.S.M's and platoon Sergts. OC Coys & other offrs on coy scheme. Kit inspection etc. A class & SGP joined the Battalion.	
	2		Brigade Church parade 9.30am and 10 a.m. for coy attd.	
	3		As before scheme in the morning 2.30 a.m. specialist training	
	4		Specialist training as before, and afternoon.	
	5		Morning protection on the move. New arms drill parts afternoon & kitting	
	6		Road-making on the morning & general specialist training. 11.30 a.m. Draft of 50R joined the Battalion	
	7		Usual field day. Got back to camp.	
	8		Co dispose in march of order. Afternoon rest.	
	9		Co dispose in perspective planes.	
	10		2 Bn & 60 or per co perspective planes.	
	11		C Coys field firing and practice advance and flank guards. A & B field firing. 3 reupl (Irishmen)	
	12		C & D Coys field firing and practice advance and flank guards. A & B field firing. 3 reupl (Irishmen) 30 R joined Battn	
	13		A & B Coy Coy exid on New advance and transport as in train. Reveille by the corp bugler.	
	14		Baptized from 6th A,5 Bn, etc. the Draws. Br the Regl organization 1915. Afternoon 1914.	
	15		8.30 out foot scheme (C-C) advance & firing rear part. Afternoon Band officers and NCO's 8 went officers & about observer cameras apparatus in the Kite Half war. In the morning and afternoon. 8 went officers & about to aeroplane at night	
	16		Usual training in the morning. 3 & D R.S.C. Mor. C D & D went 5 miles of equivalent & equiv to A MESS of ARS out Princess 110.	
	17		Retention exercise in every to the 3 & D R.S.C. Mor. C D & D went 5 miles of equiv & A MESS of ARS on or on Princess	
	18		Usual. Moved back. Reveille 6.00 am. Naval officers and men arrived & practiced spirit in the trenches	
	19		10. Rifle and Equipment inspection in the morning. Special training in afternoon 2.30 pm.	
	20		9.30 to 10 Church Parade	
	21		Serve in morning and demonstration in the morning. Specialist training in afternoon.	
	22		Advanced guard and rearguard. Officer specialist training as on one day.	
	23		R.S. Training officer inspection rank recruits. Morning Musketry middle issue on day.	

A W Critchett
Lt Col

WAR DIARY.

1st. NORTHAMPTONSHIRE REGIMENT.

2nd. INFANTRY BRIGADE.

1st. DIVISION.

OCTOBER. 1917.

WAR DIARY
or
INTELLIGENCE SUMMARY.
(Erase heading not required.)

Army Form C. 2118.

Vol. 37

OCT 1917

Instructions regarding War Diaries and Intelligence Summaries are contained in F. S. Regs., Part II. and the Staff Manual respectively. Title pages will be prepared in manuscript.

Place	Date	Hour	Summary of Events and Information	Remarks and references to Appendices

[Handwritten entries illegible]

WAR DIARY or INTELLIGENCE SUMMARY

Army Form C. 2118.

1/5th Northampton Yeomanry (?)

Place	Date	Hour	Summary of Events and Information	Remarks and references to Appendices
Bulford	18		Specialist Training	
	19		"	
	20		Fired to Trench Attack. Proceeded on voyage abroad	
	21		1970 to on jetty. Boys proceed to Moascar	
Ismailia	22		Battalion inspected by Lt Gen Sir B.T. Righam, draw kit at Ordnance ??	
	23		Battalion equipment for Turkey	
	24		Coys B Novelin proceed near Belmontos ?? an outpost draws kits & enfield rifle & bayonet	
Hill 70	25		March to H 70 by rail. No foreringers ??	
Hill 70	26		W.O. and platoon drill. Dumps up camp.	
"	27		See about ???	
"	28		?? Church Parade Battalion ??	
	29		Battalion received A.C.A. 12 - pm. J.M.D ??	
	30		Battalion inspection by ??	
	31		Battalion and ?? in night operations.	

WAR DIARY.

1st. NORTHAMPTONSHIRE REGIMENT.

2nd. INFANTRY BRIGADE.

1st. DIVISION.

NOVEMBER.1917.

Army Form C. 2118.

WAR DIARY
of 1st Northamptonshire Regt.

INTELLIGENCE SUMMARY.
(Erase heading not required.)

Instructions regarding War Diaries and Intelligence Summaries are contained in F.S. Regs., Part II and the Staff Manual respectively. Title pages will be prepared in manuscript.

Place	Date	Hour	Summary of Events and Information	Remarks and references to Appendices
SCHOOLS CAMP NR ST OMER	Nov. 1st		Corps of deposit & try soldiers for individual training & musketry.	
	2		Physical Recreation and Specialist training.	
	3		Inoculation 1st dose.	
WM, POPERINGHE	4		10 Officers and 10 NC Officers proceeded to London (2nd A.R.D.B.H.)	
	5		10% and 44 OR for Church Parade. Remainder attended parades for the morning. Preparation for the march.	
			Assembly in Square for Marching.	
		11am	21.10.72nd returned taken on marching. Cap T.S. Martie proceed on leave	
			Battalion moved to POPE RINGHE. Cap T. Delauix left at transport lines & Officers' Rest came. Lieut. S.D. Dehails reported at Station of 3rd Corps.	
POPERINGHE	6		Battalion moved to METEORINE Ref map (28.I) Sheet 28 Fauquissart on billeting of Storn.	
	7		(Camp Poss. Moved up by train to WIEME V26242 (Reynart's SPRIET V26247 (Reynart) Mtr HYDE HALL (V26247 (Reynart)	
HELTER ON SEA	8		First returning the Perham attachment. Helton 58 of POSTKAPEDAE B.N. Pay Burns Moje V26247 (Reynart) A.R.R. (Brahms front with M.B. Armentières and	
	9		Relieved 2nd K.R.R. in the line 58 of POSTCAPEDAE. B.N. Pay Munich First was about 1 to 2 hundred and the trench was bad.	
		(1000)	Relief complete 1100. Regt. Of attacks was much 1500.	
	10		3rd Bde attacked on the left. 2 of Cdr. Scott, PT G. Cuthbert, was wounded. Length & front about 300yds. Moved back to 2 lines for relief B.N. 2nd Canadian Bn moved 27 killed.	
			Men on these positions not held a line of trenches but a series of posts. 70/80 Casualties on 10 and 11th.	
	11		Relieved by 1st R.R.R. Relief complete about 9:30. So sent up with from Canadians Portfolio and left fallen position to 1.2.6.A sent 5 to assist H.T. Canal.	
			Unwounded at duty, not held to complete 9.15pm. Relieved 7 or men admitted to hospital.	
HILL TOP FARM			Relieved by 1st R.R. Relieved about 9.15pm. Rally complete about 9:30. Sent 5 to assist in 126A position 9am.	
			About 70 men admitted to hospital. All owing to conditions. Still owing to be made.	
	12		Relieved 2nd K.R.R. again in the same front. Relief complete 12 M.N.	
	13		Relieved 2nd K.R.R. and 1 DY 11 Snipers and 11 MRS Position.	
			17MG Two platoons under 2nd MATTHEWS and DY11 5th Berks. Completed. Advance relief flank attack, some hand by 5 Rifle bombers also shortly.	
	14	11pm	Near front. Still hill up at thick. Position 294. B. Fred by Lieut 6 Rice & G. Beck. Rally. Taken over and suitable relief by 2nd Welsh by and DY11 G. Berkshire 2nd Lt. R.D. Martin gassed in same way.	
	15		Relieved by 2nd Welsh Reg., and DY11 G. Berkshire. Snipers and 2 Lt R.D. Martin yesterday.	
DOMBRE Camp	16		Moved back to DOMBRE Camp 3274. Snipers arranged Enlist officers lost in dispersion. Mostly have seen 9 hour Mediterranean.	
	17		Number of our men gassed. Cleaning up & rest. Communication of the train of the water	
	18		Battalion talked on 11th morning. Battalion Church Parade. Capt. A.B. Marriage returns from a wound Exchange.	

A.F. Godwin Lt Col.

10th Box W. W4973/M687 750,000 8/16 D.D. & L. Ltd. Forms/C.2118/13.

Army Form C. 2118.

WAR DIARY
of 1/7th Argyll & Sutherland Highlanders Regt.
INTELLIGENCE SUMMARY.
(Erase heading not required.)

Instructions regarding War Diaries and Intelligence Summaries are contained in F. S. Regs., Part II. and the Staff Manual respectively. Title pages will be prepared in manuscript.

Place	Date	Hour	Summary of Events and Information	Remarks and references to Appendices
HILLTOP	19.		Battalion route to HILL TOP FARM. Details go back to RETIRED Camp.	
	20.		Rub feet with whale oil etc.	
	21.		Relieved 2nd R.R. in the line. S.W. of PASSCHENDAELE. N.Z. on right flank on our left the 51st Battalion. Right wing at AT D.W. front line. 2 platoons (C Coy) at KRON PRINZ Farm D.3.c.5.4 (Spriet Wood). Qr Mr and Coy about V.2.B.8.0 N.E. About V.29.d.2.m Quiet morning in no landmen. Intn left coy Copy about V.2.B.8.0 N.E. About V.29.d.2.m Quiet morning in no landmen. The two reserve platoons (C Coy)	
	22.		Rt front company shelled during the afternoon. Heavily to our no casualties. Carry party heads for the REAR at night. At 11pm we got word of a probable German attack at dawn & several flares opened fire. Nothing happened. Next morning, owing to wireless messages intercepted. Wounded Rest. Left with orders the line. Rifles cleaned and ammunition issued. Relief complete by 7pm. Relief complete by 7pm with orders ready.	
	23.		Stand to 4.30am till 7am. Nothing doing by the Scots. Hanover of. Batt. Relieved by 7th R.H. Regt. whilst relation occurred during one and two. Cooks one. Zonit out. Returned to hill Farm. Motor bus to hill Farm.	
			Trucks (lorries) to another corner of the farm. Then about 11pm.	
	24.		Went by train at 10pm to training station near SERAINCOURT. Arrived at 6.30pm everyone to bed very tired. Picked up details at RUGHPLEET Detrained Entrained at F. JEAN. Everyone of 3 to No. 11 lorry. And Marched to TUNNELING Camp where found the main road between FUPER and 22	
TUNNELING CAMP			PROVEN. 10 OR. Found hot dinner.	
	25.		Kit and equipment inspection.	
	26.		Physical Training, close order drill etc.	
HERZEELE	27.		Marched to HERZEELE. Battalion 1.30 p.m. 2nd FURNISHED joined.	
	28.		Coy and platoon drill. Co. commander Capt JEAN Rennee M.C. awarded end of Oct. NC. Earle McTeggar	
	29.		Appl Q.O in cmd.	
	30.		Paraded also 3 subaltern.	

A5834 Wt. W4973/M687 750,000 8/16 D. D. & L. Ltd. Forms/C.2118/13

WAR DIARY
of 1st Matabeleland Rhodesia Regt
INTELLIGENCE SUMMARY

Army Form C. 2118

(Erase heading not required.)

Place	Date	Hour	Summary of Events and Information	Remarks and references to Appendices
		full day	The Battalion had had 3 days in the forest since the month. The food was bad, the forest full of leeches & the rain was very bad, and the whole side entailed the men were carrying more weight than the pipers and drummers. The spirit was good. They were 1,500 rating the ammunition. The 2nd and 3rd blew how the 15 cwt lorries were always kept off from the dumped men at night and like ambushes. Het rough conditions were always kept off by small parties then was no continuing after a time, and the people was had to be more perpetual. Muc Top Jamm the Caints, to which we came first which seemed to be more perpetual. After being in the line was continually being moved, changed one road morning, slept & and even aft the tunnel carried one way. Godding over next morning & down hill and then do much damage, but were paths frightened. Jamtu Camp was built the lines of the tin Camps, & the retreat from was burned on the place. There was a big count of the tin Camps & one about fell over & sat. It is a service you get more ammunition sleeping out for the Camps always seems to pour clear promising to get to the two Camps, that ammunition dumps always seems to pour clear promising to get the two Camps that, the camps. The total evacuation for the period which the battalion has been in the line were 28 killed 65 wounded 13 missing	

A.J. Cockwell

WAR DIARY.

1st. NORTHAMPTONSHIRE REGIMENT.

2nd. INFANTRY BRIGADE.

1st. DIVISION.

DECEMBER. 1917.

1st Northampton Regt

WAR DIARY
or
INTELLIGENCE SUMMARY.
(Erase heading not required.)

Army Form C. 2118.

Vol 39

Place	Date	Hour	Summary of Events and Information	Remarks and references to Appendices
HERZEELE Area	1.12.17.	9am.-12noon	Bgn. training.	
	2.12.17.	9am.	Divine Service 2 Officers and 60 O.R's. per Coy attended.	
			2/Lt W.C. Twinniger off. to attend a 3 days course at PROVEN (War Front's except up to for times to fire C+D)	
	3.12.17	9am.-12 noon	Coy. Training (Close order drill, Gas order drill, Bayonet Fighting) A+B Coys	
		2pm - 3pm	Specialist training A+B Coys + H.2. details inspected by Comd'g Officer.	
	4.12.17		A+B Coys. Night Operations (Compass Marching + Platoon Raids).	
		9am - 11am	C+D Coys inspected by Comd'g Officer.	
			C+D Coys. Night Operations	
	5.12.17	9am-12noon	Coy. Route March. Specialist Training. Following N.C.O's	
		2.0-3.0 pm	and men awarded the Military medal.- No. 7777 L/Cpl P. Hearn. No 25/78 Pte E. Pears. No 3/104 20 Pte L.C. Jackson No.17737 Pte. I. Findley No. 7890 Pte. O.E. Morgan No. 31037 Pte W. Allen No. 9741 Pte. H. Pease.	
	6.12.17	9am - 12.30pm	Coy. Training. A Regtl Amusement Committee formed of one officer per Coy.	
	7.12.17	10.30am.	13th moved to French Internment camp at WAAYEMBURG	
WAAYEMBURG REF.MAP. SHEET 19. X. 14. C.	8.12.17	9am-10am.	Cleaning up huts + camp. 10.30am-12.30 pm. Close order Drill + Musketry.	
		2.0pm - 3.0pm	Specialist training. I.N.C.O + 11 O.R. Ptes. att'd to XIX Corps Works. Bn.	
	9.12.17		Preparations for move. 3.30pm. Voluntary Church Service. Moved to ZUIDEVIS Internment camp in EIKHOEK area at 10 am.	

A/G Williams

Army Form C. 2118.

WAR DIARY
or
INTELLIGENCE SUMMARY.
(Erase heading not required.)

Instructions regarding War Diaries and Intelligence Summaries are contained in F. S. Regs., Part II. and the Staff Manual respectively. Title pages will be prepared in manuscript.

Place	Date	Hour	Summary of Events and Information	Remarks and references to Appendices
WOESTEN CAMP.	20.12.17		Preparations for move. Bn. moved to B²n in support. B² H.Q. at U.14.c.6.0.44. Coys. in pill boxes and shelters in vicinity. Relieving 2nd K.R.R.C.	
B²n H.Q.	21.12.17		Large working and carrying parties provided every night for B²n in the line	
LA CHAUDIERE	22.12.17		Fort-washing. Carrying & working parties for forward lines	
U.14.C.6.6	23.12.17		Same as previous day.	
(R.er.MAP. BIXCHOOTE)/10,000	24.12.17		Relieved 2nd K.R.R.C. in front line. Relief complete by 8 p.m. Right 13=of Bn. with 57th Bn. on right. A + D Coys. in front line in organised shell-holes. B + C Coys. in organised posts in main line of resistance. B²n front about 1200 yds. B²n and Coy H.Q in pill boxes. Conditions good owing to frost.	
B²n H.Q.	25.12.17		Everything very quiet. Work done on main line of resistance, especially wiring. One man particularly wounded.	
U.9.d.14.6.	26.12.17		Ditto. 11 p.m. B + C Coys. relieved A + D in front line.	
	27.12.17		Ditto. One man slightly wounded. Great work done on wire.	
	28.12.17		Ditto. 10 p.m. Relieved by 1st Cameron Highlanders. Moved back to WOESTEN CAMP.	
WOESTEN CAMP.	29.12.17		Moved at 9.30 a.m. to ZUIDHUIS CAMP. Details and transport moved B²n	
ZUIDHUIS CAMP.	30.12.17		10.30 a.m. Divine Service.	
	31.12.17		Inspections & refitting under Coy arrangements.	

Army Form C. 2118.

WAR DIARY
or
INTELLIGENCE SUMMARY.
(Erase heading not required.)

Instructions regarding War Diaries and Intelligence Summaries are contained in F.S. Regs., Part II. and the Staff Manual respectively. Title pages will be prepared in manuscript.

Place	Date	Hour	Summary of Events and Information	Remarks and references to Appendices
ZUIDEMS Camp.	10.12.17		Morning. Clearing up of huts and camp. Afternoon. Rifle & Lewis Gun inspection. 2/Lt A. Gallen joined 2/5th Mortar Battery for duty.	
REF B24G 1/40 SHEET 20. S.28.a.	11.12.17		9am – 12.30 pm. Coy training (Close order Drill. Physical & Bayonet 2/5th Kemp. Musketry). Afternoon. Recreational training.	
	12.12.17		9am – 12.30 pm. Coy training. D.L.H. Mackenzie (5 A. by) + 6 O.R's joined D=	
	13.12.17		1 pm. 113= moved to camp in Support Area 7.25.d.6.8. Transport moved to lines at S.24.a (Shut 20.)	
WOESTEN 8"H 8 at T.25.d.6.4 (Shut 20)	14.12.17		9 – 11am. Cleaning up of billets. 11.0am – 12.30pm. Physical training. Afternoon. Inspection of rifles and Lewis Guns. One Officer per Coy went up to reconnoitre forward area.	
	15.12.17		9 – 12.30 am. Coy training. Afternoon. Specialist training. Working party of one Officer + 50 other Rks ⅛ per Coy.	
	16.12.17		10.30 am. Voluntary Church Service. Morning – Lewis Gun classes fired on miniature range. 2/Lt O.A. Moll was posted to 7th B= Northamptonshire Regt.	
	17.12.17		Working party of 1 Officer and 50 other Rks. Remainder Coy. training.	
	18.12.17		Morning. Coy training. Afternoon. Baths.	
	19.12.17		Working party 2 Officers + 150 other Rks per Coy.	

1st Division
2nd Brigade
Northamptonshire Regt.
1918 From 1st January, To 31st ~~December 1918~~ 1919 MAY

2nd Brigade
1st Division.

1st BATTALION

NORTHAMPTONSHIRE REGIMENT

APRIL 1918.

Army Form C. 2118.

WAR DIARY
or
INTELLIGENCE SUMMARY.

1st Battn. Northamptonshire Regiment

(Erase heading not required.)

Place	Date	Hour	Summary of Events and Information	Remarks and references to Appendices
ZUIDHUIS CAMP.	1/1/18	11am.	Divine Service. Celebration of Xmas.	
	2.1.18		9am – 12.30pm. Coy. training. 2pm – 3pm. Specialist training. Bathing.	
	3.1.18.		9am – 12.30pm. Coy. training.	
	4.1.18.		Comdg. Offrs. inspection of A & C Coys. Coy. & Specialist training.	
	5.1.18		" " " of B " " "	
	6.1.18.		" " Remainder of Bn. "	
Camp at WOESTEN.			Moved to Support Area. B Coy. attached for work to 26th Field by R.E. Transportmen. WOESTEN.	
T.25.d.6.4.	7.1.18.		Coy. training. Working party of 2 officers + 101 O.R.	
	8.1.18.		" " " " " 4 officers 200 O.R.	
	9.1.18.		" " " " " " "	
	10.1.18.		" " " " " " "	
	11.1.18.		1 day for training " " 5 officers & 310 other Rks.	
Bn. H.Q. at	12.1.18		Coy. training " " 2 officers & 100 O.Rks.	
	13.1.18		" " " " " " "	
U.14.c.4.0.	14.1.18.		Moved into Support relieving 2nd K.R.R.C. Coys. situated as before.	
BINCHOOT	15.1.18.		Foot washing. Large working parties every night for Bn. in the	
H.Q.MO.	16.1.18.		Much snow + rain, conditions bad. B Coy moved to U.8 central.	
H.Q. at	17.1.18.		Large carrying & working parties at night.	
U.9.d.3.3.			Relieved 2nd K.R.R.C. Relief completed about 9pm. 3 Coys. in front line and one in Reserve. Bn. only 1 platoon per Coy. in front support line to deal with an extra 6op front Taken over on left, an 12 B- Yold Dwuon at front.	

Army Form C. 2118.

WAR DIARY
or
INTELLIGENCE SUMMARY.
(Erase heading not required.)

Instructions regarding War Diaries and Intelligence
Summaries are contained in F. S. Regs., Part II
and the Staff Manual respectively. Title pages
will be prepared in manuscript.

Place	Date	Hour	Summary of Events and Information	Remarks and references to Appendices
H.Q. at U.9.d.3.3	18.1.18.		Conditions much worse owing to thaw and rain. Work chiefly being done on wire, new shelters & improvement of old ones. Patrol nightly.	
	19.1.18.		Trenches still very great. Into platoon relief.	
	20.1.18.			
	21.1.18.		Relieved by 1st Cameron Highlanders. Relief complete 6.40 pm. Moved back to T.25.d.6.4. Casualties during tour, Gas 2, wounded. Duty turn to their admission to hospital.	T.25.d.6.4.
T.25.d.6.4.	22.1.18.	10 am.	Moved to ZUIDHUIS CAMP	
ZUIDHUIS CAMP.	23.1.18.		Regimental & general cleaning up.	
	24.1.18.		Coy. training in morning. Freshest training in the afternoon	
	25.1.18.	"	"	Working parties & offrs. [illegible] R.
	26.1.18.	"	"	
	27.1.18.		Draft of 57 other Ranks joined Bn.	
	28.1.18.	10 am.	Divine Service at 10 am. Bathing	
T.25.d.6.4.	29.1.18.		Inspection by G.O.C. 2nd Bde. Moved to T.25.d.6.4.	
	30.1.18.		Coy. cleaning.	
	31.1.18.	"	"	

WAR DIARY 1st Northamptonshire Regt.
INTELLIGENCE SUMMARY. 1.2.18 – 9.2.18.

Army Form C. 2118.

Instructions regarding War Diaries and Intelligence Summaries are contained in F.S. Regs., Part II. and the Staff Manual respectively. Title pages will be prepared in manuscript.

(Erase heading not required.)

Vol 71

Place	Date	Hour	Summary of Events and Information	Remarks and references to Appendices
VANDAMME CAMP. WOESTEN.	1.2.18		Coy. training during morning. Recreational training in afternoon. Supper at 9 oth Regimental.	
	2.2.18		Coy. training. Recreational training. Working party of 1 officer + 50 other Ranks for work in forward area.	
	3.2.18		Divine Service + Baths. Address given by Bishop Kent Lordship of Killaloe.	
	4.2.18		Usual Coy. + Recreational training.	
	5.2.18		" " " "	
			Divisional Railroad.	2nd Lt A.R. WHITE reported rejoining officers
	6.2.18		Usual Coy. and Recreational training.	
	7.2.18		" " " "	
	8.2.18		Entrained at ONDANK at 2pm, detraining at WIELTJE, marching from there to Front Line. Bn H.Q. at HUBNER FM. D.1.C.4.6. (Bart 28 1/40000) Blue Dogs in front line, and one in support. Frontage about 1500 yds. Relieved 11th Royal Scots. Transport and details moved to B.E.G. CAMP ELVERDINGE. Bays in line about 100 yds. Front very flat. Changed from November 1917. Infantry little military and weather conditions much better. No enemy had shown down recently - Early my men shelters created. Consequently wiring and creation of shelters taken in hand. Very time posts while being improved upon.	
Bn H.Q. HUBNER FM. P.t.C.4.6 Part 28 1/40000	9.2.18		Coy old and shellig lightly - from front-line LEKKERBOTERBEEK and PADDEBEEK. 2 men wounded.	

Army Form C. 2118.

WAR DIARY /s/ 1st Hampshire Regt
or
INTELLIGENCE SUMMARY. No. 2.18. — Mar. 2. 18

(Erase heading not required.)

Instructions regarding War Diaries and Intelligence Summaries are contained in F.S. Regs., Part II. and the Staff Manual respectively. Title pages will be prepared in manuscript.

Place	Date	Hour	Summary of Events and Information	Remarks and references to Appendices
HUBNER FM. D.1.C.4.6.	10.2.18		Front quiet. No casualties. Relieved by 2nd Royal Fus. Moved back to H.Q. in support. Bn. H.Q. at HUGGETT HALLES C.11.2.3.6 (sheet 28 /40,000). 2 Bty at U.30.D.5.3 (sheet 20SW and SE /20,000) and 2 Btys at U.30.D.5.3 (sheet 20SW and SE /20,000).	
H.Q at C.11.2.3.6 (sheet 28/40,000)	11.2.18		Small carrying and working parties provided.	
	12.2.18		Relieved 2nd K.R.R.C. in POELCAPPELLE sector. Bn H.Q. at NORFOLK HOUSE V.19.a.6.2 (sheet 20SW&SE /20,000) 3 Btys in front line, one remaining at U.30.D.5.3 organ. Line a system of shell-holes. POELCAPPELLE itself formed Coy area. B2 frontage about 1500 yds.	
H.Q at NORFOLK HOUSE V.19.a.6.2 (sheet 20SW+SE) /20,000	13.2.18		Very quiet with very little shelling. Ground very wet, but gradually improving. Wiring of front line carried out and additional shelters for support platoons erected.	
	14.2.18		Two men wounded. Ground much better owing to front line proper main line of resistance organised about 500 x behind outpost line firing position for this dug and large proportion wired. Work on front continued at night.	
	15.2.18		Relieved by 2nd Royal Sussex. Relief completed by 8.30 p.m. Only 3 casualties in 4 days tour.	
	16.2.18		Returned to Bn in support as on 10.2.18	
Bn H.Q at C.11.2.3.6	17.2.18		Small working and carrying parties. Fortunately 1 man wounded.	
	18.2.18		Relieved 2nd K.R.R.C. in night B2 sector. Weather still good. Sector very quiet.	

A5834 Wt. W4973/M687 750,000 8/16 D.D. & L. Ltd. Forms/C.2118/13.

WAR DIARY or INTELLIGENCE SUMMARY.

Army Form C. 2118.

1st Northampton Regt
19.2.18 — 28.2.18

Place	Date	Hour	Summary of Events and Information	Remarks and references to Appendices
HUBNER FM. (B" H.Q.)	19.2.18.		5 men wounded. 2nd Bn Northamptonshire Regt. 5th Div. on the night. Ground hard owing to frost. Wiring of front line still carried on.	
	20.2.18.		Relieved by 1st E.Y. Lancashire Regt. 1st Bn. Entrained at MIEJT proceeded to HOSPITAL CAMP ELVERDINGHE. arriving about midnight. Details and transport went there in afternoon.	
HOSPITAL CAMP	21.2.18.		General cleaning up. 2/Lt. MOORE proceeded to England for 6 months Ian of duty.	
ELVERDINGHE.	22.2.18.		Bathing cleaning up and inspections.	
	23.2.18.		Close order drill and inspections. Platoon for football competition commenced.	
	24.2.18.		Divine Service.	
	25.2.18.		Coy and Recreational training.	
	26.2.18.		" " " a draft of 18 other Ranks joined Bn.	
	27.2.18.		" " " 2nd Lt. Sharp and 14 other Ranks attached to Lewis and M.G. Sy.	
	28.2.18		" " " Inspection of transport by O.R.C. 2nd Inf. Bde.	

Army Form C. 2118.

WAR DIARY
or
INTELLIGENCE SUMMARY.
(Erase heading not required.)

Instructions regarding War Diaries and Intelligence
Summaries are contained in F. S. Regs., Part II.
and the Staff Manual respectively. Title pages
will be prepared in manuscript.

Place	Date	Hour	Summary of Events and Information	Remarks and references to Appendices
HILLTOP FARM	12-3-18			
	13-3-18			
	14-3-18			
	15-3-18			
	16-3-18			
ALICE HOUSE	17-3-18			
	18-3-18			
HUGHES FARM Dis H.Q.	19-3-18			
	20-3-18			

Instructions regarding War Diaries and Intelligence Summaries are contained in F. S. Regs., Part II. and the Staff Manual respectively. Title pages will be prepared in manuscript.

WAR DIARY
or
INTELLIGENCE SUMMARY.
(Erase heading not required.)

Army Form C. 2118.

Place	Date	Hour	Summary of Events and Information	Remarks and references to Appendices
HUBNER FARM DIC 4.6	21-3-18		[illegible] Brigadier [illegible] wounded in leg. Col. Robinson [illegible] to [illegible] Brigade [illegible] commanding [illegible] [illegible] [illegible] again [illegible] [illegible] The night was [illegible] clear and [illegible] bright. The patrol advanced with extreme caution until an enemy [illegible] [illegible] point [illegible] plainly apparent in the moonlight. Pausing here a few moments to decide on a plan of action the leader suddenly observed a man who came out of the [illegible] and walked away in an easterly direction. Keeping as close to him as the light permitted the patrol saw him enter an enemy post. Presently he was joined by two others and the three stood outside the post talking. The enemy post was carefully examined and a weak point eventually found. The patrol formed up, and at a whispered word from the leader made a rush for the post. ~~[illegible]~~ The three men bolted and a bomb was thrown into the shelter, from which a man emerged hurriedly with his hands above his head. The patrol seized him and returned as quickly as they might. Though fired upon the whole way back by MGS all returned unharmed and the prisoner was safely delivered to Brigade	
	22-3-18		The day passed fairly quietly. We were relieved by the 2nd K.R.R. Corps and moved back into support as before with Bn HQ at HUGEL HALLES	

J. C. Gentlemen? Lieut.
1st Northamptonshire Regt.

Army Form C. 2118.

WAR DIARY
or
INTELLIGENCE SUMMARY.
(Erase heading not required.)

Instructions regarding War Diaries and Intelligence Summaries are contained in F. S. Regs., Part II. and the Staff Manual respectively. Title pages will be prepared in manuscript.

Place	Date	Hour	Summary of Events and Information	Remarks and references to Appendices
HUGEL HALLES	23-3-18		[illegible handwritten entry regarding 8th Bn and the Emergency... reserve Bn Battalion... Brigade... 2nd R. Berks...	
	24-3-18		8th Bn Suffolk relieved with 8th Bn (D) of DELTA TRIBES in support. During the night heavy HE & Gas shells... Germans attacked and fell back... The night passed quietly...	
NORFOLK HOUSE V.19.a.6.2 (St ROSM (S.W)) (HQ.org)	25.3.18		Machine gunned incessantly. 1 O.R. killed and 5 wounded. FERDAN HOUSE (A Coy HQ) was evacuated. CSM Mayes and 2 O.R.s (1 signaller and 1 Tel Personnel) were killed, and 4 O.R. wounded. D Coy were at POEL HOUSE and proceeded to DELTA... and the patrols were carefully made... keep front... Put no units to keep in touch. A patrol of 1 above Lt SPRIET ROAD Right flank kept killed a few... was fired upon. They opened fire. MG fire. Rifle fire and...	
	26-3-18		FERDAN HOUSE attacked during the night. Various parts of the line shelled and heavy rifle and MG fire during the night. Enemy in chief and light. Relieved by our own Battalion of Tyne... during the night our patrols encountered two enemy patrols one at [illegible] 14 and one at 30. There were exchanges and the enemy...	

WAR DIARY
or
INTELLIGENCE SUMMARY.

(Erase heading not required.)

Army Form C. 2118.

Place	Date	Hour	Summary of Events and Information	Remarks and references to Appendices
NORFOLK HOUSE	27-3-18		Part of the train under Lieut. Knights & 2/Lt and I RMC proceeded from 3 am train	
Vigo 6.7 & 2 O.S.H. (B.S.E.) 1/1/1,2,3,0,0,0	28-3-18		Said but no personnel for entrainment arrived at the Transit Camp and was Camped Late. Fellow companies 2/8th into the Base Rain commenced to fall & we were asked to dig in & Kember	
KEMPTON PARK	29-3-18		"D" Coy now at left of PHEASANT TRENCH. They started morning & undulate rifle & Lewis were full occupied throughout morning. The new Company ammunition parade & Lt Lingo hung a bank on the Battalion decided to allow many men into the Bath present not to have sufficient time. Working parties (on Battle Zone) but any other company turned were turned out during the day to Carry arms & ammunition.	
	30-3-18		C.C.G. + Captain Butterfield + 96 Prisoners & four captured Germans & 6 and twelfth over the line of G&? for and leaves at Lille & suffering first day of passed. KIRBY struck off strength from hospital in England.	

J. Graham Lt 1st Batt

Army Form C. 2118.

WAR DIARY
of 1/5 Northamptonshire Regt.

INTELLIGENCE SUMMARY.
1st April – 8th April 1918

(Erase heading not required.)

Instructions regarding War Diaries and Intelligence Summaries are contained in F. S. Regs., Part II. and the Staff Manual respectively. Title pages will be prepared in manuscript.

Place	Date	Hour	Summary of Events and Information	Remarks and references to Appendices
HERRION PARK	1/4/18		Bayonet fighting and Physical training. Working parties from B.H.Q. Lt. Col. Hammond, Pte Sickness and young men available enlisting medium for a few days.	
	2		Raid, in which they took part. Yesterday Coy. Lieut. Harrison in same town.	
	3		Trench-fas. for yesterday. 5 O.R. joined. Following S.P.s & S.A.A. guns sent in. Military Gov.	
	4		Great firing and working parties. Orders received to move up on the 5th to relieve 10 Hunts at an advanced position.	
AVESNES	5		on 10 ? baingham BOESINGHE to 6/10 ?? Rd gram Battalion moved off at 3:30 and reached its allotted position.	
	6		Colonel and Coy Commander went up to reconnoitre the line as it was decided by Brigade that Bttn would go further forward. Narrow [illegible] (53rd Division) Quiet Stay.	
CURREY	7		Very Quiet day	
	8		Very quiet day [illegible]	R.P. Thornewill [illegible] Lt. Col. Comdg. 1/5 [illegible]

1st North'n Cyclist Regt.
9th April – 14th April 1918.

WAR DIARY
or
INTELLIGENCE SUMMARY.
(Erase heading not required.)

Army Form C. 2118.

Instructions regarding War Diaries and Intelligence Summaries are contained in F. S. Regs., Part II. and the Staff Manual respectively. Title pages will be prepared in manuscript.

Place	Date	Hour	Summary of Events and Information	Remarks and references to Appendices
CUINCHY	9.4.18.		Fairly heavy Bombardment from 4.20 a.m. with gas shells, H.E. and T.M.s, increasing in violence between 5 am and 9 am. Under cover of heavy mist the enemy attacked the 55th Div: N. of LA BASSÉE CANAL, & succeeded in establishing himself in GIVENCHY. Mist made it impossible to see what was happening from S. of CANAL. During the afternoon the 55th Bn. counter-attacked & drove the enemy back to his former position. The mist having lifted A Coy on the S. side of CANAL were able to bring Lewis Gun and Rifle fire to bear on retiring enemy with considerable success. Pte. Ingles wounded + 25 O'Rks casualties during bombardment. The details and transport at LE QUESNOY were shelled during the morning. Transport received orders to move back to BETHUNE about 11 am.	
REP MAP GORRE 1/20,000	10.4.18.		Fairly Quiet. Every one very much on the qui vivre + very keen, expecting enemy to attack. Scheme of defence for our Sector & arrangement & schemes made for holding crossings over canal if Bn. on our left were forced to retire. Transport at FOUQUEREUIL. Details at BURBURE.	
	11.4.18. 12.4.18.		Work carried on in improvement of defensive Weather conditions good all the time. Details at MAR DES MINES.	
	13.4.18.		Relieved by 2nd Royal Fusiliers & moved back into billets in CAMBRIN. (Except of the probability of enemy attempting to billow a few of the new forms then in use) Two Platoons of B Coy remained in support with Fusiliers & 2 Platoons went to 2nd K.R.R.C.	
CAMBRIN	14.4.18.		Defensive scheme for CAMBRIN taken in hand. An all round defensive system formed by means of defensive localities. No organised defence seems to have been made until about 2 wks ago. Nothing apparently done for past 3 years. The civilians in CAMBRIN had been evacuated, + had left behind almost all household goods, which Bn. detailed to collect and police.	

R. Inch Lt Col

1st Northamptonshire Regt. WAR DIARY 15th April – 20th April 1918.

Army Form C. 2118.

Instructions regarding War Diaries and Intelligence Summaries are contained in F.S. Regs., Part II. and the Staff Manual respectively. Title pages will be prepared in manuscript.

INTELLIGENCE SUMMARY.
or
(Erase heading not required.)

Place	Date	Hour	Summary of Events and Information	Remarks and references to Appendices
CAMBRIN	15.4.18 → 16.4.18		Work on defences of CAMBRIN. Details and transport at GOSNEY. C Coy relieved B Coy in the immediate support positions to 2nd R.Fusiliers & 2nd K.R.R.C.	
REF MAP. GORRE 1/20,000.	17.4.18. 18.4.18.		All very quiet. Details and transport at VERQUIN. About 11am an heavy bombardment commenced North of the canal. This gradually spread to 12th sector S. of Canal and to CAMBRIN area which was shelled with 8", 5.9" & gas. Coyns all stood to. From 5am. About 7am a strong attack launched at GIVENCHY and FESTUBERT front on 1st & 3rd BDES. At 10am. 1 platoon D Coy moved to VAUXHALL BRIDGE to take up position and told brigaded if necessary. 11.30am remainder of details moved up and relieved a Coy of CAMERON HIGHRS at PONT FIXE N. At about same time 3 platoons of A Coy went to WESTMINSTER BRIDGE. Enemy held up on front 1st & 3rd BDE fronts on main line of resistance. Evening of 18/4th. Notts. & Derby 46th Div. 1st & 3rd BDE fronts on main line of resistance. Evening of 18/4th. Notts. & Derby 46th Div. came up and took over duties of support Bn at CAMBRIN. A + C Coys withdrawn to CAMBRIN to rest prior to counter-attack N. of Canal. 8pm. B Coy. moved up to relieve a Coy of CAMERONS at VAUXHALL and WESTMINSTER Bridges.	
	19.4.18		Commanding Officer + O.C. A + C Coys (Capt. Pickering M.C. + Capt. Batley) went up to reconnoitre high ground in front of GIVENCHY - make arrangements for counter attack. The high ground in front of GIVENCHY comprised roughly of a couple of lines of trenches from about 450 yds and depth about 300 yds. This ground was very important as it overlooked surrounding country. This part of front was held by 1st Black Watch. Map + operation orders issued by Lt. Col. Robinson M.C. late.	
	20th		Battle H. Qrs. + A + C. Coys moved from CAMBRIN at 1am into GIVENCHY trenches	

Army Form C. 2118.

WAR DIARY
or
INTELLIGENCE SUMMARY.

1st Northamptonshire Regt.
20th April 1918

(Erase heading not required.)

Place	Date	Hour	Summary of Events and Information	Remarks and references to Appendices
GIVENCHY Ref MAP GORRE 1/20,000	20.4.18		The Coys formed up at 4.30 am, A Coy on the right and C Coy on the left, and moved forward to the attack at 4.45 am as dawn was breaking. By 5.5 am the Coys were established in final objective. The position was fairly strongly held, but most of the enemy rallied on the approach of our men, but quite a large proportion of them were killed. 16 prisoners were taken, and 5 more in the afternoon. The enemy opposed the advance with fairly heavy M.G. fire and after position was taken there was a considerable amount of sniping with Lgt M.G. and rifles, & at close range. The enemy also made some half-hearted attempts both on the left & right to break in but through eager leading from the craters in front which the enemy held. These attempts were easily repulsed. During the morning 2 platoons of B Coy went up to re-inforce, one going to A Coy + 1 to C Coy. The men did their share extremely well, especially as the ground was absolutely new to all, and as the attack was at dawn it was most difficult to keep direction. No organised counter attack was made but during evening trench was rather heavily bombarded. Casualties were A Coy Lt Cockerill and 2/Lt Still wounded and 40 other Rks. casualties. Capt Pickering M.C. was wounded in the hand but remained at duty. C Coy had 2/Lt Falkner Fox killed + Mr Coldwell missing and 57 other Rks. casualties. During the period 17-20th. D Coy had 36 other Rks casualties at PONT FIXE IV.	

WAR DIARY
or
INTELLIGENCE SUMMARY.

(Erase heading not required.)

1st Northamptonshire Regt. Army Form C. 2118.

20th April — 30th April.

Place	Date	Hour	Summary of Events and Information	Remarks and references to Appendices
GIVENCHY Ref Map GORRE 1/20,000	20.4.18.		No. 15 platoon D Coy went over the country with 4 guns teams of M.G.C. They were especially thanked for their good work by M.G.C. Coy Comdr. Only 3 casualties. Batt H.Q. moved back to CAMBRIN at 5 p.m. Details at RAINBERT. Comparatively quiet.	
Bn H.Q. A.14.a.5.5.	21.4.18.		Relieved 1st CAMERON HIGHrs who were support Bn. of 1st Bde. B Coy at Windy Corner area. C Coy attd. to Cameron in front line. A & D Coys on CANAL BANK.	
	22.4.18.		Comparatively quiet. Lt. RAMSAY killed.	
LA BOURSE	23.4.18.		Relieved by 1st L.N. Lancs. 55th Div. Moved back for night to LA BOURSE.	
CAMBRIN	24.4.18.		Moved at 3 pm + relieved 1st GLOSTERS in CAMBRIN locality. 10tal casualties from 9th Apr. 5 officers and 200 other Rks. Loss of these being cause of gas, the effects of which some cases took about a week to become apparent.	
Bn H.Q. A.28.d.5.3	25.4.18.		Preparations to move into line. Details at BOIS de FROISSART.	
	26.4.18.		Relieved 2nd K.R.R.C. on S.E. main LA BASSEE - CAMBRIN Rd. Line practically same as in CUINCHY area. Outpost line + Main line of Resistance manned by 2 Coys. — 2 Coys in Reserve. Extent of front 1000 yds. 1 Royal Scots on Right. 3rd Bde on Right.	
	27.4.18.		⎫	
	28.4.18.		⎬ Entire ordinarily quiet.	
	29.4.18.		⎪	
	30.4.18.		⎭	

R.P. Shanton ?

WAR DIARY

1st Northamptonshire Regt. 1st May 1918 – 7th May

Army Form C. 2118.

or

INTELLIGENCE SUMMARY

(Erase heading not required.)

Place	Date	Hour	Summary of Events and Information	Remarks and references to Appendices
Ref: MAP: GORRE 1/20,000 B.H.Q. A.20.d.5.3.	1.5.18.		Everything quiet. Following M.M.s for work on 20th April. Bar to M.M. 3/10420 Cpl. Swinn. M. A Coy. 6696 Pte. Markham. D. Coy. M.Military Medal to 9055 Sgt. Adams A Coy. 31172 Pte. Bedlington A Coy. 31273 Pte. Moreley A Coy. 204866 Pte. Barham A Coy. 31039 " Aylmer " 31012 " Stansfield " 20551 " Jones B Coy. 8293 Cpl. Morris C Coy. 9/10147 Pte. Halliwell C Coy. 43408 Pte. Beckett " 46308 " Chapman " 7636 " Flamman D Coy. 40872 " Addleham D Coy.	
Nouex les Mines	2.5.18.		Relieved by 1st L.N. Lancs. + moved back to billets at Nouex les Mines.	
	3.5.18.		Inspections + cleaning up. Baths. No.8091 C.S.M. Barker awarded the Italian Bronze Medal for military valour.	
	4.5.18.		Coys on the Range.	
	5.5.18.		Church parade. Following officers joined 2/Lt. J.S. Fowler. 2/Lt. J.S.T. Hampor. 2/Lt. W. Ellis. 2/Lt. H. Knight. 2/Lt. Eastwood.	
	6.5.18.		Coys moved up to 36 CAMBRIN – 16 VILLAGE LINE in front. These coys under orders of 1st Black Watch. H.Qu. and details remained at Nouex.	
	7.5.18.		Training for H.Q. + details.	

Army Form C. 2118.

1st Northamptonshire Regt.

WAR DIARY
or
INTELLIGENCE SUMMARY.

(Erase heading not required.)

8th May – 21st May 1918

Instructions regarding War Diaries and Intelligence Summaries are contained in F.S. Regs., Part II. and the Staff Manual respectively. Title pages will be prepared in manuscript.

Place	Date	Hour	Summary of Events and Information	Remarks and references to Appendices
NŒUX LES MINES	8.5.18.		C Coy returned. Remaining Coys staying at CAMBRIN working on its defences.	
	9.5.18.		Range fire H.Q. details and C Coy.	
	10.5.18 11.5.18	}	Training " " " "	
	12.5.18.		Church services in morning. Relieved 1st GLOSTERS as Bn in support in ANNEQUIN & Coys coming from CAMBRIN. Transport at NŒUX LES MINES. Details at BOIS d'OHLAIN.	
ANNEQUIN.	13.5.18.		Men billeted in cellars of houses. Defence scheme consisted of a series of mutually supporting posts which made an all round defence for the village. LT. A.P. WHITE (attd. R.E.) wounded. Zeppelin shelled. 2 casualties only.	
	14.5.18.		All quiet. Bar to Military Cross awarded to Capt. A.C. Pickering M.C. Military Cross to Capt. H.C. Betley & Lt. R.D. Martin. D.C.M. to 8393 Sgt. A Jolly A Coy.	
	15.5.18			
	16.5.18.		Relieved 2nd KRRC in front line in Left Hohenzollern sector. 2 Coys in front line, 1 in support + 1 in Reserve. Same system of defence as in previous sector in this area	
Bn H.Q at A.25.d.8.2.	17.5.18. 18.5.18	}	Everything very quiet. Normal work done on defences. Weather exceedingly hot.	
REGINA TORRE (1/20,000)	19.5.18 20.5.18			
	21.5.18		6 casualties. All quiet.	

Army Form C. 2118.

1st Northamptonshire Regt. WAR DIARY 22nd — 31st May 1917.

or

INTELLIGENCE SUMMARY.

(Erase heading not required.)

Instructions regarding War Diaries and Intelligence
Summaries are contained in F. S. Regs., Part II.
and the Staff Manual respectively. Title pages
will be prepared in manuscript.

Place	Date	Hour	Summary of Events and Information	Remarks and references to Appendices
Rt. Map. IL GORRE/46cm	22.	5.18.	Comparatively little shelling & casualties.	
	23.	5.17.		
B - H Q at	24.	5.17.	Gas successfully projected other night. 5 casualties.	
H 25.d B.2.	25.	5.17.	Relieved by 2nd R. Innis Regt. Moved back to Annequin & Cambrin.	
ANNEQUIN	26.	5.17.	Baths.	
	27.	5.17.	Training.	
	28.	5.17.	Relieved by 1st Cameron High. and moved back to Moeuvres Mines.	
	29.	5.17.	Inspections & Cleaning. 5 Cheuringle turned up 28/5 Regt 1/2 Cheuringle one 30th Reinforcement.	
MOEUX MINES	30.	5.17.	Manual & gas training.	
	31.	5.17.		

Avon. W. w18139/M293 75000. 1/17. D D & L Ltd. Forms/C2118/4.

Army Form C. 2118.

1st Northamptonshire Regt. WAR DIARY 1st June 1918 —
or
INTELLIGENCE SUMMARY. 16th June 1918.

(Erase heading not required.)

Instructions regarding War Diaries and Intelligence
Summaries are contained in F. S. Regs., Part II.
and the Staff Manual respectively. Title pages
will be prepared in manuscript.

Place	Date	Hour	Summary of Events and Information	Remarks and references to Appendices
Noeux les Mines	1.6.18.		Moral Coy training including Range.	
	2.6.18.		Bathing and Church Parade.	
	3.6.18.		Coy training including firing on Range. Reconnaissance of line by 2/Lt Combe & 2/Lt F.C. Cockerill re-joined.	
	4.6.18.		Coy training. Lt (A/Capt.) B.C. Carey awarded M.C. for gallantry in the field.	
Bn. H.Q. A.20.d.	5.6.18.		Moved from Noeux les Mines and relieved 1st/4th Gloster's on the S. side of La Bassée Rd. Echelon "B" (Details) to Bois d'OHLAIN. Everything very quiet but attack expected any day. Draft of 13 other Rks.	
Ref Map Gmn 1/40,000	6.6.18		⎫	
	7.6.18		⎬ Everything very quiet. Expected attack failing to materialize.	
	8.6.18		⎭ Draft of 94 other Rks joined. Work improvement of defenses.	
	10.6.18			
	11.6.18		⎫	
	12.6.18		⎬ Comparatively quiet. 5 casualties.	
	13.6.18		⎭ Inter-Coy Relief.	
	14.6.18		⎫	
	15.6.18		⎬ Quiet. 6 casualties.	
	16.6.18		⎭ A kind of influenza fever began to spread apparently only affecting men a few days. 2 Lt. Kempson and 9 other Rks. to hospital with this fever.	

1st Northamptonshire Regt. WAR DIARY
17th June — 30th June 1918
INTELLIGENCE SUMMARY
(Erase heading not required.)

Army Form C. 2118.

Place	Date	Hour	Summary of Events and Information	Remarks and references to Appendices
B.H.Q.	17.6.18		Details affected by fever, about 50 cases	
A.20.d.	18.6.18		1 x (eight) Tetley and 2/Lt Ellis and 8 other Rks to hospital. Everything quiet in the line. Draft of 26 O.Rks.	
Ref Map GORRE 1/20000	19.6.18		5 more to Hospital with fever. Draft of 11 O.Rks. D.A.I. Ward went to England to join M.G.C. gun	
	20.6.18		No. 9636 Sgt. A.E. Teeling awarded Meritorious Service Medal	
	21.6.18		Relieved by 1st Black Watch & moved back to Noeux les Mines where details regrouped. 4 casualties on way out.	
Noeux les Mines	22.6.18		Fever still prevalent but arrangements made to keep them some where returning from hospital. Inspections & cleaning up.	
	23.6.18		Church Parade.	
	24.6.18		Baths and platoon training	
	25.6.18		1830 out from 8am to 8pm on tactical scheme at Bois d'Olhain	
	26.6.18		Coy training. Draft of 16 other Rks.	
	27.6.18		Coy training. No. 9781 Cpl. J. Butts B Coy awarded D.C.M.	
	28.6.18		Coy training	
	29.6.18		Rehearsal at Bois du Dameshun BRUAY for Bn. inspection of 2nd Bde by H.R.H. The Duke of Connaught	
	30.6.18		Cleaning up for inspection. About 35 other Rks admitted to hospital during week with fever.	

Army Form C. 2118.

1st Northamptonshire Regt. WAR DIARY 1st July 1918 – 16th July.

INTELLIGENCE SUMMARY.

(Erase heading not required.)

Instructions regarding War Diaries and Intelligence Summaries are contained in F.S. Regs., Part II. and the Staff Manual respectively. Title pages will be prepared in manuscript.

Place	Date	Hour	Summary of Events and Information	Remarks and references to Appendices
Noeux les MINES	1.7.18		The 2nd Inf. Bde. was inspected by H.R.H. The Duke of Connaught at the Bois de DAMES (near BRUAY) + all three Bns were complimented by him on their turn-out smartness.	
ANNEQUIN	2.7.18		Bn moved into support + relieved 1st GLOSTER REGT. at ANNEQUIN. Details to BOIS D'OHLAIN. A draft of 15 O.Rks. joined.	
	3.7.18		Everything very quiet. Normal routine followed – Working parties and	
	4.7.18		a certain amount of platoon training.	
	5.7.18			
	6.7.18			
FRONT LINE LEFT HOHENZOLLERN SECTOR.	7.7.18.		Moved into front line relieving 2nd K.R.R.C. Feelin very quiet and practically unchanged from last tour in this front. The front line simply held now for observation purposes. Draft of 30 O.Rks joined	
	8.7.18.		Everything quiet. Normal work on improvement of defences. Normal trench Warfare.	
	9.7.18			
	10.7.18			
	11.7.18			
	12.7.18		Lieut. Coy retnd. Lt. A.P. Palmer joined the Bn + posted to D Coy.	
	13.7.18			
	14.7.18		Lt. F.C. Cockrill struck off strength, + proceeded to an Instructors Course at Aldershot	
	15.7.18			
	16.7.18		Drafts amounting to 75 O.Rks. joined Bn between 9th + 17th.	

Army Form C. 2118.

1st Northamptonshire Regt.

WAR DIARY 17th July.
or
INTELLIGENCE SUMMARY.
(Erase heading not required.)

Place	Date	Hour	Summary of Events and Information	Remarks and references to Appendices
ANNEQUIN.	17.7.18.		Moved back to ANNEQUIN as Bde in support. A Coy stayed in front line to enable Coy of 2nd R. Sussex to practice & execute a raid.	
	18.7.18			
	19.7.18		Normal routine of Working Parties & platoon training.	
	20.7.18			
	21.7.18		Moved back into NOEUX LES MINES.	
NOEUX les MINES.	22.7.18.		Baths and cleaning up. Lt. F.C. Papworth posted to 2nd Bn Northamptonshire Regt. Platoon now formed into 1 Lewis gun section & 3 with 2 guns.	
	23.7.18		Coy training at Bois d'OHLAIN. & 2 other sections.	
	24.7.18		Coy training.	
	25.7.18.		-do- -do-	
	26.7.18.		Training at "Bois d'OHLAIN".	
	27.7.18.		Unable to carry out Sports owing to weather. Special Regimental dinner for men & Sergts to celebrate TALAVERA.	
	28.7.18.		Church Parade. Major J.R. Frayth-Forrest left Bn to take over command of 1st L.N. Lancashire Regt. Major G.G. Gould Durham Light Infantry joined and assumed duties of 2nd in Command vice Major Forrest.	
	29.7.18.		Coy training.	
	30.7.18.		Coy training. I Lewis Sports carried out in afternoon & evening.	
	31.7.18.		Bn moved up & relieved 2 WELCH REGT in RIGHT CAMBRIN SECTOR.	

Army Form C. 2118.

August, 1916.

WAR DIARY
or
INTELLIGENCE SUMMARY.
(Erase heading not required.)

1st Bn The Northamptonshire Regt

Instructions regarding War Diaries and Intelligence Summaries are contained in F. S. Regs., Part II. and the Staff Manual respectively. Title pages will be prepared in manuscript.

Place	Date	Hour	Summary of Events and Information	Remarks and references to Appendices
CAMBRIN	1.8.16		Battalion in the front line in right sector CAMBRIN.	
	2.8.16		" " " " " " " "	
	3.8.16		" " " " " " " "	
	4.8.16		" " " " " " " "	
	5.8.16		" " " " " " " "	
	6.8.16		" " " " " " " "	
	7.8.16		" " " " " " " "	
	8.8.16		" " " " " " " "	
	9.8.16		" " " " " " " "	
	10.8.16		Battalion moves into support at CAMBRIN.	
	11.8.16		" " " " " "	
	12.8.16		" " " " " "	
	13.8.16		" " " " " " Capt & Quarter Master E.S. Hibbert joined Battn.	
	14.8.16		" " " " " " Capts Quarter Master proceeded to be given an appt as A.D.C.
	15.8.16		Capt F.G.S. MARTIN wounded. Capt Hofman joined Battn.	
	16.8.16		Lieut A.J. Tongue joined Battn.	
	17.8.16		Battalion in support at CAMBRIN.	
	18.8.16		Battalion moves into front line in left sector CAMBRIN area.	
	19.8.16		Lieut Legg wounded.	
	20.8.16		Battn in front line in left sector CAMBRIN area.	
	21.8.16		Battalion move by Bus to BOURS for a rest. Relieved by 18th Gloucester Regt of 16th Division. Transport move by road.	

Army Form C. 2118.

WAR DIARY
or
INTELLIGENCE SUMMARY. 1st Bn. The Northamptonshire Regt

(Erase heading not required.)

Instructions regarding War Diaries and Intelligence Summaries are contained in F. S. Regs., Part II. and the Staff Manual respectively. Title pages will be prepared in manuscript.

Place	Date	Hour	Summary of Events and Information	Remarks and references to Appendices
BOURS	22.8.18		General re-organisation of Battn.	
	23.8.18		Demonstration attack by 5th Bde details for Officers.	
	24.8.18		Platoon training. Following Officers joined the Battn. Lieuts I.A. Bellamy, W.P. Gibbs, C. Smeathers	
	25.8.18		Platoon Training. Capt A.B. Phillips & Lieut G. D. Aclanson joined the Battn.	
	26.8.18		-do-	
	27.8.18		Company training. Officers class for Tactical Schemes	
	28.8.18		-do- -do- -do-	
	29.8.18		-do- & Range -do-	
	30.9.18		-do- & Range practice	
ARRAS	31.9.18		Battalion entrained & entrain at Pernes. Detrain at ARRAS	

W.C. Cumming Col.
Lieut for Lt Col.
Commanding 1st Bn Northamptonshire Regt

Army Form C. 2118.

WAR DIARY
of 1st Northamptonshire Regt.
INTELLIGENCE SUMMARY.
(Erase heading not required.)

Instructions regarding War Diaries and Intelligence Summaries are contained in F. S. Regs., Part II. and the Staff Manual respectively. Title pages will be prepared in manuscript.

Place	Date	Hour	Summary of Events and Information	Remarks and references to Appendices
ARRAS	Sept 1		Arrived ARRAS at 2 am from DIEVAL. Battn in billets	
	2		Kit Inspections and marched to WANCOURT. Dinner on arrival to ChauMarque. 178	
			3rd Bn in Support 80 on the left, remainder on the right. Turned forward Bay to Support	
			Paraded to CHRISTIAN road in relief from work on OB LIFE SUPPLY	
	3		Relieved Kings Own 4th Divn at 10 pm in SUPPORT line in JAUNT-BLA	
			supporting 8 Albuera & DROUART DURANTHE, 18 Cameronians	
	4	4.30		
	5		Relieved by 1st London Scottish	
	6		Moved by CAMBRAI road and entrained to HERMANVILLE arrived at about 6.45	
	7		March CAMBRAI 22nd and 1000 to HAUTAVESNES, Battn Billet	
	8		One Coy (Y Company) moved at 1800 to...	
	9		Battn had Clean up	
	10		Divn at 9 am on trainings NCRW Manoeuvre Dismiss 6.45 1/2 ho...	
			Returned about 2 night	
	11		In the Butts in Schoolings	
	12		Cleaning up. Rain prevented any Parade	
	13		Field Day PLYMT & Mules and JHELOO 2nd to HAPPENCOURT. Turned Y	
			Issued Bd PLYMT SD MULES, and JHELOO 2nd to HAPPENCOURT. Turned Y	
	14		Battn 8 Bn Bivouacked in...	
	15		March 6.45 to tram...	
			March at 5.30 in Brace NEPTEN. TRY	

D.K. K...

Army Form C. 2118.

WAR DIARY
or INTELLIGENCE SUMMARY.

of 1st Battalion the [?]

September, 1916.

Vol. 4

(Erase heading not required.)

Instructions regarding War Diaries and Intelligence Summaries are contained in F.S. Regs., Part II. and the Staff Manual respectively. Title pages will be prepared in manuscript.

Place	Date	Hour	Summary of Events and Information	Remarks and references to Appendices
Origine Huts	16		Battalion moved from TERTRY to a wood at [?] HUMBERCOURT B.20.c.2.) Ref. map 62cSE.	
	17		Worked on aeroplane bombers. Loaned to 3rd Canadian Div. 32 men. Strong nor-easterly wind. Gale with rain. Several of the men without overcoats and rifles. Battalion moved down to assembly [?] in B.15.d.7.2, in support of the 2nd Royal Sussex Regt. was attacked at 5:20 am by the Germans and drove off by R.S.R. Enemy [?] the trenches were 2 officers and 23 other ranks	
	18		During the day 2 officers and [?] relieved in the evening (Appx 77 + [?])	
	19		On R.B. billets (rest movement)	
	20		Battalion in support. Behind the 2nd R. Sussex on support.	
	21		Came out of trenches at midnight, relieved by [?] (Appx 78), moved by road to O35), camped in [?]	
	22		6th Oxford Bde inc.) Wind storm & rain.	
	23		Cleaning up and [?] equipment	
			At 2:30 pm Battalion marched to Ancaster brigade	
			14/12/13	

B.C. Smart
Lt Col
13

WAR DIARY
INTELLIGENCE SUMMARY.
(Erase heading not required.)

Army Form C. 2118.

Hour, Date, Place	Summary of Events and Information	Remarks and references to Appendices
1st Oct. 1918 GAULAINCOURT.	The Battalion was encamped in LAKE WOODS EAST OF GAULAINCOURT, resting after the operations of the 24th September. On the 9th orders were received to stand by ready to move and on the 10th the Battalion proceeded by route march through MAISSEMY, PONTRUET and BELLENGLISE to MAGNY-LA-FOSSÉ	
10th Oct 1918 MAGNY-LA-FOSSÉ.	The companies were bivouaced in a line of disused trenches and Bn. H.Q in the ruined chateau. Six days were spent here in company training and battalion schemes. On the morning of the 16th the Battalion marched through LE VERGIER, SEQUEHART, FRESNOY-LE-GRAND and bivouaced at 2 p.m. about one kilomètre NORTH OF BOHAIN	
16th Oct 1918. 1 Kilm. N of BOHAIN.	Orders were received that the Battalion would attack next morning and pass thro' the 1st BUFFS. 18 Bde. on the first objective and continue the advance and capture LA VALLEE MULÂTRE and WASSIGNY. At 1 a.m. 17th Oct the Battalion moved through BECQUIGNY to its assembly points at LES FAUX VIVIERS in the BOIS DE BUSIGNY. At Zero 5.20 a.m. the attack commenced under a creeping barrage.	

WAR DIARY
or
INTELLIGENCE SUMMARY.
(Erase heading not required.)

Army Form C. 2118

Hour, Date, Place	Summary of Events and Information	Remarks and references to Appendices
	Attached is an account of the operations of the 17th	
	Officer Casualties.	Casualties in O.Rs.
	2/Lieut R.S. STRANGE } Killed in action " F.A. GEORGE	91 including 12 killed.
	Lieut A. SI & COLDWELL 2/Lieut A. FULLEN (2nd L.M.B) } Wounded. 2/Lieut R. LEWIS " J.T. ROBERTS " B.L. KEESHAN } Gassed.	
18th Oct. 1918.	Battalion rested for the night at BOIS ST PIERRE.	
19th Oct. 1918.	and next day moved at 4.30 p.m. thro' VALLÉE MULATRE and RIBEAUVILLE to MAZINGHIEN where it relieved the	
23rd Oct. 1918.	At 1.20 a.m. the Battalion attacked under a creeping barrage and took objectives EAST of the CANAL DE LA SAMBRE A L'OISE. and CATILLON. Attached is an account of the attack. The Battalion was relieved in the evening by the 1st Royal Highlanders and went back to LA VALLÉE MULATRE.	

Army Form C. 2118

WAR DIARY
or
INTELLIGENCE SUMMARY.

(Erase heading not required.)

Instructions regarding War Diaries and Intelligence Summaries are contained in F.S. Regs., Part II. and the Staff Manual respectively. Title pages will be prepared in manuscript.

Hour, Date, Place	Summary of Events and Information	Remarks and references to Appendices
	Officer Casualties on the 23/10/18.	
	Lieut L T D STABLES } Killed in action	
	2nd Lieut G.O. TIMMINS }	
	2nd Lieut E H ANSCOMB wounded.	
	Casualties O.Rs	
	66.	
	12 killed.	

WAR DIARY
or
INTELLIGENCE SUMMARY.

(Erase heading not required.)

Army Form C. 2118.

Instructions regarding War Diaries and Intelligence Summaries are contained in F. S. Regs., Part II. and the Staff Manual respectively. Title pages will be prepared in manuscript.

Place	Date	Hour	Summary of Events and Information	Remarks and references to Appendices
LA VALLÉE MULATRE	24–27/X/1918.		Battalion resting and reorganising.	
	27/X/1918.		Battalion moved up by route march through RIBEAUVILLE and relieved the 1st BLACK WATCH. EAST of MAZINGHIEN. A coy had 12 casualties from shell fire during the relief.	
	28/X/1918		Dispositions of the Battalion. A coy. left coy. B coy centre coy. C coy right coy. D coy support. During the day the Battalion endeavoured to to reach the line of the CANAL DE LA SAMBRE A L'OISE by peaceful penetration. The right company reached the canal without opposition but the centre company met with strong opposition from machine guns and snipers.	
	29/X/1918.		At 8.00 the centre coy attacked under a barrage and gained all its objectives except a strong point on the right flank by 8.25. 15 prisoners + several M.Gs were captured in this attack. Prisoners were of the 78. R.I.R.	

WAR DIARY
or
INTELLIGENCE SUMMARY

Army Form C. 2118.

(Erase heading not required.)

WD (Cancel 5th Commanding) 1/5th N. Hampshire Regt
For LV

Place	Date	Hour	Summary of Events and Information	Remarks and references to Appendices
	29/X/1918	14.15	The entire coy again attacked, and gained all its objectives by 14.30.	
		16.55.	The Boche counter attacked in strength and pushed the right of the left company and also the left of the centre company.	
		5.03.	The Boche again counter attacked in force and pushed back the right flank slightly. The enemy attacked in two parties, one hastily attacked the left coy. from the direction of CATILLON, and the other enveloped the centre coy. by a ridge by the barrage and attacked the right of the entire company.	
		12.00	The left and centre companies again attacked under the cover of a creeping barrage (100 yds. in 4 minutes) but were again held up by M.G. fire from the strong point on the right flank. All objectives were gained by 16.20 and at 19.00 the Battalion was relieved by the 1st Bn. the Gloucestershire Regt on the line of the canal. The left company had formed a defensive flank south of	
	30/X/1918			

Army Form C. 2118.

WAR DIARY
or
INTELLIGENCE SUMMARY.

(Erase heading not required.)

Place	Date	Hour	Summary of Events and Information	Remarks and references to Appendices
CATILLON.	30/X/1918		The Battalion marched out to VAUX ANDIGNY through HAZINGHIEN, L'ARBRE de GUISE and MOLAIN.	
VAUX ANDIGNY.	31/X/1918		Casualties for 29/30th 4/5 R.P.Bgde Killed in action. 15 O.R. do 39 O.R. Wounded. 13 O.R. Missing.	

WAR DIARY

INTELLIGENCE SUMMARY

of 1st Bn The Northamptonshire Regt.

Army Form C. 2118.

Place	Date	Hour	Summary of Events and Information	Remarks and references to Appendices
VAUX ANDIGNY	1-11-18		Battalion resting.	
	2-11-18		Five Officers posted to the Bn, belonging to the Bedford & Bucks Light Infantry. Viz: MORTEN, COBBOLD, DRAYTON, SPOKES, STEVENS. Also a draft of 10 O.R.	
MAZINGHIEN	3-11-18		At 5.30 p.m. the Bn marched up to & bivouaced near MAZINGHIEN preparing for attack – marched off again at 11pm to assembly positions just E. of Sambre-Oise Canal.	
	4-11-18		At 5.20 the 1st Division attacked to cross Canal. 1st Bde on left. Second Bde on Right, 3rd Bde to capture CATILLON. 32nd Division on left B. 1st Division – French chasseurs Divn on right. Bn in support to Bde. 60th on Right, R. Sussex on left. Attack launched under cover of a heavy bombardment. Morning misty. Enemy retaliation heavy on support line – R. Sussex crossed Canal at lock with 60th in spite of heavy opposition from enemy M.G. in lock buildings. Bridges were thrown over by 409 Field Coy R.E. & assisted by 28 men under 2/Lt MANSFIELD from the Bn. At 6 am the R. Sussex & 60th Bn crossed the Canal. The Bn crossed about 6.15 am.	A/C Lieutenant H. S. Humphreys P/C Bdg 1st Northants Bde [illegible signatures]

WAR DIARY

of 1st Bn Northamptonshire Regt

INTELLIGENCE SUMMARY

Army Form C. 2118.

Place	Date	Hour	Summary of Events and Information	Remarks and references to Appendices
MAZINGHIEN	4.11.18		line over the Canal there was slight opposition. The Battn took up position in support just W of L'ERMITAGE Road, when two companies were sent forward to support the R. Sussex Regt. The 1st Objective was gained everywhere by 9am & attack pushed forward to the second objective which was also successful. The French on the right & the 1st Bde on the left had meanwhile also pushed on & were across the Canal everywhere at about 2pm. The Bn went forward to capture the village of FESMY & link up with the French Division on the right. B & D Coys pushed forward & cleared the village with the exception of the East end where the enemy put up a determined resistance with his machine guns. Eventually supported by trench mortars the whole village was cleared by 4.30 p.m. By this time it was becoming dark. A pocket of M. Gs was still holding out on our right making liaison with the French impossible. Patrols were pushed forward to the intentional ~~intentional~~ post for me arranged at La Justice & Patrols but failed to find French patrols.	

W.C. Furmenger
Lt Col
Comdg 1st Northamptonshire
Regt.

Army Form C. 2118.

WAR DIARY of 1st Bn. Northamptonshire Regt.
INTELLIGENCE SUMMARY

Instructions regarding War Diaries and Intelligence Summaries are contained in F.S. Regs., Part II. and the Staff Manual respectively. Title pages will be prepared in manuscript.

(Erase heading not required.)

Place	Date	Hour	Summary of Events and Information	Remarks and references to Appendices
Gd FESMY.	4.11.18		A right defensive flank was therefore formed to the Bole by the Batn with B. Do Coys & Coy remaining in support.	
	5.11.18		At 5 am we were in touch with the French & post prearranged at LA JUSTICE Xroads. Our defensive flank was swung forward by B Coy. ~~Capt~~ O.C. Coy came back into support. It was found that the enemy had retired in the night & except for slight artillery fire all was quiet. The 46th & a new French Division continued the attack through the 1st Division & eventually about 3 pm the Bole was squared out through the 46th & the French joining hands. About 4.30 pm orders were given for the Bn to march back to billets in LA VALLÉE MULATRE & WASSIGNY.	TOTAL CASUALTIES MISSING 2/Lieut L.J. MORTEN and 7 O.Ranks KILLED IN ACTION 2/Lieut R.W. COBBOLD and 31 O.Ranks WOUNDED { 2/Lieut R.J. TONQUET M.M. Lieut R. FARRELL 2 Lt Jennings N. joined 15 CET 2nd Lt for Northamptonshire Regt 29 E.T.
LA VALLÉE MULATRE 6.11.18 FRESNOY.			The Bn billeted in LA VALLÉE MULATRE & continued the march back to FRESNOY where they restarted B the 1st Division were concentrated & out of the line for a rest.	

WAR DIARY of 1st Bn. The Northamptonshire Regt.
INTELLIGENCE SUMMARY.

Army Form C. 2118.

Instructions regarding War Diaries and Intelligence Summaries are contained in F.S. Regs., Part II. and the Staff Manual respectively. Title pages will be prepared in manuscript.

(Erase heading not required.)

Place	Date	Hour	Summary of Events and Information	Remarks and references to Appendices
FRESNOY	7.11.18		Battalion clean up.	
	8.11.18			
	9.11.18		Extensive training	
	10.11.18		Church Parade.	
	11.11.18		Armistice signed.	
	12.11.18		Bn. Training. Draft of 5 & 8 O.R.	
FAVRIL	13.11.18		Battn. move by bus to FAVRIL. Capt. T.E.M. Pierson & 25 O.R. move up per Rail.	
	14.11.18			
	15.11.18		} Battn. remain at FAVRIL.	
	16.11.18		Battn. commence the "march to the Rhine" & march to SARS POTERIES.	
SARS POTERIES	17.11.18		Draft of 11 O.Rs. Capt. A.G. McNaught, 2Lt Irons, C.S.M. Adams, Sgt Rogers & Sgt Jones proceed to England to receive the Regtl Colours.	
	18.11.18		Remain at SARS POTERIES.	
	19.11.18		Bn. march through SOLRE le CHATEAU - HESTRUD - BEAUMONT to STRÉE. First batch of released prisoners pass through us — English, French & Italians. One man from our own battn passed us having been captured on Oct 28th 1918.	
STRÉE				
PRY	20.11.18		Bn. march through CLERMONT & RODNEE to PRY.	
	21.11.18		} Remain at PRY. Battalion parade for ceremonial.	
	22.11.18			

W.G. Gurney Lt Col
Comdg 1st Northampton Regt

Army Form C. 2118.

WAR DIARY
of 1st Bn. The North amptonshire Regt.
INTELLIGENCE SUMMARY.

(Erase heading not required.)

Instructions regarding War Diaries and Intelligence Summaries are contained in F. S. Regs., Part II. and the Staff Manual respectively. Title pages will be prepared in manuscript.

Place	Date	Hour	Summary of Events and Information	Remarks and references to Appendices
MORIALMÉ	23.11.18		Bn. march through CHASTRES to MORIALMÉ.	
FALAEN	24.11.18		Bn. march through FLORENNES – CORENNE – FLAVION to FALAEN. The whole village turn out to welcome us.	
	25.11.18		The Band perform in the village square & the formation? Ladies thoroughly enjoy dancing on the pebbles.	
	26.11.18		Bn. ceremonial drill. Lt. Col. G. St. G. Robinson awarded the D.S.O.	
	27.11.18			
	28.11.18		2/Lt H. G. Brown, 2/Lt S. G. Bedford & 2/Lt Scotding join the Battn.	
	29.11.18		Capt. G. C. Martin rejoins Battn. & takes over command of D-Coy. 2/Lt B. A. Hill rejoin Bn. & posted to B Coy.	
	30.11.18		Bn. ceremonial parade.	

W.C. Spurcroft
Lieut. Col.
Lieut Col.
Comdg 1st Northamptonshire Regt.

WAR DIARY of 1/5 Bn Northamptonshire Regt
INTELLIGENCE SUMMARY

Honours & Awards for month of November.

D.S.O. Lt Col. G. L. G. Robinson M.C.   26.11.18.

M.C.
- 2/Lt C. Smeathers   15.11.18
- 2/Lt W. J. N. Taylor   15.11.18
- 2/Lt A. E. S. Bayley   15.11.18
- 2/Lt J. H. Knight   15.11.18

D.C.M.
- 7324 C.S.M. H. Roughton D.C.M. 15.11.18.
- 9055 C.S.M. Adams. R.   M.M.   15.11.18
- 3/10420 Sgt Dwen. C. M.M. 9 bar 21.11.18
- 49640 Pte Dye A.H.   21.11.18

M.M. 9 bar.
- 9348 Sgt Perkins J.   M.M.
- 40703 Cpl Burns M.   M.M.
- 10308 Pte Chapman A. M.M.

M.M.
- 59323 Pte Bleese J.
- 37092 - Fawden T.
- 315712 - Wills R.
- 32847 Cpl Acton V.J.
- 6414 Pte Reynolds M.
- 24365 - Read J.
- 31209 L/Cpl Hedden H.
- 15905 Pte Littlemore J.
- 28337 - Wright W.C.
- 43333 Cpl Hayes R.
- 16599 Sgt Walpole C.
- 204857 Pte Jewell H.
- 40725 - Callaghan T.
- 23085 Sig Mitchell J.
- 40900 - Howard H.
- 3/10232 L/Cpl Arrowsmith A.

N.J. Jennings
Lt for 15 CO
Comdg 1/5 Northamptonshire Regt.

WAR DIARY 1st Bn Northamptonshire Regt
INTELLIGENCE SUMMARY.

(Erase heading not required.)

Army Form C. 2118.

Vol 51

Place	Date	Hour	Summary of Events and Information	Remarks and references to Appendices
SOMMIÈRE	1/11/18		Battn march route to SOMMIÈRE.	
MIRANDA CHATEAU	2/11/18		Battn march route through DINANT to MIRANDA CHATEAU.	
			Battn march over the MEUSE the bridge across the MEUSE at DINANT playing by the Regimental Band.	
VILLERS SUR LESSE	3/11/18		march to VILLERS SUR LESSE. The villagers turn out to greet us.	
	4/11/18 5/11/18 6/11/18		Battalion ceremonial parades. Village band plays the King to the C.O. Cure & Burgomaster introduced. Drinks all round. Dance in the evening for N.C.Os & men. Young ladies of the village invited. C.O. presented with a bouquet from the Curates de CUINCHY. Colour party return from NORTHAMPTON with the colours.	
	7/11/18		Battn march to CHEVETOGNE ABBEY. The last colours carried on the march for the first time since the war. The Abbey inhabited by monks & nuns of the Benedictine Order. Unfortunately they were unable to produce any legume of that ilk.	

N.C. Jermyn Lt/Col
Comdg 1st Northampton Regt

WAR DIARY
or
INTELLIGENCE SUMMARY

1st Bn Northamptonshire Regt.

Army Form C. 2118.

Place	Date	Hour	Summary of Events and Information	Remarks and references to Appendices
CHEVETOGNE ABBEY.	8/12/18		Bn. remained billeted in CHEVETOGNE ABBEY. A Ceremonial Parade was held at 11.00 and the Colours which were handed over to the Depôt on the outbreak of war in August 1914 for safe custody, having been brought out from England by a special Colour Party sent home from the Bn, were handed over on parade to the Battn. The Battalion was drawn up in line and the colour party who brought out the Colours (Capt. A.G. McNaught, 2nd Lt. F. Irons, R.S.M. Adams, Sgts. Rogers & Jones) marched on parade with the Colours at the Carry. The Battn. presenting arms, Colours were then handed over to a new Colour Party and Bn. again presented arms. Bn. then formed up & remarched past, first in Column & afterwards Close Column of Coys. The G.O.C. 2nd Bde. being present on parade took the Salute. On completion of the March Past the Bn. piled arms & fell out. The Colours were carried over a Pile of Rifles at the Saluting Base & men were allowed to go up & inspect them. Divine Service was held on the same ground at 12.15. Parade for Northamptonshire Regt.	Capt. 1st Northamptonshire Regt.

WAR DIARY 1st Bn. Northamptonshire R.t.

Army Form C. 2118.

or

INTELLIGENCE SUMMARY.

(Erase heading not required.)

Instructions regarding War Diaries and Intelligence Summaries are contained in F. S. Regs., Part II. and the Staff Manual respectively. Title pages will be prepared in manuscript.

Place	Date	Hour	Summary of Events and Information	Remarks and references to Appendices
SINSIN	9/12/18		Bn. moved by March Route to SINSIN (about 6 miles) punched at 10.30 + arrived in billets 12.30. Rained whole time on march - roads very bad.	
HOTTON	10/12/18		Bn. moved by March Route to HOTTON (about 12 miles) punched 10.30 + arrived in billets 14.40.	
EREZÉE	11/12/18		Bn. moved by March Route to EREZÉE - CLERHEID area (about 9 miles). Paraded at 09.30 and arrived in billets 13.00. Bn. H.Q. billeted in EREZÉE. A & B coys in ERPIGNY. C & D coys CLERHEID. Bn. very scattered. Rained during the march - roads bad.	
	12/12/18		On command in Billets in EREZÉE, CLERHEID area. spent the day in generally cleaning up, arms, equipment + transport - threshed weather. Rained hard the whole morning.	
MALEMPRÉ	14/12/18		Bn. moved by March Route to MALEMPRÉ (about 9 miles). Paraded at 09.30 + arrived in billets 13.30. Billets poor + great amount of sickness among civilian population.	(signed) 2/Lt (acting) L? Col for Lt Col. comdg 1st Northamptonshire R?

WAR DIARY
1st Bn Northamptonshire Regt
INTELLIGENCE SUMMARY

Army Form C. 2118.

Place	Date	Hour	Summary of Events and Information	Remarks and references to Appendices
SART	13/12/18		Bn moved by March Route to SART (10 miles). Paraded at 09.30, arrived in billets 13.15. Bn HQ, C & D Coys in PETIT SART. A & B Coys & Transport in GRAND SART.	
ROGERY	14/12/18		Bn moved by March Route to ROGERY (about 6 miles). Paraded at 09.35, arrived in billets at 12.00. Rained the whole morning.	
NEIDINGEN	17/12/18		Bn moved by March Route to NEIDINGEN & BREITFELD (about 15 miles) via K.06 near BEHO. The frontier was crossed at K.06 near BEHO. The 3/6 1st Divn Cav shared on the frontier & a Union Jack was hoisted. The Bn marched and unit Colours flying & all the army Equipment issued on Victorious marching the salute was given. Band & Drums who went ahead of the head of the Bn immediately after crossing the frame wheeled to the left turned & played the "Bn past" to the Bn onward in billets at 14.00. Very very regimental march. Bn arrived in billets and expressed himself as entirely satisfied with them.	

Army Form C. 2118.

WAR DIARY 1st Bn Northamptonshire Regt.
or
INTELLIGENCE SUMMARY.

(Erase heading not required.)

Instructions regarding War Diaries and Intelligence Summaries are contained in F. S. Regs., Part II. and the Staff Manual respectively. Title pages will be prepared in manuscript.

Place	Date	Hour	Summary of Events and Information	Remarks and references to Appendices
MANDERFELD	12/12/18		Bn moved by March Route to MANDERFELD via (REMMEL (about 15 miles) Paraded at 8.30 arrived in billets at 15.00 Route NEIDINGEN - ST VITH - SCHONBERG. Rain fell the whole day. Billets good.	
DAHLEM	19/12/18		Bn moved by March Route to DAHLEM (about 12 miles) Paraded 8.50; arrived in billets at 14.00 Very cold day, slight snow. Billets good, whole Bn together	
	20/12/18		Bn remained in billets in DAHLEM.	
BLANKEN-HEIMERDORF	21/12/18		Bn moved by March Route to BLANKENHEIMERDORF. (about 9 miles) Paraded at 8.30 arrived in billets 11.45. Cold day but day. Ground covered with snow.	
MUNSTEREIFEL	22/12/18		Bn moved by March Route to MUNSTEREIFEL (about 12 miles) Paraded 8.30, arrived in billets at 14.00. Fine clear day. Fine scenery.	2/Lt [illegible] 1st Bn [illegible] Northamptonshire Regt. [illegible]

WAR DIARY 1st Bn. Northamptonshire Regt Army Form C. 2118.
or
INTELLIGENCE SUMMARY.
(Erase heading not required.)

Place	Date	Hour	Summary of Events and Information	Remarks and references to Appendices
ODENDORF	23/12/18		Bn. marched by March Route to ODENDORF (8 miles) Paraded at 9.25 arrived in billets at 13.00	
DUISDORF	24/12/18		Bn. moved by March Route to DUISDORF (8 miles) the final destination a large sized village some few miles from BONN. Billets easy quartered in the school. Bn. all in good billets, Coy in private houses very scattered but very comfortable. A, B & D coys. Three large halls were discovered. Two of which have been fitted up as dining halls. One for A & B coy & one for C & D. The third is being used as a recreation room.	W (ounded) 2/L for L.Cpl Northamptonshire Regt. early L Northamptonshire Regt
	25/12/18		Church Parade in the Recreation Room	
	26/12/18		Day was spent in settling down & cleaning up	
	27/12/18		Inspections, cleaning up	
	28/12/18		Officers dinner in C+D's dining hall	

WAR DIARY 1/2 Bn Northamptonshire Regt.
or
INTELLIGENCE SUMMARY.

Army Form C. 2118.

(Erase heading not required.)

Instructions regarding War Diaries and Intelligence Summaries are contained in F. S. Regs., Part II. and the Staff Manual respectively. Title pages will be prepared in manuscript.

Place	Date	Hour	Summary of Events and Information	Remarks and references to Appendices
DUISDORF	29/12/18		Mens dinner + Sergts dinner + smoking concert in the evening	
	30/12/18		Draft of 171 men joined. Divisional Conference on Education. Entrain Siegburg to Bonn. Bn proceeded to Ruhen in Bonn	
	31/12/18		Bn was lectured by the C.O. on the educational scheme. One Q.M.S. and four sergts were ordered to two periods R.W. en route for England to join demobilization camp	2nd Cavend 2 W. Col / Cd / at Northampton for Northampton Cavendy

WAR DIARY
of 1st Bn the N. Hampshire Regt

Army Form C. 2118.

INTELLIGENCE SUMMARY.

(Erase heading not required.)

Instructions regarding War Diaries and Intelligence Summaries are contained in F.S. Regs., Part II. and the Staff Manual respectively. Title pages will be prepared in manuscript.

Place	Date	Hour	Summary of Events and Information	Remarks and references to Appendices
DUISDORF	1/1/19		Twenty three men with over four years service abroad were sent to dispersal stations in England for demobilization.	
			The band played the party into BONN	
	2/1/19		Training under company arrangements and recreational training in the afternoon.	
	3/1/19		Company training.	
	4/1/19		Two men demobilised. In the afternoon a team from A and B Coys lost C+D Coys at football	
	5/1/19		Church Parade. Recreational training in the afternoon.	
	6/1/19		On training and Education scheme started. Lectures given by platoon commanders on various subjects.	

Army Form C. 2118.

WAR DIARY
of 1st Bn Hertfordshire Regt
INTELLIGENCE SUMMARY.

(Erase heading not required.)

Instructions regarding War Diaries and Intelligence Summaries are contained in F. S. Regs., Part II. and the Staff Manual respectively. Title pages will be prepared in manuscript.

Place	Date	Hour	Summary of Events and Information	Remarks and references to Appendices
DUISDORF	7/1/19		Coy Training & Education	
	8/1/19		Eight men went to demand station in England for demobilization	
	9/1/19		Battalion route march to BONN and fell out onto banks of the Rhine and returned to billets at 12.15. Coy Training. Recreational Train in afternoon.	
	10/1/19		Coy Training	
	11/1/19		Coy Training	
	12/1/19		Church Parade. 2 Officers & 38 O.Rs went to Cologne & DUREN to proceed to dispersal stations in England for demobilization.	Lt/Col (Comd. Bn.) for Lt Col CF Candy 1st Bn Hertfordshire Regt
	13/1/19		Lecture on demobilization	
	14/1/19		Coy Training, one coy firing on miniature range	
	15/1/19		Coy. Training	
	16/1/19			
	17/1/19			

Army Form C. 2118.

WAR DIARY of 1st Bn. The Northamptonshire Regt

INTELLIGENCE SUMMARY.

(Erase heading not required.)

Instructions regarding War Diaries and Intelligence Summaries are contained in F.S. Regs., Part II. and the Staff Manual respectively. Title pages will be prepared in manuscript.

Place	Date	Hour	Summary of Events and Information	Remarks and references to Appendices
DUISDORF	18/1/19		Played Regimental team played 2nd K.R.R.C. at Association football result 7-2 against	
	19/1/19		2 Officers and 17 O.Rs. went to Demobilization Camp at DÜREN & proceeded to England for final demobilization. Church Parade. Regimental team played 2nd Royal Sussex Regiment at Hockey. Result 2-2. Drums.	
	20/1/19		to Concert Party of the 2nd K.R.R.C. performed in O & D Messing hall at 18.30.	
	21/1/19		31 O.Rs. proceeded to the Concentration Camp at DÜREN to proceed to England for demobilization	
	22/1/19		Battn. route march & educational training	
	23/1/19		Coy Training & education	
	24/1/19		— Lecture on "Canada" by Lieut Summers Canadian Dett.	
	25/1/19		Battn play R Sussex Regt at Association T. Won 1-0	McJunior Lieut / Adjt 1st Bn Northamptonshire Regt

Army Form C. 2118.

WAR DIARY of 1st Bn. The Northamptonshire Regt

INTELLIGENCE SUMMARY.

(Erase heading not required).

Place	Date	Hour	Summary of Events and Information	Remarks and references to Appendices
DUISDORF	26/1/19		Coy training & education. 20 men proceeded to England for demobilisation. Hockey Battn versus Royal Sussex won 2-0.	
	27/1/19		First round of Bde coy team competition results. (A) team A coy v 2nd R. Sussex B coy. won 2-0. (B) -"- v -"- lost 5-2 (A) team B coy v 2nd Bde H.Q. lost 1-0. (B) -"- v -"- won 9-0 (A) team C coy v 2nd K.R.R.C. won 2-1 (B) -"- v -"- lost 2-0. (A) team D coy v 2nd Field Ambulance draw 3-3 (B) -"- v -"- won 5-2. This day was a whole holiday In the afternoon Commander Lord Broome gave an interesting lecture with lantern slides on the work of the Navy during the war as played by every type of vessel including Aeroplanes	NC Furnivair Lieut for Lieut Col. Northamptonshire Regt

WAR DIARY of 1st Bn. The Northamptonshire Regt.

INTELLIGENCE SUMMARY.

Army Form C. 2118.

(Erase heading not required.)

Place	Date	Hour	Summary of Events and Information	Remarks and references to Appendices
DUISDORF	28/1/19		Company & Educational Training. Lecture by Captain H. Towse V.C. on "The Comrades of the Great War Association".	
"	29/1/19		Battalion scheme in Street Fighting. Battalion played the 2nd Field Ambulance at Association & won 4-0.	
"	30/1/19		Company & Educational Training. All leave stopped owing to congestion of traffic at the Base.	
"	31/1/19		Second round of the Brigade inter-company Association Football competition. Results: "A" teams: "A" Coy v 2nd KRRC "C" Coy. lost 0-3. " " : "C" " v 2nd R. Sussex "B" Coy. won 2-0. " " : "D" " v 2nd Field Ambulance. lost 1-2. "B" teams: "B" Coy v 2nd R. Sussex "A" Coy. won 4-1. " " : "D" " a Bye. Leave re-opened. 2 Gunns H.C. proceeds on leave.	A. C. Bertranges Lieut. Col. 1st Bn. Northamptonshire [Regt]

WAR DIARY
of 1st Bn The Northamptonshire Regt
INTELLIGENCE SUMMARY

Army Form C. 2118.

Vol 53

Place	Date	Hour	Summary of Events and Information	Remarks and references to Appendices
DUISDORF	1/2/19		Coy + Educational Training. First game of the inter-unit football (association) competition played. Bath v Royal Sussex Regt. Draw 1 – 1.	A.F.W. 3118 submitted to Bde HQ. Study for Northamptonshire Regt.
	2/2/19		Church Parade. 2 offrs + 60 OR's per coy attended.	
	3/2/19		Result of semi-final of Bde inter-coy football competition. C coy v 2 Field Ambulance Draw 0 – 0. B " v R. Sussex Regt "D" Won 5 – 0. D " v " "B" Lost 1 – 2.	
	4/2/19		Company route marches. Replay of inter-coy C coy v 2 Field Ambulance Lost 0 – 1. Lt Tipler & 2Lt Stevens proceed to demobilisation centre.	
	5/2/19		Bn route march. Inter-unit football compt – Bn v 2nd KRRC won 3 – 0.	

Army Form C. 2118.

WAR DIARY
or
INTELLIGENCE SUMMARY.
(Erase heading not required.)

Instructions regarding War Diaries and Intelligence Summaries are contained in F. S. Regs., Part II. and the Staff Manual respectively. Title pages will be prepared in manuscript.

Place	Date	Hour	Summary of Events and Information	Remarks and references to Appendices
DUISDORF	6/7/19		Educational & Company Training. Bde football competition. The final of the inter coy Bde football competition. "B" Coys 2nd team win versus R. Sussex Regt "3" Coy. Score 7-0.	
	7/7/19		Educational & Coy Training. Lt TIPLER & Lt STEVENS proceed to demobilisation camp.	
	8/7/19		Final of the Bde inter-unit football competition. Bn v No 2 Field Ambulance. Bn won 2-1. A Cup is to be presented to the Bn.	
	9/7/19		Church Parade B 1 Offr & 40 O.R. per company.	
	10/7/19		Coy & Educational Training. Brig-Gen Kelly D.S.O. present - also the won cup to "B" Coy for winning Football Cup to the Battn - the inter-coy Bde football comp't.	
	11/7/19		Battn route-march. Lts A & G Colwell & A.W. Kinsley proceed to England on 2 mths furlough prior to serving abroad with the 58th	Lieut A.C. Jamieson proceed to Northampton Regt

WAR DIARY of 1st Northamptonshire Regt.

INTELLIGENCE SUMMARY

Army Form C. 2118.

Place	Date	Hour	Summary of Events and Information	Remarks and references to Appendices
DUISDORF	13/7/19		Bde Cross country run – 1st Camerons 1st Scottish 6th Place	
	14/7/19		Coy & Educational Training. Bde Tug of War competition. Results – Bns 110 above winners 1st Northamptonshire Regt. Under – : – No 2 F. Ambulance	
	15/7/19		Capt Preston proceeds to Demobilisation Camp. Battn band arrives Bandmaster W Cresswell + 27 ORs. complete mit 2½ tons of Kit.	
	16/7/19		Church Parade 15β + 40 URs per coy attended Bishop Fordham lectures on German & English colonies compared.	
	17/7/19		Divisional cross-country run (distance 4 miles) 1st Camerons 10th place. L/Cpl Harding 11th place.	
	18/7/19		Coy & Educational Training	
	19/7/19		Bn beat Divl Engineers in Tug of War 1st Divisional Championship 4 to 0. Football: Officers v Sergeants 3–1	

Army Form C. 2118.

WAR DIARY
of 1st Northamptonshire Regt
INTELLIGENCE SUMMARY.
(Erase heading not required.)

Place	Date	Hour	Summary of Events and Information	Remarks and references to Appendices
DUISDORF	20/7/19		Coy of Educational Training	
	21/7/19		—	
	22/7/19		Semi-final of Divnl Football competition. The Battn versus the Divnl Engineers. Score 1-1.	
	23/7/19		Battn Church Parade.	
	24/7/19		Battn inspected by the G.O.C. 2nd Bde. Bde Boxing Tournament in the evening. Winner of welter weight - Pte Middlemiss. Winner of light weight L/Cpl Pilcher - both of the battn.	
	25/7/19		Replay of the football semi-final - score 0-0. Extra time was played. There was no score. Teams played for 2 mins 10 mins.	
	26/7/19		Replay of semi-final lost 4-0.	

Army Form C. 2118.

WAR DIARY
of 1st Northamptonshire Rgt
INTELLIGENCE SUMMARY.
(Erase heading not required.)

Instructions regarding War Diaries and Intelligence Summaries are contained in F. S. Regs., Part II. and the Staff Manual respectively. Title pages will be prepared in manuscript.

Place	Date	Hour	Summary of Events and Information	Remarks and references to Appendices
DUISDORF	27/2/19		A whole holiday for the Division. Football, Boxing & Rugby War finals in BONN.	
	28/2/19		Lecture by Lieut B. HAKE on "The contending forces in Europe"	

A.G. Summary for 1st N.T.T.C
Cmdg 1st Nor Hamptonshire Rgt

Army Form C. 2118.

WAR DIARY
or
INTELLIGENCE SUMMARY.
(Erase heading not required.)

Instructions regarding War Diaries and Intelligence Summaries are contained in F.S. Regs, Part II. and the Staff Manual respectively. Title pages will be prepared in manuscript.

Vol 54

Place	Date	Hour	Summary of Events and Information	Remarks and references to Appendices
DUSDORF	1/3/19		Church Parade 10:30 & 1:30 SRs.	
	2/3/19		Usual training	
	3/3/19		Preparations for relief were made.	
	4/3/19		Battalion relieved by 52nd Welsh. Move to LENGSDORF at 17.00 hrs.	
LENGSDORF	5/3/19		70 men demobilised	
	6/3/19		Divisional General bid farewell in a speech to the Battalion	
	7/3/19		Usual training	
	8/3/19		200 of the Battalion went for a trip up the Rhine as far as Andernach. The band went also	
	9/3/19		Church Parade 10:30, 11:30 SRs	
	10/3/19		Usual training	
	11/3/19		The Doctor (Capt F.D.T. Hayes) leaves the Battalion & is attached to the 52nd Welsh.	

Army Form C. 2118.

WAR DIARY
or
INTELLIGENCE SUMMARY.
(Erase heading not required.)

Instructions regarding War Diaries and Intelligence Summaries are contained in F.S. Regs., Part II. and the Staff Manual respectively. Title pages will be prepared in manuscript.

Place	Date	Hour	Summary of Events and Information	Remarks and references to Appendices
LENGSDORF	12/3/19		As usual.	
	13/3/19		7 Officers & 300 ORs proceed to be attached to the 53rd Bedford Regt at WAHN on boat cuise of the Rhine. The Band played the party to Bonn.	
	14/3/19		1 Off & 6 ORs Transferred to 53rd Bedfords.	
	15/3/19		3 Offrs & 40 proceed on a Trip up the Rhine as the paddle boat ELDERBERG. The day was very cold & the trip not appreciated to its full extent.	
	16/3/19		Church Parade	
	17/3/19		Battalion amalgamated into one company. 27 ORs demobilised	
	18/3/19		1 Officer & 10 ORs proceed to join the 53rd Bedford R.P.	
	19/3/19		As usual.	
	20/3/19		Semi final of the Army football competition. Cameron Highlanders Won 2-0 against 10 Corps R.E.	
	21/3/19		10 ORs proceed to Demobilisation Camp.	
	22nd		5 ORs	

WAR DIARY

or INTELLIGENCE SUMMARY.

Army Form C. 2118.

1st Bn. The Northamptonshire Regt

(Erase heading not required.)

Place	Date	Hour	Summary of Events and Information	Remarks and references to Appendices
KENGSDORF	23/3/19		Church Parade. Checking all Mobilization stores. Preparing for Ordnance board (held at 10 am)	
	24/3/19		Semi-final of Army football competition. 1 Bn Q.O. Cameron's beat representatives of 10th Corps. Score 4-1. Gutmen Packery up of Mobilization stores. Preparing for move.	
	25/3/19		5 O.R's proceed to Demobilization camp DUREN.	
	26/3/19		All available men were employed in preparation for move.	
	27/3/19		Officers versus the Battalion at Basket ball. Officers won 9-3.	
	28/3/19		6 O.R. proceed to Demobilization Camp Duren. Final of the Army Cup football competition at Cologne between the Q.O. Cameron's + 9th Royal Highlanders. Score 2-1. R.S.M. J. BLAKE awarded the Meritorious Service Medal.	
	29/3/19		5 O.Rs proceed to Demobilization Camp, Duren.	
	30/3/19		Church Parade. 2 O.Rs proceed to Demobilization Camp.	
	31/3/19		Final of Divisional Hockey Competition won by R. Sussex Regt.	

WAR DIARY

of 1st Bn. The Northamptonshire Regt.

INTELLIGENCE SUMMARY

Army Form C. 2118.

Instructions regarding War Diaries and Intelligence Summaries are contained in F.S. Regs., Part II. and the Staff Manual respectively. Title pages will be prepared in manuscript.

(Erase heading not required.)

Place	Date	Hour	Summary of Events and Information	Remarks and references to Appendices
LENGSDORF	1/4/19		5 O.R. demobilised	
	2/4/19		12 O.Rs demobilised. Battalion Baths. Accounts of the Battalion audited	
	3/4/19		2 O.Rs demobilised. 4 O.R. demobilised from Bde H.Q.(attached)	
	4/4/19		3 O.Rs —	
	5/4/19		5 O.Rs transferred to 52nd Welch Regiment	
	6/4/19		Lt/Capt F.G.S. Martin & G/Capt L.H.R. Mackenzie relinquished their acting rank on ceasing to command a coy owing to the Battn being reduced to cadre strength. Church Service. Officers v NCOs Band at Basket Ball. Officers won 28–3. 1 O.R. transferred 6.32nd Welch Rgt.	Allowances to W/O/1 for staff study 1st Bn. The Northamptonshire Regt.
	7/4/19		2 O.R. proceeded to Demobilisation camp.	
	8/4/19		Basket-ball match B.H.Q. Officers v the rest of the Battalion Baths. Officers won 13–8.	
	9/4/19		Sgts' mess meeting	
	10/4/19		Bn H.Q. Officers versus Officers at Basket Ball. Bn H.Q. won 9–8.	
	11/4/19		All N.C.O.s then on fatigue at B.M. Stores.	
	12/4/19		As for 11th.	

Army Form C. 2118.

WAR DIARY
or
INTELLIGENCE SUMMARY.
(Erase heading not required.)

Instructions regarding War Diaries and Intelligence Summaries are contained in F.S. Regs., Part II. and the Staff Manual respectively. Title pages will be prepared in manuscript.

Place	Date	Hour	Summary of Events and Information	Remarks and references to Appendices
LENGSD	Sept 13th/19		Lt Col G.O.G. Atkinson D.S.O. Inf. proceeds to England to take up an appointment at the Royal Military College Sandhurst. Band performs at 9th Corps.	
	14/9.		4 Officers proceed to England on leave prior to Battalion talks rejoining the Battalion on their return to the depot. 1 Officer + 1 O.R. transferred to 53rd Bedford Regt.	
	15/9.		4 Officers proceed on leave prior to reporting to the depot.	
	16/9.		2 O.R.s transferred to Bde H.Q.	
	17/19.		1 Officer — " — to 53rd Bedfordshire Regt.	
	18/9.		No 5184 RSM. J. Blake permitted to continue in the service, after completing 21 years, to complete 5 years as Warrant Officer class I.	
	19/9.		9 Other Ranks proceeded to Concentration Camp DUREN for Demobilisation. Band proceeded by lorry to EUSKIRCHEN (9th A.R.D. H.Q.) and played a At Home. Programme on the Square. (march appended)	
	20/9		Cadre proceeded to Baths at DUSDORF	
	21/9		Band played at a 52nd Light Regt. Sports DUSDORF in the afternoon. Lt FUCHINGER proceeded En Route to England	

(A7092). Wt. W12830/M1293. 75,000. 1/17. D.D. & L., Ltd. Forms/C2118/14.

WAR DIARY
or
INTELLIGENCE SUMMARY.

(Erase heading not required.)

Army Form C. 2118.

Place	Date	Hour	Summary of Events and Information	Remarks and references to Appendices
LECHENICH	22/5/19		Still awaiting Orders to proceed home.	
	23/5/19		Band proceeded to EUSKIRCHEN for Funeral.	
	24/5/19		Quiet day. Still awaiting Orders to Move. Band played at Brigade H.Q. Sports at DUISDORF in the afternoon. Maj Govier + Capt Bletsoe proceed to WEISBADEN on 48 Hours Leave	
	25/5/19		Quiet day. Still awaiting Orders to Move.	
	26/5/19		Band practice for Medical Inspection; Maj Govier + Capt Bletsoe returned from WEISBADEN	
	27/5/19		Divine Service held at 6pm (Voluntary)	
	28/5/19		Ordinary Routine. Quiet day.	
	29/5/19		Coms + Band practice + Baths at DUISDORF	
	30/5/19		Band attended Inspection at 2=15 by the Commander in Chief at DUISDORF. 2/Lt H.G.S. MARTIN Grants 14 days leave to U.K. due to leave from BOULOGNE on the 2nd May	

H.G. Stanflt-Caplin. a/cy
1/N'hamptonshire Regt

Army Form C. 2118.

1st BN NORTHAMPTONSHIRE REGT
WAR DIARY
or
INTELLIGENCE SUMMARY.
(Erase heading not required.)

CENTRAL REGISTRY
HEADQUARTERS
WIMEREUX
22 MAY 1919

A. H. Bowditch - Capt - actg
1/ Northamptonshire Regt.

Place	Date	Hour	Summary of Events and Information	Remarks and references to Appendices
LENGSDORF	1/5/19		Battn still at LENGSDORF working parties to Divisional Horse	
	2/5/19		" " " Bread Ration Convoy no Mudical Inspection at 10.30 a.m.	
	3/5/19		" " " Bann arrived at EUSKIRCHEN & played a them tournamt	
	4/5/19		" " " Battn still at Divisional & Bn Corps DISPORT	
	5/5/19		" " " Divisional Parade	
	6/5/19		" " "	
	7/5/19		" " "	
	8/5/19		" " "	CREED
	9/5/19		" " " 5 & 150 Regts under the Capt. 2nd march to Euskirchen	
	10/5/19		" " " Proceeded out Training & Drill in the morning	
	11/5/19		" " " Kings Birthday Parade Cancelled owing to heavy rain	
	12/5/19		" " " Divisional Service of Thanksgiving	
12 & 13/5/19			" " " Othr Battalion of the Brigade & of Consolidation camps for other Ranks proceeding home Demobilisation in Divisions	
			" " " In the evening Day Spent in Preparing to depart Battn	
	14/5/19		CADRE left LENGSDORF at 12.30 p.m. & proceeded to EUSKIRCHEN by road. Arrived at EUSKIRCHEN about 2 P.M. loaded vehicles, & train arrived left EUSKIRCHEN about 6 P.M. Arrived at ANTWERP about 9 A.M. unloaded vehicles transport & turned into No 6 Camp. Head of Staal Authority. Remain at ANTWERP for about a week	

Army Form C. 2118.

1st / 5th NORTHAMPTONSHIRE REGT

WAR DIARY
or
INTELLIGENCE SUMMARY.
(Erase heading not required.)

Instructions regarding War Diaries and Intelligence Summaries are contained in F. S. Regs., Part II. and the Staff Manual respectively. Title pages will be prepared in manuscript.

Place	Date	Hour	Summary of Events and Information	Remarks and references to Appendices
ANTWERP	15/5/19		CADRE remained at ANTWERP. Vehicles & Baggage cleared during the morning. Men were allowed out in PARIS to visit ANTWERP.	
—	16/5/19		Still at ANTWERP. Roll Call & Guard mounting at 9 am. Inspection of quarters immediately afterwards. Organisation of the Camp very good. Men quite comfortable & awaiting movements. Good bathing in the waters of the MOAT near Camp.	
—	17/5/19		Still at ANTWERP awaiting embarkation. Men were paid out.	
—	18/5/19		" " Orders received to the effect that we entrain Embark on the 19.12 or 20.7	
—	19/5/19		" " Orders received to entrain tomorrow 20th	
—	20/5/19		Vehicles & Baggage loaded on S.S. "SICILIAN" Embark at 3.30 pm on S.S. "SICILIAN" Cadre embarking consists of 4 officers and 70 o/Ranks including the Band. The officers being A/Major J.D. Enser M.C. Capt & Adj J.G.H. Taylor M.C. Capt H.F. PITCHER M.C. & Lieut & Q.M. E.E. HILBERT.	Lt. H. Boult Captain 1/Northamptonshire Regt

www.ingramcontent.com/pod-product-compliance
Lightning Source LLC
Chambersburg PA
CBHW080810010526
44113CB00013B/2354